MW01253390

PERSONALITY, COGNITION, AND EMOTION

WARSAW LECTURES IN PERSONALITY AND SOCIAL PSYCHOLOGY
Published in cooperation with the Warsaw School of Social Sciences and
Humanities, Warsaw, Poland

PERSONALITY, COGNITION, AND EMOTION

Edited by

Michael W. Eysenck
Roehampton University
Whitelands College
London, United Kingdom

Małgorzata Fajkowska
Warsaw School of Social Sciences and Humanities and
Polish Academy of Sciences
Warsaw, Poland

Tomasz Maruszewski
Polish Academy of Sciences and
Warsaw School of Social Sciences and Humanities
Warsaw, Poland

ELIOT WERNER PUBLICATIONS, INC.
CLINTON CORNERS, NEW YORK

Library of Congress Cataloging-in-Publication Data

Personality, cognition, and emotion / edited by Michael W. Eysenck, Malgorzata
Fajkowska, Tomasz Maruszewski.
p. cm. — (Warsaw lectures in personality and social psychology ; v. 2)
Includes bibliographical references and index.
ISBN 978-0-9797731-7-4
1. Personality and cognition. 2. Personality and emotions. 3. Personality. 4.
Cognition. 5. Emotions. I. Eysenck, Michael W. II. Fajkowska, Malgorzata. III.
Maruszewski, Tomasz.
BF698.9.C63P476 2011
155.2 — dc23

2011025450

ISBN-10: 0-9797731-7-2
ISBN-13: 978-0-9797731-7-4

Copyright © 2012 Eliot Werner Publications, Inc.
PO Box 268, Clinton Corners, New York 12514
http://www.eliotwerner.com

Printed in the United States of America

Contributors

Ewa Domaradzka • Interdisciplinary Center for Applied Cognitive Studies, Warsaw School of Social Sciences and Humanities, Warsaw, Poland

Michael W. Eysenck • Department of Psychology, Roehampton University, Whitelands College, London, United Kingdom

Małgorzata Fajkowska • Institute of Psychology, Polish Academy of Sciences, Warsaw, Poland; Warsaw School of Social Sciences and Humanities, Warsaw, Poland

Angela N. Fellner • Department of Psychology, University of Cincinnati, Cincinnati, Ohio, USA

Nico H. Frijda • Department of Social and Behavioral Sciences, University of Amsterdam, Amsterdam, The Netherlands

Alina Kolańczyk • Warsaw School of Social Sciences and Humanities, Faculty in Sopot, Sopot, Poland

Elizabeth Malouf • Department of Psychology, George Mason University, Fairfax, Virginia, USA

Debra Mashek • Department of Humanities and Social Sciences, Harvey Mudd College, Claremont, California, USA

Gerald Matthews • Department of Psychology, University of Cincinnati, Cincinnati, Ohio, USA

Tomasz Maruszewski • Warsaw School of Social Sciences and Humanities, Warsaw, Poland; Institute of Psychology, Polish Academy of Sciences, Warsaw, Poland

Keith Oatley • Department of Human Development and Applied Psychology, University of Toronto, Toronto, Canada

William Revelle • Department of Psychology, Northwestern University, Evanston, Illinois, USA

Grzegorz Sedek • Interdisciplinary Center for Applied Cognitive Studies, Warsaw School of Social Sciences and Humanities, Warsaw, Poland

Jeff Stuewig • Department of Psychology, George Mason University, Fairfax, Virginia, USA

June Price Tangney • Department of Psychology, George Mason University, Fairfax, Virginia, USA

Szymon Wichary • Interdisciplinary Center for Applied Cognitive Studies, Warsaw School of Social Sciences and Humanities, Warsaw, Poland; Department of Psychology, University of Basel, Basel, Switzerland

Bogdan Wojciszke • Warsaw School of Social Sciences and Humanities, Warsaw, Poland

Foreword

The first Biennial Symposium on Personality and Social Psychology (BSPSP), organized by the Warsaw School of Social Sciences and Humanities, was arranged in the hope that we would be able to gather internationally recognized researchers in the fields of personality and social psychology to exchange ideas and discuss possibilities for future collaboration in these areas of research. Małgorzata Fajkowska accepted the challenge to organize the BSPSP, with results that have surpassed our expectations. Only after the first meeting did the idea mature to publish the most interesting and significant intellectual fruits of this meeting. I am glad we were able to convince the organizers that the only way to have the results of our symposia internationally disseminated is to publish them in English, but as psychological monographs rather than conference proceedings. I am pleased that Eliot Werner agreed to publish selected papers presented in the symposia in the form of extended chapters in a series Warsaw Lectures in Personality and Social Psychology, and hope Eliot shares my impression that this was a sound decision.

The first three volumes—*Personality From Biological, Cognitive, and Social Perspectives*, this one, and the third one in preparation (*Personality Dynamics: Embodiment, Meaning Construction, and the Social World*, based on the third biennial meeting that took place in 2010)—convinced us that our decision, strongly influenced by the well-known series Nebraska Symposia on Motivation, was right. Indeed, we were able to generate interest in our symposia among highly recognized researchers and experts in personality and social psychology. To mention only a few of them who have taken part in our symposia and contributed to the volumes: Susan Andersen, John Cacioppo, Daniel Cervone, Michael Eysenck, Nico Frijda, Hubert Hermans, Shulamith Kreitler, Gerald Matthews, Risto Näätänen, Paula Niedenthal, Keith Oatley, Ernst Pöppel, William Revelle, Robin Vallacher, and Frank Van Overwalle.

I am pleased that Volume 2 is now in the hands of the reader. The book is divided into two parts: Part I, "Differential Approaches to the Study of Cognitive and Affective Processes"; and Part II, "Self in Social Behavior and Emotional Expression." As stated by the editors in their introduction, "Part I is concerned with the effects of individual differences and emotion on cognitive processing and performance," whereas "Part II is concerned with emotions and with the relationships between emotional states and various aspects of individual differences and cognitive processes."

To some extent the uniqueness of this volume has its roots in the provocative question posed by Robert Zajonc, "Which occurs first, feeling or thinking?" to which he answered, "Feeling before thinking." This was probably the first well-grounded empirical approach aimed at studying the relationship between cognition and emotion. In this volume evidence is presented showing that there are reciprocal relationships between both variables under discussion: feeling influences cognition and, inversely, cognition influences emotions; and the same is true if we take into account the mutual relationships among the triad cognition-emotion-behavior. Further, in most of the chapters the reader will find extensive theoretical discussions—much broader than those in typical journal articles—in the context of which data are presented. The concluding chapter (with over one hundred references) written by William Revelle shows the broad empirical and theoretical context within which the chapters in this volume are discussed.

After perusing the chapters included in Volume 2, edited by Michael Eysenck, Małgorzata Fajkowska, and Tomasz Maruszewski, I am firmly convinced that researchers and students interested in personality and social psychology will find this book both challenging and exciting. My congratulations to all those who contributed in different ways to this significant work.

Jan Strelau, Pro-Rector for Research
Warsaw School of Social Sciences and Humanities

Contents

**PART II.
SELF IN SOCIAL BEHAVIOR AND EMOTIONAL EXPRESSION**

Chapter 6 • Emotions in the Individual Mind, in Relationships, and in Reading Fiction 107

Keith Oatley

Chapter 7 • Agency and Communion as Basic Dimensions of Social Cognition 123

Bogdan Wojciszke

Chapter 8 • Emotions and Morality: You Don't Have to Feel Really Bad to be Good 141

June Price Tangney, Elizabeth Malouf, Jeff Stuewig, and Debra Mashek

PART III.
EPILOGUE: TOWARD A COMMON PARADIGM

PERSONALITY, COGNITION, AND EMOTION

Relations Among Personality, Cognition, and Emotion

Michael W. Eysenck
Małgorzata Fajkowska
Tomasz Maruszewski

HISTORICAL PERSPECTIVE

This volume, which grows out of a symposium held in Warsaw in 2008, is the second in what is intended to be an open-ended series. The first volume (based on a symposium held in Warsaw in 2006) focused on personality from biological, cognitive, and social perspectives. The third volume (based on a symposium held in Warsaw in 2010) is tentatively entitled *Personality Dynamics: Embodiment, Meaning Construction, and the Social World*. The intended readership of this second volume consists of professionals and graduate students who have a keen interest in the areas of personality, cognition, and emotion. It is also our avowed intention to demonstrate to our readers that these are intellectually exciting times in those areas, and that rapid progress at both the theoretical and empirical levels is being achieved.

The primary goal of the Warsaw Lectures in Personality and Social Psychology is to focus on broad, advanced themes that are discussed by outstanding researchers internationally recognized in their particular field. Although this series of volumes possesses unique features in terms of comprehensiveness and scope, it bears some similarity to the long-running Nebraska Symposia on

Personality, Cognition, and Emotion edited by Michael W. Eysenck, Małgorzata Fajkowska, and Tomasz Maruszewski. Eliot Werner Publications, Clinton Corners, New York, 2012.

Motivation. These annual symposia started in 1953 and 2010 saw the 58th
Nebraska Symposium on Motivation. Of course we cannot guarantee to match
that number, especially since our conferences are biennial rather than annual, and
so our 58th symposium and accompanying volume would be scheduled for the
year 2120! However, we have already emulated that very successful series by
attracting international authorities as participants.

Throughout most of the history of psychology, it has been the norm for theories and research to be limited in scope. Thus, for example, we have theories of
emotion, theories of personality, and theories of cognition. This approach is
intrinsically limited because it fails to acknowledge sufficiently one of the central
truths in psychology—that personality, emotion, cognition, motivation, and so on
interact in very complex ways. One of the main implications is that approaches
within psychology need to be comprehensive in order to accommodate such interactions. Of central importance in the Warsaw Lectures in Personality and Social
Psychology (including this volume) is precisely this emphasis on crucial interactions among areas of psychology that have too often been regarded as separate
from each other.

We can illustrate the above argument by considering the cognitive approach,
which has become increasingly dominant within psychology. A recent review of
the literature on human cognition (Eysenck & Keane, 2010) concluded that there
is still a dearth of research assessing the impact of emotional states and individual differences in personality on cognitive processing and performance. This is
puzzling. Research on the effects of emotional states—including anxiety, depression, anger, and positive affect—has typically found that they influence attention,
comprehension, problem solving, and reasoning (see Blanchette & Richards,
2010, for a review). In similar fashion, research on individuals high and low in
the personality dimension of trait anxiety has consistently revealed differences in
attentional processes involving threat-related stimuli and the interpretation of
ambiguous stimuli and events (see Eysenck, 1997, for a review).

There has been increasing interest in understanding emotions from the cognitive perspective. Much of the original impetus in this area came from Lazarus
(e.g., 1991), who argued convincingly that the emotional states we experience
depend on our cognitive appraisal of the current situation (see Frijda, this volume).

This approach has been developed and extended by recent research within
cognitive neuroscience. Forms of cognitive appraisal that are effective in producing emotional regulation typically involve high levels of activation in the prefrontal cortex, followed by reduced amygdala activation (Ochsner & Gross, 2008).
The implication of such findings is that higher-level cognitive processes within the
prefrontal cortex play an important role in the control of emotional states.

We have seen that there has been some progress in understanding the effects
of cognition on emotion and of emotion on cognition. The same is true (but possibly to a lesser extent) of the effects of cognition on personality, of personality
on cognition, of emotion on personality, and of personality on emotion. As a consequence, there is much scope for integrative theory and research to elucidate the

interrelations of cognition, personality, and emotion. Some of the main fruits of such endeavors are discussed in this volume.

WHAT'S AHEAD IN THIS BOOK

The ambitious nature of this volume has already been made clear. Indeed, there are those who might argue that what we are attempting here is too ambitious. However, our strong opinion is that attempts at theoretical integration within the broad scope of cognition, personality, and emotion research are timely. Why is that the case? The amount of relevant research (although not great) has increased considerably in recent years. As a result, it is much truer now than in the past that there are sufficient findings to provide the basis for integrative theories, some of which are discussed in detail in this volume.

The eight substantive chapters in this volume are divided into two parts, each of which deals with a wide variety of important topics. In general terms, however, Part I is concerned with the effects of individual differences and emotion on cognitive processing and performance. By contrast, Part II is concerned with emotions and with the relationships between emotional states and various aspects of individual differences and cognitive processes. What all the contributions have in common is that they are thought provoking, and we hope they will encourage readers to join in the exciting task of enhancing our psychological understanding of personality, cognition, and emotion.

Part I: Differential Approaches to the Study of Cognitive and Affective Processes

As already indicated, Part I deals with the ways in which individual differences and emotions influence human cognition. As we will see, several major dimensions of individual differences are considered. More specifically, two of the chapters (Michael Eysenck; Gerald Matthews and Angela Fellner) deal with personality dimensions (trait anxiety and emotional intelligence, respectively). Another chapter (Szymon Wichary, Ewa Domaradzka, and Gregorz Sedek) deals with the impact of aging on cognition, and the final chapter (Alina Kolańczyk) deals with various individual differences influencing creative intuition.

Part I begins with a chapter by Michael Eysenck entitled "Anxiety and Cognitive Performance." The central theme that he explores is that of understanding some of the differences in cognitive processing between individuals high and low in the personality dimension of trait anxiety. This is an important goal in part because of the considerable evidence that students high in trait anxiety—or the closely related dimension of test anxiety—typically have lower levels of academic achievement than those low in trait anxiety (Hembree, 1988).

There are several reasons why high levels of trait anxiety might be associated with impaired cognitive performance. The theoretical approach that is the main focus of Eysenck's chapter is attentional control theory (Eysenck, Derakshan, Santos, & Calvo, 2007). According to this theory, it is important to distinguish between two major types of attentional control stemming from the seminal research of Miyake et al. (2000) on executive functions. One is negative attentional control, which involves inhibiting attention being directed toward task-irrelevant stimuli or responses. The other is positive attentional control, which involves shifting or switching attention optimally within and between tasks to maximize performance. It is assumed within attentional control theory that the efficiency of negative and positive attentional control is impaired in anxious individuals.

According to attentional control theory, there is an important distinction between performance effectiveness and processing efficiency. Performance effectiveness refers to the quality of performance (e.g., percent correct answers), whereas processing efficiency refers to the relationship between performance effectiveness and the use of processing resources. The distinction can be exemplified by considering two individuals A and B. They have a comparable level of performance effectiveness on a given task, but A has expended more processing resources than B. Thus A has less processing efficiency than B. According to attentional control theory, the adverse effects of anxiety are greater on efficiency than on effectiveness. Anxious individuals "peddle harder" than nonanxious ones (i.e., have a higher level of motivation) and this reduces the negative impact of anxiety on effectiveness. As a consequence, measures of performance effectiveness may camouflage effects of anxiety on processing efficiency. In other words, anxiety may occur "hidden costs."

Eysenck discusses the research literature of relevance to attentional control theory, which provides reasonable support for its major hypotheses. So far as the future is concerned, there is exciting potential in using brain imaging and EEG measures—in addition to behavioral ones—to provide more precise assessment of differences between high- and low-anxious groups in processing efficiency.

The second chapter in Part I, by Gerald Matthews and Angela Fellner, has as its title "The Energetics of Emotional Intelligence." There has been considerable interest in emotional intelligence in recent years and it has been the subject of numerous research studies (see Zeidner, Matthews, & Roberts, 2009, for a review). Emotional intelligence is generally assumed to have trait-like qualities and to involve the ability to manage one's own emotions and interact successfully with others. An issue here is that measures of emotional intelligence often correlate positively with extraversion and negatively with neuroticism. Thus it is important to show that any measure of emotional intelligence possesses incremental validity when account is taken of its relationship to extraversion and neuroticism.

It has been argued that there are many important differences between individuals high and low in emotional intelligence. For example, those high in emotional intelligence experience more positive affect and less negative affect than those low in emotional intelligence. As Matthews and Fellner point out, such individual differences in emotional state can mediate differences in cognitive performance.

What did Matthews and Fellner discover? Somewhat surprisingly, they found that emotional intelligence was a poor predictor of objective performance on a range of tasks concerned with perception, attention, and learning even with emotional stimuli. However, there were interesting effects of emotional intelligence on subjective state during task performance. More specifically, a high level of emotional intelligence was associated with low levels of distress and worry.

The approach taken by Matthews and Fellner provides an admirable example of how personality, emotion, and cognition can be studied together. In essence, they show how personality (emotional intelligence) impacts on emotional state (e.g., distress, worry) and how emotional state then impacts on cognitive performance. This approach can readily be adapted to study a range of personality traits, emotional states, and cognitive processes and tasks.

The third chapter in Part I is by Szymon Wichary, Ewa Domaradzka, and Grzegorz Sedek. Its title is "The Impact of Aging on Information Integration in Reasoning and Decision Making." There is overwhelming evidence that aging has significant (and often substantial) negative effects on complex cognition (e.g., Sedek & von Hecker, 2004). As Wichary et al. point out, among these negative effects are difficulties with conflict and error processing, goal maintenance, set switching, and the rapid processing of contextual information.

Several explanations for impaired cognitive performance in older adults have been put forward. In their chapter Wichary et al. discuss three of the main ones. First, older individuals have cognitive slowing and in addition may exhibit limitations with memory retrieval. Second, older adults have impairments of inhibitory processes, making them more susceptible to distraction and to producing dominant (but incorrect) responses. Third, older individuals often use less efficient cognitive strategies than younger adults.

It has often been assumed that older adults simply accept these limitations on their cognitive processing ability. However, Wichary et al. argue persuasively that this is by no means the case. Instead, older adults make use of various compensatory strategies to mitigate the adverse effects of those limitations. Of particular importance, older adults experience less of a need for cognitive closure when confronting reasoning and decision-making problems. In addition, older adults are more inclined than younger ones to engage in deliberative integration of information on complex problems in order to produce correct solutions.

The fourth and final contribution to Part I is a chapter by Alina Kolańczyk, "Building Bridges in Psychology as Exemplified by Creative Intuition." There has been a disproportionate emphasis on convergent thinking throughout most of the history of psychology. However, there are encouraging signs that divergent thinking and creative intuition are starting to attract the research attention that they deserve (Dijksterhuis & Aarts, 2010). One of the major reasons why creative intuition has been relatively neglected is undoubtedly because it is a difficult topic. It is difficult because it is hard to find tasks that permit the use of creative intuition and because it is hard to identify the underlying processes, many of which are unconscious in nature.

Kolańczyk's main contribution to our understanding of creative intuition is contained within her trifactor model. This is a complex model, and so only a few key components will be mentioned here. First, there is meta-motivation, which involves adopting the appropriate mindset for creative intuition. Second, there is attention state. In general terms, creative intuition is most likely to occur in individuals whose attention is extensive and who adopt a global mode of information processing. Third, there is the notion of an affective map. Affect influences which contents are processed by attention, and individuals tend to process and integrate information associated with positive affect. This can facilitate the creative process.

The trifactor model provides a very useful theoretical framework within which to consider creative intuition. Kolańczyk discusses several research findings providing support for this model. For the future the numerous hypotheses incorporated within the model provide the basis for additional research studies. Another potential focus for future research should be further exploration of individual differences in creative intuition, as exemplified by the distinction between intuitionists and rationalists.

Part II: Self in Social Behavior and Emotional Expression

The main focus of Part II is on emotions considered from various perspectives. There are several issues of major importance to emotion researchers. First, there is the complex issue of the essential nature of emotion, and of the combination of elements that are involved. It is also important to identify the antecedents of emotional states. In other words, what factors determine the nature and intensity of emotional experience? Another important issue is to predict the consequences of emotional states. In other words, how is an individual's behavior changed as a result of being in a given emotional state?

Two of the chapters in Part II (Nico Frijda; Keith Oately) address the above issues with respect to emotions in general rather than at the level of specific emotional states. By contrast, the remaining two chapters (Bogdan Wojciszke; June Price Tangney et al.) are somewhat more specific in their focus. Wojciszke concentrates on the two dimensions of agency and communion, and Tangney et al. deal with the two related emotions of shame and guilt.

Part II starts very appropriately with a chapter by Nico Frijda entitled "How Emotions Work." Frijda has long been at the forefront of theorizing and research on emotions and this chapter provides an overview of his major ideas on emotions (see also Frijda, 2007). According to Frijda, cognitive processes relating to appraisal of the current situation typically play some role in the initiation of an emotional state. However, his central contention is that there are close links between emotions and motivation, and this is especially the case with relatively intense emotional states. More specifically, emotions involve motive states and they have control precedence, meaning that they change the individual's priorities. As a consequence, emotions produce a state of action readiness (e.g., attend, care for, possess, reject, dominate) that varies from emotion to emotion. We can observe various emotions in other people's facial expressions, but aspects of action readiness can also be perceived from those expressions.

Why is a state of action readiness a vital component of emotion? According to Frijda, emotions serve the valuable function of safeguarding individual concerns. This function can typically best be served by means of an active involvement with the world.

An important challenge for the future is to understand more of the ways in which the various components of emotion (e.g., appraisal, motivation, action readiness) are combined and integrated. Frijda discusses brain imaging studies that reveal evidence of synchrony or integration of various relevant brain areas during emotional experience, but we need to know more about the processes permitting such integration. The good news is that as a result of Fridja's efforts, we know the nature of the major components of emotion that require integration.

The second chapter in Part II is by Keith Oatley and is entitled "Emotions in the Individual Mind, in Relationships, and in Reading Fiction." This chapter is rich in theoretical ideas and speculations, and only a few of the main ones will be mentioned explicitly here. First, there is the powerful notion that there are close connections between our goals and our emotional states (Johnson-Laird & Oatley, 2000). In other words, there is an intimate relationship between emotion and motivation. For example, happiness is the typical emotion that we experience when we perceive ourselves to be making progress toward a current goal, whereas we experience sadness when a goal is lost or has to be abandoned.

Second, Oatley addresses the issue of how to account for the existence of numerous emotional states. In essence, he argues persuasively that there is a strictly limited number of basic emotions. However, there are also many complex emotions that result from a blending of two or more basic emotions.

Third, Oatley emphasizes the important point that most emotional states emerge within a social context. There are several ways in which this can happen, but empathy plays a fundamental role in many of the social emotions. It is a fascinating possibility that empathy may depend in part on mirror neurons (see Welberg, 2010, for a review). These neurons are activated when an organism performs an action or observes another organism performing the same action. Another intriguing idea is that empathy can be fostered by reading novels: it may be easier to understand the emotional makeup of a fictional person than that of a real person, and the empathy thus experienced may transfer to real life.

The third chapter in Part II is "Agency and Communion as Basic Dimensions of Social Cognition" by Bogdan Wojciszke. The main thrust of this chapter—as implied by the title—is to demonstrate the central importance of the dimensions of agency and communion in many different areas within social psychology (see Wojciszke & Abelc, 2008).

There are substantial overlaps among agency, masculinity, individualism, the independent self, task-oriented leadership, and intellectual activities, and among communion, femininity, collectivism, the interdependent self, relation-oriented leadership, and social activities. These overlaps suggest that agency and

communion are of fundamental importance. Wojciszke has provided strong support for this assumption in several research studies, finding that 90% of the variance among several variables could be accounted for by two independent dimensions of agency and communion (Abele & Wojciszke, 2007). Note that this
study—and most others—have indicated that agency and communion are independent rather than opposite dimensions.

Apart from showing very clearly the very general applicability to the agency-
communion distinction, Wojciszke has also shed important light on some of the
factors determining which of the two factors is more important in some situations. For example, individual levels of self-esteem depend far more on the
strength of their agentic traits than on the strength of their communal traits.
Especially interesting is the finding that a given behavior is perceived in more
agentic terms when the individual focuses on his or her own behavior, but in more
communal terms when he or she focuses on the same behavior in others.

Since personality is one of the main themes of this volume, it is tempting to
speculate on the relationships between agentic and communal traits and well-
established personality dimensions such as the Big Five (e.g., McCrae et al.,
2005). For example, it is plausible that communal traits are more common in individuals high in extraversion and agreeableness than those low in those dimensions.

The fourth and final chapter in Part II is by June Price Tangney, Elizabeth
Malouf, Jeff Stuewig, and Debra Mashek and is entitled "Emotions and Morality:
You Don't Have to Feel Really Bad to be Good." Most emotions are complex and
it has generally proved difficult to provide theoretically coherent accounts of
related emotions. Tangney, Stuewig, and Mashek (2007) have shown convincingly that a major exception to this generalization concerns the negative emotions of
shame and guilt. Shame is associated with a devaluation of the self, whereas guilt
is associated with feeling bad about one's own behavior. Since it is much harder
to change your inner self than your behavior, shame is typically a more intensely
painful emotional state.

Does shame or guilt have a more beneficial effect on an individual's subsequent behavior? Tangney et al. provide a clear-cut answer to that question:
guilt is far more likely than shame to have advantageous consequences. Guilt-
prone individuals tend to be relatively high in empathy, handle anger in constructive ways, and generally behave in moral ways. By contrast, shame-prone
individuals lack empathy, experience considerable anger but deal with it inef-
fectively, and are inclined to behave in immoral and antisocial ways. For example, shame-proneness is associated with delinquency, alcoholism, drug problems, and risky sex.

One of the most impressive features of the research discussed by Tangney et
al. is that the findings are very similar regardless of whether shame and guilt are
regarded as states or trait-like proneness. It is interesting to consider how shame-
proneness and guilt-proneness are related to major personality dimensions. In
view of the fact that shame and guilt are both negative emotions, it is reasonable

to assume that they are both more prevalent in individuals high in neuroticism. The evidence is not extensive but does in general support that assumption (e.g., Kroll, Egan, Erickson, Carey, & Johnson, 2004; Tong, 2010).

Part III: Epilogue: Toward a Common Paradigm

The final chapter in the volume, and the sole chapter in Part III, is by William Revelle. Revelle focuses on the issue of providing an integration of the research areas discussed in this book. In so doing, he provides an excellent theoretical framework that will prove invaluable as a basis for further research and theory.

SUMMARY

The central unifying theme of this book is that we can only attain a comprehensive understanding of human behavior by considering the interactive influences of personality, cognition, and emotion. As we have discussed in this introduction, all the chapters in this book illustrate that theme in various ways. For example, consider major dimensions of individual differences. There are chapters focusing on the relevance to emotion and cognition of individual differences in trait anxiety, emotional intelligence, aging, agentic traits, and communal traits.

Diversity is also to be found with respect to emotion. There are chapters by Frijda and Oatley concerned with emotion in general in which the close links between emotion and motivation are emphasized. There are other chapters that focus more specifically on emotions such as shame and guilt and emotional states such as worry and distress.

Over fifty years ago, Cronbach (1957) discussed "the two disciplines of scientific psychology." These two disciplines were experimental psychology (involving well-controlled laboratory studies) and correlational psychology (focusing on individual and group variations). Cronbach argued forcefully—and we believe cogently—that it would be highly desirable for researchers to produce a synthesis by combining these two approaches. This book shows various ways in which such a synthesis might be achieved.

REFERENCES

Abele, A. E., & Wojciszke, B. (2007). Agency and communion from the perspective of self versus others. *Journal of Personality and Social Psychology, 93*, 751–763.

Blanchette, I., & Richards, A. (2010). The influence of affect on higher level cognition: A review of research on interpretation, judgment, decision making and reasoning. *Cognition and Emotion, 24*, 561–595.

Cronbach, L. J. (1957). The two disciplines of scientific psychology. *American Psychologist, 12*, 671–684.

Dijksterhuis, A., & Aarts, H. (2010). Goals, attention, and (un)consciousness. *Annual Review of Psychology, 61*, 467–490.

Eysenck, M. W. (1997). *Anxiety and cognition: A unified theory.* Hove, UK: Psychology Press.

Eysenck, M. W., Derakshan, N., Santos, R., & Calvo, M. G. (2007). Anxiety and cognitive performance: Attentional control theory. *Emotion, 7,* 336–353.

Eysenck, M. W., & Keane, M. T. (2010). *Cognitive psychology: A student's handbook* (6th ed.). Hove, UK: Psychology Press.

Frijda, N. H. (2007). *The laws of emotion.* Mahwah, NJ: Erlbaum.

Hembree, R. (1988). Correlates, causes, effects, and treatment of test anxiety. *Review of Educational Research, 58,* 47–77.

Johnson-Laird, P. N., & Oatley, K. (2000). Cognitive and social construction in emotion. In M. Lewis & J. Haviland (Eds.) *Handbook of emotions* (2nd ed., pp. 458–475). New York: Guilford Press.

Kroll, J., Egan, E., Erickson, P., Carey, K., & Johnson, M. (2004). Moral conflict, religiosity, and neuroticism in an outpatient group. *Journal of Nervous and Mental Disease, 192,* 682–688.

Lazarus, R. S. (1991). *Emotion and adaptation.* Oxford, UK: Oxford University Press.

McCrae, R. R., Terracciano, A., and 78 Members of the Personality Profiles of Cultures Project (2005). Universal features of personality traits from the observer's perspective: Data from 50 cultures. *Journal of Personality and Social Psychology, 88,* 547–561.

Miyake, A., Friedman, N. P., Emerson, M. J., Witzki, A. H., Howerter, A., & Wager, T. (2000). The unity and diversity of executive functions and their contributions to complex "frontal lobe" tasks: A latent variable analysis. *Cognitive Psychology, 41,* 49–100.

Ochsner, K. N., & Gross, J. J. (2008). Cognitive emotion regulation: Insights from social cognitive and affective neuroscience. *Current Directions in Psychological Science, 17,* 153–158.

Sedek, G., & von Hecker, U. (2004). Effects of subclinical depression and aging on generative reasoning about linear orders: Same or different processing limitations? *Journal of Experimental Psychology: General, 133,* 237–260.

Tangney, J. P., Stuewig, J., & Mashek, D. J. (2007). Moral emotions and moral behavior. *Annual Review of Psychology, 58,* 345–372.

Tong, E. M. W. (2010). Personality influences in appraisal-emotion relationships: The role of neuroticism. *Journal of Personality, 78,* 393–417.

Welberg, L. (2010). Mirror neurons: Mirrors, mirrors, everywhere? *Nature Reviews Neuroscience, 11,* 374.

Wojciszke, B., & Abele, A. E. (2008). The primacy of communion over agency and its reversals in evaluations. *European Journal of Social Psychology, 38,* 1139–1147.

Zeidner, M., Matthews, G., & Roberts, R. D. (2009). *What we know about emotional intelligence: How it affects learning, work, relationships, and our mental health.* Cambridge, MA: MIT Press.

PART I

Differential Approaches to the Study of Cognitive and Affective Processes

CHAPTER 1

Anxiety and Cognitive Performance

Michael W. Eysenck

INTRODUCTION

There is a considerable volume of research over the years indicating that anxiety (whether regarded as a personality dimension or as an emotional state) is associated with impaired performance on a wide range of cognitive tasks and on broader assessments of academic achievement. For example, Hembree (1988) carried out a comprehensive meta-analysis based on hundreds of studies. He reported that there was an overall correlation of –0.29 between test anxiety and academic achievement or aptitude. Such evidence, of course, is suggestive rather than definitive because it is only correlational in nature.

The causality issue can be addressed appropriately by means of intervention studies designed to reduce the level of anxiety. Schwarzer (1990) reported meta-analytic findings from more than one hundred intervention studies. He discovered that test performance and grade point average (a global measure of academic achievement) were significantly higher for individuals who had undergone an intervention designed to reduce anxiety than for those who were assigned to a placebo or waiting list group. The implication is that high levels of test anxiety have a detrimental effect on cognitive performance. However, it is also possible that poor levels of academic achievement may tend to enhance an individual's level of test anxiety, rather than high test anxiety impairing performance.

Several theories to explain the negative effects of anxiety on cognitive performance have been put forward. However, most of these theories are limited in that they lack specificity with respect to the mechanisms involved. For example,

Personality, Cognition, and Emotion edited by Michael W. Eysenck, Małgorzata Fajkowska, and Tomasz Maruszewski. Eliot Werner Publications, Clinton Corners, New York, 2012.

in his cognitive interference theory, Sarason (1988) argued that worry is an important component of anxiety, and that it leads to impaired performance because it interferes with attention to the ongoing task. It is probable that worry is relevant to an explanation of the effects of anxiety on performance. However, its effects on attentional processes need to be specified more precisely. In addition, some of the available evidence is inconsistent with the theory. According to cognitive interference theory, the most obvious prediction is that high anxiety will have a detrimental effect on performance whenever it is associated with greater levels of worry than is low anxiety. However, although there are several studies (e.g., Blankstein, Flett, Boase, & Toner, 1990; Blankstein, Toner, & Flett, 1989) in which high-anxious participants had substantially more worrying thoughts than low-anxious ones (based on self-report data), there was no difference between the two groups in terms of their level of performance. Such findings indicate clearly that the relationships among anxiety, worry, and performance are more complex than envisaged within cognitive interference theory.

In what follows the emphasis will be on the attentional control theory put forward by Eysenck, Derakshan, Santos, and Calvo (2007) and by Derakshan and Eysenck (2009). This theory represents an extension and development of the earlier processing efficiency theory (Eysenck & Calvo, 1992). Both theories were designed to elucidate the mechanisms underlying the effects of anxiety on efficiency and effectiveness. One of the distinctive features of these theories—and of the research designed to test them—is that the emphasis is on specific cognitive processes and on relatively "process pure" tasks. The underlying assumption is that the optimal way of understanding the effects of anxiety on cognitive processing and cognitive performance is to use conceptually simple tasks. When conceptually complex tasks are used, it is extremely difficult to interpret the findings unequivocally. However, other factors are also important in determining whether a task is process pure. For example, a task that is process pure for an individual who possesses much relevant knowledge and experience may not be so for one who lacks such knowledge and experience.

ATTENTIONAL CONTROL THEORY

The rapid progress made by cognitive psychology in recent decades has provided very useful theoretical frameworks within which to consider the effects of anxiety on cognitive performance. Eysenck and Calvo (1992), in their processing efficiency theory, focused on Baddeley's (1986) working memory model. According to this model, working memory is involved in the processing and temporary storage of information, and so is used across a very wide range of cognitive tasks. In early versions of the model, the working memory system consisted of three components. The most important component was the central executive, which is attention-like and possesses limited capacity. The other two components were regarded as "slave" systems. One of these slave systems was the phonological loop, which is used in the rehearsal and transient storage of verbal information. The other slave system was the visuo-spatial sketchpad, which is used in the processing and temporary storage of visual and spatial information.

According to processing efficiency theory, the adverse effects of anxiety mostly involve the central executive rather than the phonological loop or the visuo-spatial sketchpad. There is some support for this assumption. Eysenck, Payne, and Derakshan (2005) considered performance on the Corsi Blocks Test by individuals low and high in trait anxiety. This task was in different conditions accompanied by a concurrent task that involved the central executive, the phonological loop, or the visuo-spatial sketchpad. The key finding was that performance on the primary task (the Corsi Blocks Test) was only adversely affected by high trait anxiety when the secondary task involved use of the central executive. This pattern of findings suggested that anxiety only impaired the functioning of the central executive. Similar findings using a different methodology were reported by Christopher and MacDonald (2005). There is scope for more research on this topic, perhaps involving attempts to directly influence the functioning of the central executive.

The single most important assumption built into processing efficiency theory (and subsequently also incorporated within attentional control theory) revolved around a distinction between performance effectiveness and processing efficiency. In essence, performance effectiveness is simply the quality of performance as assessed by, for example, the percentage of correct responses produced on a task. Processing efficiency is a more complex notion based on the relationship between performance effectiveness on one hand and use of resources or effort on the other. Thus there would be poor processing efficiency if there were a low level of performance effectiveness accompanied by a high use of resources.

Inhibitory and Shifting Functions: Theory

There are several differences between processing efficiency theory on one hand and attentional control theory on the other. However, we will focus here on what is perhaps the single most consequential difference, which relates to the effects of anxiety on the central executive. As we have seen, it is assumed within processing efficiency theory that the main effects of anxiety on performance are mediated by the central executive. That was a reasonable theoretical assumption at the time, because little was known of the major functions of the central executive. However, it now seems somewhat general and vague in light of the increased understanding of the workings of the central executive. As a result of this increased understanding, attentional control theory is based on more specific assumptions about the executive functions most affected by anxiety.

Before discussing the assumptions of attentional control theory in more detail, it is necessary to discuss the issue of the number and nature of functions within the central executive. There has been a certain amount of controversy surrounding this issue (see Eysenck & Keane, 2010, for a review). However, approaches based on systematic empirical research are preferable to those lacking a solid basis in experimental findings. The empirical approach of Miyake et al. (2000) and Friedman and Miyake (2004) has been especially influential. These researchers made use of latent-variable analysis to identify the main executive functions underlying performance across several different tasks. Inhibition, shifting, and updating functions emerged from this analysis. The inhibition function is used to prevent task-irrelevant stimuli and responses from disrupting performance. The shifting function is used to allocate attention flexibly and optimally to those task stimuli that are currently most relevant. The updating function is used to update and monitor the information that is currently within working memory and important for various short-term memory tasks.

According to attentional control theory (Eysenck et al., 2007), the adverse effects of anxiety center on the efficiency of the inhibition and shifting functions rather than that of the updating function. It is assumed that the inhibition and shifting functions involve different types of attentional control. The inhibition function involves negative attentional control in that it minimizes the allocation of attention to nontask stimuli (e.g., distractors). By contrast, the shifting function involves positive attentional control in that it involves the optimal allocation of attention within a given task or between two tasks (e.g., in a task-switching paradigm; see Monsell, 2003).

There is another difference between attentional control theory and processing efficiency theory that should be mentioned at this point. The former theory (but not the latter theory) assumes that the adverse effects of anxiety on processing efficiency are likely to be greater in tasks involving negative emotional stimuli rather than neutral ones and in tasks involving self-relevant processing. The relevant research evidence is discussed fully by Eysenck et al. (2007).

In sum, there is reasonable support for the assumption that inhibition and shifting are two of the most important executive functions within the central executive. However, there may also be additional functions (see Fournier-Vicente, Larigauderie, & Gaonac'h, 2008).

Inhibitory and Shifting Functions: Experimental Evidence

Eysenck et al. (2007) reviewed the evidence on the effects of anxiety on the inhibition and shifting functions and there is no need to provide a detailed review here. The review by Eysenck et al. indicated that there was much evidence that anxiety impairs the efficiency of the inhibition function. However, there were practically no studies directly addressing the effects of anxiety on the shifting function.

What I will do here is to mention briefly some relevant recent research not included in Eysenck et al.'s (2007) review. While several studies (mostly involving distraction) have provided support for the hypothesis that anxiety impairs the inhibition function, they do not reveal the mechanisms responsible for the greater susceptibility to distraction among high-anxious individuals. This issue was considered in two experiments by Derakshan, Ansari, Hansard, Shoker, and Eysenck (2009), who made use of the antisaccade task. On this task participants must respond as rapidly as possible to a visual cue presented to the left or right of the fixation point with a response on the other side.

The key assumption was that successful performance of the antisaccade task involves use of the inhibition function in order to prevent relatively automatic orienting to the cue. Thus it was predicted that high-anxious individuals would take significantly longer than low-anxious ones to produce a correct saccade on the antisaccade task. That finding was obtained in both experiments.

Ansari and Derakshan (2010) replicated the findings of Derakshan, Ansari et al. (2009). They introduced an additional refinement into their experimental design in order to clarify the interpretation of the finding that high-anxious individuals take significantly longer than low-anxious ones to make a correct saccade on the antisaccade task. The adverse effects of anxiety were predominantly on inhibitory control rather than on volitional action generation, which supports the prediction that anxiety impairs inhibitory control.

I turn now to the very limited amount of research relevant to the prediction from attentional control theory that anxiety impairs the efficiency of the shifting function. The task-switching paradigm provides an effective way of assessing the shifting function (see Monsell, 2003). At the simplest level, this paradigm involves the use of two tasks and two conditions. In one condition the participants have to switch backward and forward between the two tasks, a requirement that necessitates use of the shifting function. In the other condition, there are solid blocks of trials, with each block involving only one task. In this control condition, the shifting function is not required. The prediction from attentional control theory is that anxiety will impair performance in the task-switching condition to a greater extent than performance in the control condition.

Derakshan, Smyth, and Eysenck (2009) used the task-switching paradigm with the participants being exposed to pairs of tasks (e.g., multiplication and division; addition and subtraction). In the switching condition, there was a regular alternation of tasks on each trial. In the nonswitching or control condition, only one task was performed within each block of trials. The problems used were the same in the switching and nonswitching conditions. Various findings supported attentional theory. However, the most important finding was a highly significant interaction between anxiety and task switching. In this interaction the high-anxious participants performed much more slowly in the task-switching condition than in the control condition. By contrast, the performance speed of the low-anxious participants was similar in the task-switching and control conditions. Additional support for the prediction that anxiety impairs the efficiency of the shifting function was reported by Ansari, Derakshan, and Richards (2008) using the antisaccade task.

EFFICIENCY VERSUS EFFECTIVENESS: BRAIN-IMAGING RESEARCH

There is a substantial amount of research supporting the hypothesis that anxiety impairs processing efficiency to a greater extent than performance effectiveness (see Eysenck et al., 2007, for a review). However, a limitation of most of the older research is that it relied on rather indirect and imprecise measures of processing efficiency. More specifically, these measures were behavioral in nature and open to various interpretations. As a result, the focus here will be on recent research that makes use of nonbehavioral evidence and that potentially can provide more definitive evidence concerning the effects of anxiety on processing efficiency.

What research approach would be most appropriate for studying the theoretically predicted effects of anxiety on processing efficiency with respect to the inhibition and shifting functions? In principle, patterns of brain activation in high- and low-anxious individuals performing tasks involving specific executive functions can be of great value in assessing processing efficiency as a function of anxiety (Derakshan & Eysenck, 2010). More specifically, an appropriate experimental paradigm is as follows. Participants low and high in anxiety perform two tasks that vary in their demands on the inhibitory (or shifting) function. Suppose that anxiety does not have a significant effect on performance effectiveness with either task. The expectation is that brain activation in areas associated with attentional control should be greater with the more demanding task. Of crucial importance, it is predicted that the increase in relevant brain activation from the less to the more demanding task should be greater for individuals high in anxiety than for those low in anxiety. This is based on the assumption that there is an inverse relationship between processing efficiency and increases in brain activation for any given level of performance.

Research at least approximately consistent with the above experimental paradigm has been reported by Fales et al. (2008), Bishop (2009), and Savostyanov et al. (2009). In the study by Fales et al., there was no effect of anxiety level on performance of a known working memory task (the N-back task) on which participants had to decide whether each word presented corresponded to the one presented three words previously. In spite of the lack of any effect of anxiety on performance, participants high in anxiety had greater transient brain activity in regions such as the dorsolateral and ventrolateral prefrontal cortex that are known to be associated with attentional control. Thus the overall pattern of findings suggested that anxiety impaired processing efficiency (especially related to attentional control) but not performance effectiveness.

Bishop (2009) reported complex findings using a target-detection task. This task was performed under conditions of low or high perceptual load and with or without distraction. The findings with high perceptual load were as predicted by attentional control theory. In this condition distracting stimuli had comparable effects on the performance effectiveness of individuals low and high in trait anxiety. However, the increase in activation in the dorsolateral prefrontal cortex (associated with attentional control) produced by distracting stimuli was greater for high-anxious than for low-anxious individuals. Thus high trait anxiety was associated with impaired processing efficiency but not impaired performance effectiveness. If it is assumed that resisting the effects of distracting stimuli required use of the inhibitory function, then the findings suggest that anxiety impaired the efficiency of that function. For reasons that remain unclear, the findings from the condition involving low perceptual load differed substantially from those from the condition involving high perceptual load.

There is one important limitation with the studies of Fales et al. (2008) and Bishop (2009). They used functional magnetic resonance imaging, a technique with reasonably good spatial resolution but relatively poor temporal resolution. As a consequence, it is difficult to decide which cognitive processes are responsible for increased brain activation. It would be preferable to use a technique with greater temporal resolution, because that would facilitate the task of relating patterns of brain activation to specific cognitive processes. Precisely this was done by Savostyanov et al. (2009) who used a measure of EEG desynchronization based on the assumption that increased EEG desynchronization reflects increased processing effort and use of resources. Their task involved categorizing stimuli as rapidly as possible. In the crucial "Stop" condition, a signal indicated that the participants should not respond (i.e., make a categorization decision) on that trial.

Savostyanov et al. (2009) found that there was no effect of trait anxiety on performance effectiveness in the "Stop" condition. However, there was considerably more EEG desynchronization (and thus increased processing effort) in the high-anxious group than in the low-anxious group. Of importance, the greater EEG desynchronization shown by the high-anxious participants was very largely confined to the time period after the presentation of the warning signal indicating that the response should be inhibited. These findings suggest (as predicted by attentional control theory) that the high-anxious participants used greater processing resources than the low-anxious participants in order to achieve the necessary inhibitory attentional control.

EFFECTS OF ANXIETY VERSUS DEPRESSION

The main focus of this chapter has been on theory and research designed to elucidate the underlying mechanisms and processes responsible for mediating the effects of anxiety on performance. We have seen that the central executive appears to be of particular importance. More specifically, there is accumulating evidence that the inhibition and shifting functions of the central executive are especially vulnerable to the effects of anxiety.

It is of value to consider research on anxiety and performance within the broader context of the effects of emotional states on performance (see Derakshan & Eysenck, 2010). Of particular importance is research on depression (including clinical depression and depressed mood) and cognitive performance. There has been some controversy concerning the precise relationship between anxiety and depression. However, there is support for the tripartite model put forward by Clark and Watson (1991). According to this model, anxiety and depression are similar in that both emotional states involve general affective distress. However, they are dissimilar in that physiological hyperarousal characterizes anxiety but not depression, and anhedonia or lack of positive affect characterizes depression but not anxiety. Note that this model is probably most applicable to clinical anxiety and depression, and in practice anxious and depressed mood states often differ relatively little from each other.

In spite of the complexities involved, it may be possible to shed some light on the extent to which anxiety and depression resemble each other by comparing the effects of depression on the functioning of the working memory system. We have seen that much of the available evidence suggests that anxiety impairs the functioning of the central executive to a greater extent than that of the other components of the working memory system (Christopher & MacDonald, 2005; Eysenck et al., 2005). The findings with respect to depression are somewhat inconsistent. Channon, Baker, and Robertson (1993) and Hartlage, Alloy, Vazquez, and Dykman (1993) obtained evidence suggesting that depression impaired the functioning of the central executive but not the phonological loop or visuo-spatial sketchpad. By contrast, Christopher and MacDonald (2005) found that depression was associated with impaired functioning of all three components of the original working memory model.

What are the effects of depression on the inhibition and shifting functions? The available evidence is not extensive but suggests that depression impairs the inhibition and shifting functions in a similar fashion to anxiety. Joormann and Gotlib (2010) studied patients who had been diagnosed with a major depressive episode. They used a negative affective priming task and found that these depressed patients showed a significant impairment in the inhibition function compared with healthy controls. De Lissnyder, Koster, Derakshan, and de Raedt (2010) used the Affective Shift Task and discovered that rumination (a major feature of depression) was associated with impaired inhibitory functioning on that task. In addition, there was a significant impairment of the shifting function on the Affective Shift Task among individuals who were moderately or severely depressed.

Much of the research on depression and the shifting function has made use of the Wisconsin Card Sorting Task. De Lissnyder et al. (2010) reviewed this research, finding that depressed patients make more perseverative errors (indicative of impaired use of the shifting function) than controls. In similar fashion Whitmer and Banich (2007) found that individuals with depressive rumination were significantly inferior to those without such rumination with respect to task-shifting set.

What conclusions can we draw from the available research? The limited evidence that is available clearly suggests that there are important commonalities between the effects of anxiety and those of depression on cognitive performance. However, there are two important qualifications that need to be placed on that conclusion. First, questionnaire and other measures of anxiety and depression typically correlate moderately highly, thus making it difficult to identify effects specific to only one of those negative emotions. Second, there is much circumstantial evidence suggesting that low motivation and general disengagement are more closely associated with depression than with anxiety (Eysenck, 1997). This motivational difference provides a basis for predicting that the adverse effects of depression on cognitive processing and performance should often be greater and more extensive than those of anxiety.

SUGGESTIONS FOR THE FUTURE

We have seen that there has been an accumulation of empirical support for the predictions of attentional control theory. This is especially the case with respect to the predictions that anxiety primarily impairs the efficiency of the central executive and that anxiety impairs processing efficiency to a greater extent than performance effectiveness. Furthermore, real progress is being made in obtaining supporting evidence for the predictions that anxiety impairs the shifting and inhibition functions of the central executive.

Miyake et al. (2000) argued that there is an updating and monitoring function as well as shifting and inhibition functions. According to attentional control theory, any adverse effects of anxiety on the updating function are generally smaller than those on the shifting and inhibition functions. The evidence that was available was reviewed by Eysenck et al. (2007) and provided some support for this assumption.

Since the latter article was published, Walkenhorst and Crowe (2009) have carried out a study using a task that is assumed to involve use of the updating function (the N-back task). What happens with this task is that several items are presented. After the last item has been presented, the participants' task is to indicate which item was presented a given distance back in the series (e.g., three back, four back). Walkenhorst and Crowe found with both verbal and spatial N-back tasks that participants high in trait anxiety tended to perform the task faster than those low in trait anxiety. Since there were no effects of trait anxiety on performance accuracy, these findings suggest that anxiety does not impair the updating function. However, it is a matter for future research to clarify whether the absence of adverse effects of anxiety on the updating function extends to all tasks primarily involving that function.

There are various other fruitful directions for future research, but I will discuss only three of them here. First, the emphasis in processing efficiency theory and attentional control theory is on the effects of anxiety on working memory. However, it is entirely possible that there are bidirectional influences of anxiety on working memory and of working memory on anxiety. For example, in a study involving several test sessions, Matthews and Campbell (2010), found that participants' emotional state (distress and task engagement) influenced working memory, and working memory also influenced emotional state. It would be of considerable value to carry out similar studies focusing more specifically on anxiety as an emotional state.

Second, there is the issue of the relationship between anxiety and motivation. The prediction that anxiety typically impairs performance effectiveness less than processing efficiency is based on the assumption that high levels of anxiety are often associated with high levels of motivation. Indeed, it is enhanced motivation that permits high-anxious individuals and low-anxious individuals to have comparable performance effectiveness in spite of the former's impaired processing efficiency. According to Eysenck and Calvo (1992), anxiety creates worry, and one of the consequences of worrying thoughts (e.g., "I am performing this task poorly"; "I am inept") is to produce enhanced levels of motivation. This is a plausible hypothesis. However, there is relatively little direct evidence on the effects of anxiety on motivation. This is one of the greatest lacunae in the research literature.

Third, there is much evidence that there is considerable heterogeneity among individuals scoring low in trait anxiety. Of particular theoretical importance is the distinction introduced by Derakshan, Eysenck, and Myers (2007) between repressive copers (low in trait anxiety but high in defensiveness) and the truly low anxious (low in trait anxiety and defensiveness). These two groups differ substantially in their behavioral and physiological responses to stressful situations. As yet, however, much remains to be discovered about differences in processing efficiency and performance effectiveness between them.

REFERENCES

Ansari, T. L., & Derakshan, N. (2010). Anxiety impairs inhibitory control but not volitional action control. *Cognition and Emotion, 24,* 241–254.

Ansari, T. L., Derakshan, N., & Richards, A. (2008). Effects of anxiety on task switching: Evidence from the mixed saccade task. *Cognitive, Affective, and Behavioral Neuroscience, 8,* 229–238.

Baddeley, A. D. (1986). *Working memory.* Oxford, UK: Clarendon Press.

Bishop, S. J. (2009). Trait anxiety and impoverished prefrontal control of attention. *Nature Neuroscience, 12,* 92–98.

Blankstein, K. R., Flett, G. L., Boase, P., & Toner, B. B. (1990). Thought listing and endorsement measures of self-referential thinking in test anxiety. *Anxiety Research, 2,* 103–111.

Blankstein, K. R., Toner, B. B., & Flett, G. L. (1989). Test anxiety and the contents of consciousness: Thought listing and endorsement measures. *Journal of Research in Personality, 23,* 269–286.

Channon, S., Baker, J., & Robertson, M. M. (1993). Working memory in clinical depression: An experimental study. *Psychological Medicine, 23,* 87–91.

Christopher, G., & MacDonald, J. (2005). The impact of clinical depression on working memory. *Cognitive Neuropsychiatry, 10,* 379–399.

Clark, L. A., & Watson, D. (1991). Tripartite model of anxiety and depression: Psychometric evidence and taxonomic implications. *Journal of Abnormal Psychology, 100,* 316–336.

de Lissnyder, E., Koster, E. H. W., Derakshan, N., & de Raedt, R. (2010). The association between depressive symptoms and executive control impairments in response to emotional and non-emotional information. *Cognition and Emotion, 24*, 264–280.

Derakshan, N., Ansari, T. L., Hansard, M., Shoker, L., & Eysenck, M. W. (2009). Anxiety, inhibition, efficiency, and effectiveness: An investigation using the antisaccade task. *Experimental Psychology, 56*, 48–55.

Derakshan, N., & Eysenck, M. W. (2009). Anxiety, processing efficiency, and cognitive performance: New developments from attentional control theory. *European Psychologist, 14*, 168–176.

Derakshan, N., & Eysenck, M. W. (2010). Introduction to special issue: Emotional states, attention, and working memory. *Cognition and Emotion, 24*, 189–199.

Derakshan, N., Eysenck, M. W., & Myers, L. B. (2007). Emotional information processing in repressors: The vigilance-avoidance theory. *Cognition and Emotion, 21*, 1585–1614.

Derakshan, N., Smyth, S., & Eysenck, M. W. (2009). Effects of state anxiety on performance using a task-switching paradigm: An investigation of attentional control theory. *Psychonomic Bulletin & Review, 16*, 1112–1117.

Eysenck, M. W. (1997). *Anxiety and cognition: A unified theory*. Hove, UK: Psychology Press.

Eysenck, M. W., & Calvo, M. G. (1992). Anxiety and performance: The processing efficiency theory. *Cognition and Emotion, 6*, 409–434.

Eysenck, M. W., Derakshan, N., Santos, R., & Calvo, M. G. (2007). Anxiety and cognitive performance: Attentional control theory. *Emotion, 7*, 336–353.

Eysenck, M. W., & Keane, M. T. (2010). *Cognitive psychology: A student's handbook* (6th ed.). Hove, UK: Psychology Press.

Eysenck, M. W., Payne, S., & Derakshan, N. (2005). Trait anxiety, visuospatial processing, and working memory. *Cognition and Emotion, 19*, 1214–1228.

Fales, C. L., Barch, D. M., Burgess, G. C., Schaefer, A., Mennin, D. S., Gray, J. R., et al. (2008). Anxiety and cognitive efficiency: Differential modulation of transient and sustained neural activity during a working memory task. *Cognitive, Affective, and Behavioral Neuroscience, 8*, 239–253.

Fournier-Vicente, S., Larigauderie, P., & Gaonac'h, D. (2008). More dissociations and interactions within central executive functioning: A comprehensive latent-variable analysis. *Acta Psychologica, 129*, 32–48.

Friedman, N. P., & Miyake, A. (2004). The relations among inhibition and interference control functions: A latent-variable analysis. *Journal of Experimental Psychology: General, 133*, 101–135.

Hartlage, S., Alloy, L. B., Vazquez, C., & Dyckman, B. (1993). Automatic and effortful processing in depression. *Psychological Bulletin, 113*, 247–278.

Hembree, R. (1988). Correlates, causes, effects, and treatment of test anxiety. *Review of Educational Research, 58*, 47–77.

Joormann, J., & Gotlib, I. H. (2010). Emotion regulation in depression: Relation to cognitive inhibition. *Cognition and Emotion, 24*, 281–298.

Matthews, G., & Campbell, S. E. (2010). Dynamic relationships between stress states and working memory. *Cognition and Emotion, 24*, 357–373.

Miyake, A., Friedman, N. P., Emerson, M. J., Witzki, A. H., Howerter, A., & Wager, T. (2000). The unity and diversity of executive functions and their contributions to complex "frontal lobe" tasks: A latent variable analysis. *Cognitive Psychology, 41*, 49–100.

Monsell, S. (2003). Task switching. *Trends in Cognitive Sciences, 7*, 134–140.

Sarason, I. G. (1988). Anxiety, self-preoccupation and attention. *Anxiety Research, 1*, 3–7.

Savoystyanov, A. N., Tsai, A. C., Liou, M., Levin, E. A., Lee, J.-D., Yurganov, A. V., et al. (2009). EEG correlates of trait anxiety in the stop-signal paradigm. *Neuroscience Letters, 449*, 112–116.

Schwarzer, R. (1990). Current trends in anxiety research. In P. J. D. Drenth, J. A. Sergeant, & J. R. Takens (Eds.), *European perspectives in psychology* (pp. 225–244). Oxford, UK: Wiley.

Walkenhorst, E., & Crowe, S. F. (2009). The effects of state worry and trait anxiety on working memory processes in a normal sample. *Anxiety, Stress, and Coping, 22*, 167–187.

Whitmer, A. J., & Banich, M. T. (2007). Inhibition versus switching deficits in different forms of rumination. *Psychological Science, 18*, 546–553.

CHAPTER 2

The Energetics of Emotional Intelligence

Gerald Matthews
Angela N. Fellner

INTRODUCTION

It is commonplace to observe that some persons appear to be full of energy and mentally alert, whereas others are typically tired and vulnerable to fatigue. However, current accounts of personality may not adequately capture individual differences in mental energy. The new construct of emotional intelligence (EI) offers a promising perspective on this issue. EI refers to a variety of personal qualities said to enhance emotional functioning. One feature of EI that is often cited is a capacity for positive emotion and enthusiasm, and using emotion to motivate action (e.g., Salovey & Mayer, 1990). Thus tests of EI may predict individual differences in energy when the person is exposed to a mental challenge.

This chapter is structured as follows. First, we consider how EI might be related conceptually to individual differences in energization processes, including the maintenance of energy and task engagement in challenging circumstances and the mobilization of general resources for task performance. It is possible that conventional personality traits do not fully capture relevant personal qualities including positive affectivity, self-confidence, sustaining motivation, and constructive mood-regulation. Following this conceptual analysis of the energetics of EI, we review four empirical studies that aimed to test whether EI relates to both subjective energy and objective task performance. These studies investigated the role of

Personality, Cognition, and Emotion edited by Michael W. Eysenck, Małgorzata Fajkowska, and Tomasz Maruszewski. Eliot Werner Publications, Clinton Corners, New York, 2012.

EI in performing highly demanding, stressful tasks; in processing facial emotion; and in learning to use emotional cues in solitary and team performance settings. We conclude that EI may have a more limited role in individual differences in energization than some proponents of the construct might claim.

INDIVIDUAL DIFFERENCES IN ENERGY

First, a brief overview of the place of energy in differential psychology is needed. In fact, the term has two rather different connotations, referring to studies of performance and emotion, respectively. Charles Spearman (1927) attributed general intelligence (g) to mental energy. He stated that "the constancy of total output shows that all the mental activity, just like the physical, consists in ever varying manifestations of one and the same underlying thing, to which may be given the name of energy" (p. 133). In more modern times, the energy metaphor for performance is expressed most directly in the resource theory of attention (Norman & Bobrow, 1975). Some attentional processes require energization through an allocation of resources from a fixed-capacity reservoir. If the demand for resources exceeds capacity, attention is impaired. Resources are hard to define precisely (Navon, 1984) and, perhaps in consequence, it has proved difficult to obtain measures of individual differences in availability. However, recent structural modeling studies suggest that resources may be related to a factor for executive control of attention, which—as Spearman would have predicted—relates to intelligence (Chuderski & Nęcka, 2010; Schweizer, 2010).

In relation to emotion, energy corresponds to a form of subjective arousal. The pivotal work of Robert Thayer (1989, 1996) differentiated energetic and tense arousal as two distinct dimensions of subjective arousal. Other psychometric studies have substantiated this model (Gorynska, 2005; Matthews, Jones, & Chamberlain, 1990). Energy contrasts feelings of vigor, alertness, and activity, with tiredness, passivity, and lack of enterprise. Thayer (1989) conceptualized energy as an index of a biocognitive system, as follows.

> Energetic arousal appears to be a general appetitive or action system that also has an important signal function for self-monitoring and decision-making. It is most readily identifiable through feelings that range from energy, vigor and liveliness to states of fatigue and tiredness. (p. 134)

Validation studies conducted in field and laboratory settings have shown that energetic arousal has distinct antecedents and consequences consistent with this definition (Thayer, 1989).

Logically, subjective feelings of energy might be different from the energization of attentional processes described by resource theory. Nevertheless, it is plausible that a general action system would support enhanced attention, and Thayer (1978, 1989) found that higher energy was related to superior performance on several tasks. The resource theory of Humphreys and Revelle (1984) provides a basis for explaining associations between energetic arousal and attention. The theory (see also Nęcka, 1997) states that high arousal increases the availability of resources for "sustained information transfer," while also reducing the quantity of resources for short-term memory. If subjective energy corresponds to Humphreys and Revelle's arousal construct, energy should be associated with increased resources.

Matthews, Davies, and Lees (1990) tested resource theory by varying the task demands of vigilance and visual searches. Consistent with the Humphreys and Revelle (1984) theory, energy predicted performance only of more demanding tasks—such as vigilance with masked stimuli—and controlled visual search. Energy was unrelated to easier tasks such as automatic visual search that are assumed to require few or no resources. This pattern of results is sharply inconsistent with traditional arousal theory (the Yerkes-Dodson law), which predicts that arousal should be relatively more beneficial to easy than to difficult tasks. Thus, while subjective energy is not a direct index of resource availability, it serves as a useful indirect index of resources.

TABLE 1. Correspondences Between Second-Order Factors and First-Order Scales on the Dundee Stress State Questionnaire

Factor	Scale	Items	Example item	Scale
Task engagement	Energetic Arousal	8	I feel ... vigorous	80
	Task Interest	7	"The content of the task is interesting"	75
	Success Motivation	7	"I want to perform better than most people do"	87
	Concentration	7	"My mind is wandering a great deal (-ve)"	85
Distress	Tension	8	I feel ... nervous	82
	Hedonic Tone (low)	8	I feel ... contented	86
	Confidence-control (low)	6	"I feel confident about my abilities"	80
Worry	Self-focus	8	I am reflecting about myself	85
	Self-esteem	7	"I am worrying about looking foolish (-ve)"	87
	CI (task-relevant)	8	"I have thoughts of ... how much time I have left"	78
	CI (task-irrelevant)	8	"I have thoughts of ... personal worries"	86

Note. CI = Cognitive interference. Based on data of Matthews, Campbell et al. (2002).

Recent work on subjective energy and attention has employed the more elaborate psychometric framework for subjective states developed by Matthews and associates (Matthews, Campbell et al., 2002; Matthews et al., 1999). It is assumed that subjective states of stress, arousal, and fatigue are experienced through the three major domains of affect, motivation, and cognition. The Dundee Stress State Questionnaire (DSSQ) comprises eleven scales, each of which relates to a single domain, as listed in Table 1. These state dimensions are themselves intercorrelated and a second-order factor analysis (Matthews, Campbell et al., 2002) extracted three broader factors, which are also shown in Table 1. Energetic arousal emerges here as a primary marker for a task engagement dimension that is also defined by high motivation and concentration. By contrast, tense arousal—along with negative mood and lack of confidence—relates to a distress dimension. The remaining first-order dimensions collectively define a worry dimension, characterized by intrusive, self-referent thoughts.

The DSSQ has been validated through studies showing that the state factors are appropriately sensitive to task and environmental stressors (Matthews, Campbell et al., 2002; Matthews, Warm, Reinerman, Langheim, & Saxby, 2010a). State response may be linked to the transactional theory of stress and emotion (Lazarus, 1999) through data showing that states relate to appraisal of task demands and choice of coping strategy (Matthews, Campbell et al., 2002). Task engagement relates to challenge appraisal and task-focused coping but is negatively associated with avoidance coping (Matthews & Campbell, 2009).

TABLE 2. Correlations Between Task Engagement and Vigilance in Six Recent Studies of Vigilance, Using Various Tasks

Study	Task/display	Duration	N	r
Matthews et al. (2010b)	Sensory: Air traffic control display	36	186	0.345**
Matthews et al. (2010b)	Cognitive: Letter transformation	36	107	0.294**
Shaw et al. (2010)	Sensory: Degraded single characters	12	210	0.222**
Matthews et al. (2010c)	Sensory (simultaneous): Military tactical display	60	110	0.350**
Matthews et al. (2010c)	Sensory (successive): Military tactical display	60	352	0.221**
Matthews & Campbell (2009)	Cognitive: Rapid information processing	15	144	0.272**

Note. **$p < 0.01$.

Like energetic arousal, the higher-order task engagement factor reliably correlates with performance of demanding vigilance tasks (see Matthews, in press; Matthews et al., 2010a, for reviews). Much of the relevant research has employed high-workload vigilance tasks that show rapid decrements in detection rate and perceptual sensitivity over time. There is considerable evidence that relates vigilance decrement on demanding tasks to depletion of attentional resources (Warm & Dember, 1998). Table 2 summarizes recent studies that show a fairly consistent correlation of about 0.30 between task engagement and perceptual sensitivity on a variety of vigilance tasks. The effect generalizes across both sensory and cognitive vigilance tasks, consistent with a resource mechanism, rather than an influence of engagement on a specific perceptual process. The demands of sensory tasks derive from the psychophysical qualities of the stimulus (e.g., degraded stimuli), whereas cognitive tasks require symbolic processing and, often, the use of working memory. High engagement also benefits both simultaneous tasks—requiring a comparison between stimulus elements to detect the target—and successive tasks, in which information must be integrated in memory across trials. Furthermore, structural equation modeling studies (Helton, Matthews, & Warm, 2009; Matthews et al., 2010b) showed that effects of energy on attention can be attributed to the higher-order task engagement factor.

TRAIT FACTORS AND ENERGY

The studies thus far discussed show that subjective energy states relate to the energization of attention described by resource theory. The next issue is what stable trait factors relate to individual differences in subjective and attentional energization. Are there some individuals who consistently react to challenging tasks with increased energy? Spearman's (1927) identification of intelligence with mental energy provided an initial answer to the question. Recent work has substantiated a link between intelligence and some general attentional resource (Schweizer, 2010), but associations between intelligence and subjective energy are inconsistent across studies (Matthews, 1985; Shaw et al., 2010).

In fact, research on traits for energy has focused on personality and, especially, extraversion-introversion. Ironically, the first major psychobiological theory of extraversion related the trait to reduced arousal and vulnerability to fatigue (Eysenck, 1967). By contrast, the dominant theory in recent years has been reinforcement sensitivity theory (Corr, 2008), which links extraversion (and impulsivity) to a behavioral activation system that regulates reward-driven, approach behavior. According to the theory, the behavioral activation system is more easily activated by reward signals in extraverts and introverts. Because the behavioral activation system is said to control positive, excited emotion, the expectation is that extraverts should tend to show greater energy than introverts. This hypothesis has been supported in a variety of studies, although there are various possible explanations for the correlation between extraversion and positive affect (Lucas & Baird, 2004; Matthews, Deary, & Whiteman, 2009).

Although extraversion is sometimes equated with "positive affectivity," this hypothesis has limitations, especially in a performance context (Matthews et al., 2009). A basic problem is that, in experimentally controlled performance environments, correlations between extraversion and subjective energy are often rather weak (Matthews & Gilliland, 1999). For example, Matthews et al. (2006) found a nonsignificant correlation of 0.08 ($N = 200$) between extraversion and task engagement during performance, but significant correlations of around 0.20 between engagement and both conscientiousness and agreeableness. Matthews et al. (2006) also found that conscientiousness is the strongest Five Factor Model (FFM) predictor of task-focused coping, a coping strategy that tends to maintain positive affect during task performance (Matthews & Campbell, 2009).

Consistent with the subjective data, extraversion is also an inconsistent predictor of attentionally demanding tasks, including vigilance (Matthews et al., 2009). Indeed, extraversion may relate to specific attentional mechanisms rather than some general resource. For example, a series of studies of dual-task performance showed that extravert-introvert differences were dependent on the exact parameters manipulated to increase task difficulty (Szymura, 2010; Szymura & Nęcka, 1998). There appears to be no general advantage for either extraverts or introverts in dual-task performance.

We may then ask if the FFM really captures those stable individual dispositions that confer high energy during performance. Perhaps standard personality theory is missing some important feature of positive affectivity. The remainder of this chapter will explore the potential of EI as a predictor of positive mood and energy, and related attentional processes. Perhaps EI represents a missing link between character and positive emotion that goes beyond current understandings of personality.

EMOTIONAL ENERGETICS AND INTELLIGENCE

Definitions and conceptualization of EI have been much debated without any precise specification of the construct emerging (Matthews, Zeidner, & Roberts, 2002). One of the more satisfactory definitions of EI has been provided by Mayer, Salovey, and Caruso (2000), who define EI in terms of four components or branches: perceiving and identifying emotion, assimilating emotion into thought, understanding emotion, and managing emotion. Some authors have also suggested that regulating emotions of self and others represents a fundamental distinction between different elements of EI (Goleman, 2001). Other qualities said to be central to EI include empathy, expressing emotion, and self-confidence (Zeidner, Matthews, & Roberts, 2009). A general difficulty here is that definitions of EI tend to be overinclusive in describing a multitude of personal qualities that may not be strongly interrelated (Matthews, Zeidner et al., 2002).

Overlapping with controversies over definition, researchers have proposed sharply different methodologies for assessment of EI. Normal practice in intelligence research would suggest that EI should be assessed by objective tests with right or wrong answers. Mayer et al. (2000) describe their model of EI as "ability based" and they have developed tests on this basis, including the well-known Mayer-Salovey-Caruso Emotional Intelligence Test (MSCEIT). For example, their emotion perception branch is assessed by tests such as recognizing facial emotion, and emotion management is assessed by asking the person to select the best course of action for dealing with an emotive situation. These tests raise two fundamental issues (Matthews, Zeidner et al., 2002). First, by contrast with standard intelligence test items, it is difficult to determine the objectively correct answer to emotional problems. Mayer and coworkers (Mayer et al., 2000; Mayer, Salovey, Caruso, & Sitarenios, 2003) recommend scoring according to group consensus, or according to expert judgment. Second, the test items assess the person's explicit knowledge of how to deal with an emotional issue, but not his or her actual skills for emotion management (Brody, 2004). For instance, a psychology undergraduate might be able to describe cognitive therapy for emotional disorder but have no actual skills for helping clients.

An alternative measurement strategy is to rely on self-reports, and there is indeed a plethora of questionnaires that purport to measure EI. The limitations of using self-report to assess ability are obvious and it is difficult to see how a questionnaire could substitute for objective testing. There are two more subtle rationales for using questionnaires in EI research. The first is that EI should be reconceptualized as an element of personality rather than ability. Proponents of trait EI (Petrides, Furnham, & Mavroveli, 2007) have proposed that personality dimensions directly related to emotional functioning can be separated as a distinct field of trait research. An overall trait EI relating effective adaptation to emotional challenges may then be defined in relation to a number of more narrowly defined traits. A second rationale is that, even if EI remains conceptualized as an ability, some specific facets of EI—

TABLE 3. Constructs Related to Energization in Current Models of EI

Source	Construct (scale and/or concept)
Goleman (1995)	"Being able to motivate oneself and persist in the face of frustrations"
Salovey & Mayer (1990)	Motivating emotions: "I believe I can do almost anything I set out to do"
Bar-On (1997)	Happiness, optimism
Sala (2002)	Achievement orientation: "Optimistic striving to improve performance"
Petrides & Furnham (2003)	Trait happiness, optimism, self-motivation
Tett et al. (2005)	Motivating emotions

such as styles of mood regulation—may be operationalized via questionnaires. For example, Salovey, Mayer, Goldman, Turvey, and Palfai's (1995) work on the Trait Meta-Mood Scale (TMMS) has validated dimensions of clarity of thinking about mood, attention to moods, and effective mood repair.

In this chapter our concern is whether it is legitimate to treat individual differences in energy as one of various facets of EI. In fact, a fairly persistent theme in conceptualizations of EI is the idea of motivating oneself through positive emotions. The person who can remain optimistic and cheerful in the face of challenges may be more emotionally intelligent than someone who is easily discouraged. Note that positive emotionality should be distinguished from variability in negative emotional responses to challenge. Remaining calm under pressure may also be an attribute of high EI, but it is distinct from positive emotion. Table 3 summarizes some of the guises under which positive emotion has been attributed to high EI.

A closer look at different conceptualizations of EI suggests four somewhat different themes:

- *Positive affectivity.* Some individuals may generally be dispositionally optimistic and happy.

- *Self-confidence and self-esteem.* Some people may have positive beliefs about their skills for managing emotion, even in difficult circumstances.

- *Achievement motivation.* People may differ in the extent to which they retain a sense of purpose and hope in adversity. Maintaining a positive mood may enhance motivation.

- *Mood regulation.* People use a variety of strategies for monitoring and regulating emotional states. Some of these strategies may be more effective than others in maintaining positive mood and energizing adaptive behavior.

However, identifying EI with positive affectivity may be problematic in that it confounds an outcome (e.g., positive mood) with the processes from which the outcome derives (e.g., superior emotion regulation). Relating EI to self-esteem may be similarly questionable. Indeed, narcissistic individuals may have high self-esteem but poor social adaptation. It seems more satisfactory to relate EI to adaptive processes such as using positive moods in the service of effective self-motivation and more effective mood repair (e.g., Salovey & Mayer, 1990).

To summarize, a case can be made that EI may be more predictive of subjective energy in demanding situations than are standard personality traits. In performance settings more emotionally intelligent individuals may be better able to maintain positive mood and task-focus even when overloaded by the cognitive demands of the task. The less emotionally intelligent person may be prone to experience fatigue and disengagement from the task. It follows that EI should also relate to objective performance of demanding tasks that are known to be sensitive to variation in subjective energy. In the next section, we summarize some recent studies that tested these hypotheses.

EMPIRICAL STUDIES OF EMOTIONAL INTELLIGENCE
AND PERFORMANCE

We will review findings from four studies that shared some common methodological features, but that also included differences in approach (see Table 4 for a summary). In each case participants performed a mentally demanding task or tasks. There were two overarching aims for these studies. The first was to investigate whether EI related to stress response and choice of coping strategy during performance. The second aim was to test whether EI related to performance. If EI is associated with higher task engagement and more effective coping, the resource model previously described (Matthews et al., 2010a) suggests that EI should also be associated with superior objective performance on a range of attentionally demanding tasks.

To investigate individual differences in subjective stress and energy, the Dundee Stress State Questionnaire (Matthews, Campbell et al, 2002) was administered before and after performance. The critical state dimension in the present context was task engagement, which includes subjective energy. It was hypothesized that EI would relate to high levels of engagement during performance. In addition, studies investigated whether EI related to lower levels of stress in the form of reduced distress and lower worry. Studies 1–3 also administered a measure of coping strategies used to deal with the challenges of the performance tasks, the Coping Inventory for Task Situations (Matthews & Campbell, 1998). It was expected that EI would relate to greater use of task-focused coping and less avoidance coping, a style of coping compatible with higher subjective engagement. We also tested whether EI was associated with emotion-focused coping, which tends to relate to distress and worry.

The rationale for choices of performance task was as follows. Conceptualizations of EI suggest that EI should facilitate performance energization but have little to say about which specific cognitive processes might be most

TABLE 4. Summary of Four Studies of EI and Performance

Study	N	Task(s)	EI measures
Matthews et al. (2006)	200	"Four task conditions: control task + three stressful tasks"	MSCEIT
Fellner et al. (2007)	129	"Facial emotion perception + controlled search for facial emotion targets"	Trait EI
Fellner et al. (2006)	180	"Discriminating learning with emotional or neutral cues"	Trait EI
Fellner et al. (2009)	300	"Discriminating learning with emotional cue: solo and two team performance conditions"	Trait EI

sensitive to EI. The resource model (Matthews et al., 2010a) suggests that high EI might enhance performance on a variety of cognitively demanding tasks. Thus Study 1 included two high-workload tasks (vigilance and working memory) that were potentially sensitive to subjective energy. Two other task conditions in Study 1 were geared toward investigating subjective response, but not performance—reading magazines (nonstressful control condition) and attempting to solve impossible anagrams.

The subsequent studies addressed the hypothesis that EI may relate specifically to tasks that require processing of explicitly emotional stimuli. Study 2 used two tasks to investigate identification and attention to facial emotional stimuli. It was hypothesized that EI would relate to faster recognition of brief "microexpressions" of emotion and to faster, more accurate visual search for specific facial emotions, such as anger and happiness. Study 3 turned from investigating attentionally demanding tasks to exploring whether EI relates to learning to use facial emotion information as a critical cue in discriminating different categories of people ("terrorists" vs. "nonterrorists"). Perhaps more emotionally intelligent persons are quicker to figure out the relevance of emotional cues in making such discriminations. Study 4 used a similar paradigm but also introduced a team performance condition. Given the importance of the social context for emotions, it was hypothesized that EI might be more strongly related to energization processes in a team rather than a solo context.

The studies also confronted two common psychometric issues for research on EI. One difficulty is that, as previously discussed, there are a variety of instruments that claim to measure EI, but none seem ideal. It is unclear whether performance-based ability tests for EI are more predictive of individual differences in energization than are questionnaires based on a trait EI conceptualization. In this research the first study made use of the Mayer et al. (2003) MSCEIT as an ability test. Since the test failed to relate to task engagement, the remaining studies switched to a trait EI approach, using questionnaire assessments of EI.

A further general problem with research on EI is that measures of the construct, especially questionnaire measures, tend to correlate substantially with general personality and/or ability measures. Reports of criterion validity for EI measures may simply be an artifact of these overlaps, and it is thus important to check that EI measures have *incremental* validity in relation to personality and ability as predictors of criteria related to emotional functioning. All the studies described here included a scale for the FFM, and all but the first one included an ability test.

Study 1: EI and Stress Response to High-Workload Tasks

Definitions of EI suggest that emotionally intelligent individuals may be especially adept at maintaining energy and performance motivation in adverse or challenging circumstances. This hypothesis was tested by Matthews et al. (2006) in a study that required participants to perform tasks that were designed to be especially stressful. Participants were randomly assigned to one of four task conditions: read-

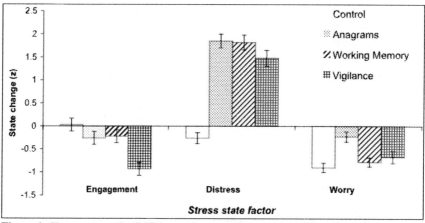

Figure 1. Change scores for DSSQ state factors in four task conditions. Error bars indicate standard errors.

ing magazines (nonstressful control condition), a difficult vigilance task requiring discrimination of the lengths of flickering lines, a working memory task in which time pressure was high, and an impossible anagrams task (the anagrams had no solution). The three stress tasks were chosen because it was believed that they would elicit qualitatively different stressful experiences. For example, it was expected that the vigilance task would provoke a decrease in task engagement. These expectations were confirmed, as seen in Figure 1, which shows the pattern of DSSQ responses to the tasks. All three tasks increased distress but only vigilance lowered task engagement. Worry was elevated by the impossible anagrams. Engagement and distress did not change in the control condition.

Table 5 shows the key data from this study—that is, associations between overall EI (as measured by the MSCEIT), and subjective state and coping. Correlations

TABLE 5. Pearson Correlations Between EI and Coping and Post-Task State Factors in Four Task Conditions

Condition	Coping Scales (CITS-S)			State Factors (DSSQ)		
	Task-focus	Emotion-focus	Avoidance	Task engagement	Distress	Worry
Control	-0.12	-0.37**	-0.36**	0.10	-0.32**	-0.41*
Anagrams	0.09	-0.14	-0.11	0.06	-0.10	-0.24
Working memory	0.04	-0.20	-0.20	0.26	0.15	-0.21
Vigilance	0.12	-0.11	-0.11	-0.02	0.18	-0.14
Whole sample	0.03	-0.18**	-0.17*	0.11	-0.02	-0.23**

Note. CIT-S = Coping Inventory for Task Situations–State. $^*p < 0.05$; $^{**}p < 0.01$.

are given for each condition and overall. There is no evidence that higher MSCEIT scores relate to higher task engagement, contrary to the energization hypothesis. EI was also unrelated to performance on the vigilance and working memory tasks. The MSCEIT related to other aspects of stress, including lower distress and worry, and reduced emotion-focused and avoidance coping. EI seemed more strongly related to lower stress in the control condition than during performance of stressful tasks. Controlling for the FFM, the MSCEIT remained associated with reduced worry and reduced avoidance coping. Thus higher-ability EI did not appear to relate to maintenance of energy and task-directed coping across a range of tasks.

Studies 2–4: Trait EI and Subjective State

The remaining studies investigated trait EI—emotional intelligence conceptualized as a set of personality traits—rather than ability EI as a predictor of subjective and objective indices of energization. Positive mood and optimism feature more strongly in accounts of trait EI than in the Mayer-Salovey model (e.g., Petrides & Furnham, 2003), and so trait EI might be more predictive of energization. These studies also used the Saucier (2002) adjectival markers to assess the FFM. Associations among trait EI, personality, and subjective state were similar in each of Studies 2–4, and so we first present data pooled across studies ($N = 609$) before looking at the performance data for each study separately.

Several trait EI measures were used in Studies 2 and 3, including selected scales from the Trait Emotional Intelligence Questionnaire (TEIQue; Petrides et al., 2007), the Schutte Self-Report Inventory (Schutte et al., 1998), and the Trait Meta-Mood Scale (TMMS; Salovey et al., 1995). These scales were substantially intercorrelated and showed similar patterns of relationships with other criteria. Here we report only data from the TMMS, which was also administered in Study 4, but results were similar for the other trait EI scales. We focused on the TMMS because it appears to be more distinct from general personality than other trait EI scales. Table 6 gives the correlations between the three subscales of the TMMS and the FFM for the pooled data. Results were broadly similar to those obtained in other studies (e.g., Warwick & Nettelbeck, 2004). Generally, superior mood regulation related to extraversion, conscientiousness, agreeableness, and open-

TABLE 6. Intercorrelations of TMMS and FFM

	E	N	A	C	O
Attention	0.23**	0.04	0.46**	0.12**	0.23**
Clarity	0.28**	-0.30**	0.28**	0.27**	0.22**
Repair	0.25**	-0.32**	0.43**	0.26**	0.16**

Note. E = extraversion; N = neuroticism; A = agreeableness; C = conscientiousness; O = openness. **$p < 0.01$. Data from Studies 2–4; $N = 608$.

TABLE 7. Intercorrelations of TMMS and Pre- and Post-Task DSSQ

| | Pre-task | | | Post-task | |
Engage	Distress	Worry	Engage	Distress	Worry
0.11**	-0.28**	0.05	0.09*	-0.03	-0.06
0.27**	-0.42**	-0.23*	0.09*	-0.25**	-0.18**
0.28**	-0.40**	-0.12**	0.10**	-0.20**	-0.09**

Note. *$p < 0.05$; **$p < 0.01$. Data from Studies 2–4; $N = 608$.

ness, although correlation magnitudes were modest. Neuroticism related to poorer clarity and mood repair but not to attention.

Table 7 gives correlations between the TMMS and subjective state, measured prior to and following task performance (tasks are further discussed below). All three TMMS scales related to higher engagement pre- and post-task, although the correlational magnitudes in the post-task data were small ($rs \leq 0.10$). The TMMS also tended to relate to lower distress and worry; clarity and repair were moderately related to lower distress. In addition, the TMMS scales tended to relate to more adaptive forms of coping (i.e., higher task-focus, lower emotion-focus and avoidance), although not all the TMMS-coping associations attained significance.

The correlations between the TMMS and DSSQ were consistent with expectations, but there is a concern that they may be an artifact of the overlap between the TMMS and the FFM shown in Table 6. To test whether the TMMS has *incremental* validity as a predictor of task engagement, two-step hierarchical multiple regressions were run. The FFM were entered at the first step, followed by the three TMMS subscales. Separate regressions were run for each pre- and post-task DSSQ factor. Table 8 shows the results. The final row of the table shows the

TABLE 8. Summary Statistics for Regressions of DSSQ Factors on FFM and TMMS Scales

| | | Pre-task | | | Post-task | |
	Engage	Distress	Worry	Engage	Distress	Worry
FMM	0.12**	0.29**	0.14**	0.03**	0.09**	0.07**
TMMS	0.03**	0.06**	0.02**	0.00	0.03**	0.01**
TMMS Sig. βs	Clarity: $\beta = 0.14**$	Clarity: $\beta = -0.16**$	Clarity: $\beta = -0.18**$		Clarity: $\beta = -0.13**$	Clarity: $\beta = -0.13**$
	Repair: $\beta = 0.13*$	Repair: $\beta = -0.18**$			Repair: $\beta = 0.12*$	

Note. *$p < 0.05$; **$p < 0.01$. Data from Studies 2–4; $N = 608$.

TMMS predictors that were independently significant in the final equation. The FFM predicted each of the state criteria. The TMMS added significantly to the variance explained for pre-task but not post-task engagement. In the pre-task data, both clarity and repair added to the variance explained. Thus the TMMS does not seem to relate to task engagement experienced during the task, with the FFM controlled. The regressions also suggest that the TMMS may be more robustly associated with other aspects of stress state. Clarity emerged as a consistent predictor of lower distress and worry. Next we consider the performance data on a study-by-study basis.

Study 2: Trait EI and Processing of Facial Emotion

The aim of Study 2 (Fellner et al., 2007) was to test whether trait EI related to more efficient perception and attention to facial emotion. A small number of prior studies have attempted to relate EI to performance on tasks requiring processing of facial emotion, with mixed results (e.g., Austin, 2005; Petrides & Furnham, 2003). In the present study, two tasks were used. The first was Ekman's (2003) Micro-Expressions of Emotion (METT) task, which requires the person to recognize the basic facial emotion shown in brief (200 ms) displays. It is thought that micro-expressions may betray the person's true emotion even when he or she is trying to conceal it. Because emotion perception is a core feature of EI, more emotionally intelligent individuals should be better at detecting micro-expressions. The METT is presented as a learning paradigm, in which the person is shown videos to train better recognition. Here recognition accuracy was measured at three points during performance. As well as trait EI and the FFM, predictors in this study included two tests of cognitive ability—the letter series and esoteric analogies tests (Stankov, 2000).

The second task tested controlled attention to facial emotion, presumed to be higher in emotionally intelligent individuals. Following the Shiffrin and Schneider (1977) paradigm, participants were required to search arrays of 1–4 faces on each trial for a target emotion, responding "Yes" or "No" by pressing one of two response keys. Targets were one of five basic emotions. The study also employed a neutral search task, searching for instances of nuts (e.g., peanut, cashew). Nuts were used because they are biological objects that are divided into familiar categories.

Correlations were computed between the predictor variables and performance indices, including mean accuracy on the METT and mean accuracy and response time (RT) on the facial emotion and neutral search tasks. No significant correlations were found between any of the trait EI scales and any performance index. However, various other trait and state predictors were obtained. The strongest trait predictor was the Esoteric Analogies ability test, which correlated with facial emotion search RT ($r = -0.248$, $p < 0.01$), neutral search RT ($r = -0.248$, $p < 0.01$), and METT recognition accuracy at all three stages of practice (range of rs: 0.279, $p < 0.01$ to 0.222, $p < 0.05$). Task engagement correlated with accuracy and speed on both facial and neutral search tasks (range of rs: 0.35, $p <$ 0.01 to 0.192, $p < 0.05$). Higher engagement also correlated with superior METT performance following the final phase of practice ($r = 0.185$, $p < 0.01$). Consistent with the introductory review of individual differences in engagement, both cognitive ability and state task engagement related to performance on these attentionally demanding tasks. However, trait EI did not predict performance.

Study 3: Trait EI and Discrimination Learning

Study 2 failed to support the hypothesis that trait EI relates to processing of facial emotion. However, EI might be more strongly related to other aspects of cognition. Study 3 (Fellner, Matthews, Warm, Zeidner, & Roberts, 2006) aimed to test whether EI relates to use of facial emotion as a cue in a discrimination learning task. A limitation of standard facial emotion perception tests is that emotion signals may have different meanings in different contexts. We may learn that one friend becomes withdrawn when sad, whereas another friend appreciates conversation. It is plausible that more emotionally intelligent persons are faster to learn what a facial emotion signifies in a specific context.

Participants in Study 3 were asked to judge whether 3-D animated characters, generated by a virtual reality program, were terrorists. Characters could be programmed to display realistic, fairly mild facial expressions. Three alternate cues were available to indicate that a character was a "terrorist": happy emotion, sad emotion, or a neutral, nonemotive cue (shape of hat). Participants were randomly allocated to one of three conditions, which varied in the single specific cue that identified terrorists. Participants were required to learn by trial and error. Initially, participants guessed whether the character was a terrorist, and following each trial they were provided with feedback on whether their choice was correct. There were one hundred trials, analyzed as four successive blocks of 25 trials. The method was otherwise similar to that of Study 2.

Initial data analyses showed that participants learned more effectively with the two emotion cues than the neutral cue, although all cues were psychophysically matched for stimulus salience. Subsequent analyses tested correlations between the predictor variables and discrimination accuracy in the first and last block of trials. In fact, correlations between the trait EI scales and performance did not exceed chance levels. In the final block (block 4), all correlations between the EI scales and accuracy were nonsignificant. The personality and general intelligence measures also failed to predict performance. By contrast, the DSSQ state scales did relate to learning. Although state was initially uncorrelated with the DSSQ factors, in block 4 task engagement related to higher accuracy and distress related to poorer performance (varying somewhat across cue condition). Again, data suggest that high engagement indexes more effective processing of emotional stimuli, whereas trait EI is irrelevant to performance.

Study 4: Trait EI and Team Performance

Previous studies failed to confirm that trait EI predicts performance, but EI may be more relevant in a team situation than during solo performance. Conceptualizations of EI tend to overlap with social competence and several trait EI scales include facets defined by social functioning, such as social awareness and social skills (Schutte et al., 1998). Organizational psychologists (e.g., Jordan, Ashkanasy, & Ascough, 2007) have especially emphasized the role of EI in teamwork. Emotionally intelligent individuals are said to be more aware of the emotions of others and better able to manage interpersonal emotion, qualities that enhance the cohesiveness and performance of teams. Thus high EI should relate to greater task engagement and more effective performance in team settings.

Study 4 ($N = 300$; Fellner et al., 2009) employed the same discrimination learning task as did Study 3, except that the critical cue was always the positive emotional face and the reference to terrorists was removed. Subjects were allocated to one of three conditions, including a solo performance condition. In the remaining conditions, participants performed in two-person teams. In the cooperation condition, they worked together to learn the discrimination, whereas in the competition condition participants worked separately but were allowed to talk to each other. Otherwise the method was similar to Study 3, except that participants in the two-team conditions also completed a scale for their subjective evaluation of the effectiveness of teamwork—the Teamwork Assessment (Zhuang et al., 2008).

Performing in a team, as opposed to solo, had two general benefits. First, performance accuracy in both team conditions was higher than solo performance. Second, team performance tended to evoke higher engagement and lower distress than the solo condition, especially in the cooperation condition. However, as in Study 3, trait EI was unrelated to performance, but high task engagement and low distress correlated with superior discrimination accuracy in both solo and team conditions. In addition to correlating with subjective state (DSSQ) similar to the associations shown in Table 7, the three TMMS subscales also correlated significantly with the Teamwork Assessment scale (range of rs: 0.303 to 0.367, $p < 0.01$). Thus, although EI was unrelated to actual performance, it did relate to perceptions of more effective teamwork. A limitation of the study is that it involved a relatively brief period of interpersonal interaction. It is possible that EI would assume more importance over more extended teamwork, as would be the case in a real-life job situation.

CONCLUSIONS

Although a variety of different performance tasks were used in this research, some consistent themes emerge. First, we could not substantiate any relationships between EI and objective performance. Although scales included some of direct relevance—such as the TEIQue emotion perception scale and the TMMS attention scale—these instruments appeared to be unrelated to perception, attention, and learning with emotional stimuli. Even in a team setting, trait EI was not related to performance. By contrast, the consistent positive associations between higher task engagement and performance match previous findings linking engagement to superior performance on a range of demanding tasks (Matthews et al., 2010a). Ironically, in Study 2 cognitive ability was a better predictor of emotional information processing than trait EI, consistent with findings that ability relates to superior attention (Schweizer, 2010). Cognitive ability failed to relate to discrimination learning in Studies 3 and 4, however, perhaps because the processing required is more implicit in nature.

The EI measures were more predictive of subjective state and coping than they were of learning. However, EI appears to relate more strongly to distress and worry than to task engagement. With the Big Five personality traits controlled, neither the MSCEIT nor the trait EI scales predicted engagement during task performance (i.e., as assessed post-task). By contrast, the MSCEIT was uniquely associated with lower worry in Study 1, and the TMMS clarity scale related to lower post-task distress and worry with personality controlled in the analyses of the pooled data from Studies 2–4. We also found evidence that the TMMS relates to perceptions of more effective teamwork in Study 4.

Although an a priori case for relating EI to energization can be made, it was not supported by the evidence. Given that the present research could only sample tasks and social contexts for performance to a limited extent, we cannot exclude the possibility that emotionally intelligent individuals are better at maintaining energy and engagement in other circumstances, but thus far findings are not promising. As argued elsewhere (e.g., Zeidner et al., 2009), current conceptions of EI tend to be overinclusive and more restrictive definitions may be more successful. The TMMS, for example, may relate more to regulation of stress and negative emotion than to maintaining positive affect.

More generally, the research surveyed here further demonstrates the importance of individual differences in energization processes. Consistent with Thayer's (1989) view of energetic arousal as a marker for a broad-based biocognitive system, evidence shows that task engagement relates to performance on a variety of performance tasks. Findings are generally consistent with the hypothesis that energy and engagement index attentional resource availability (Matthews, Davies, & Lees, 1990). Further work might explore specific executive functions in order to clarify the nature of "resources" (Matthews et al., 2010a, 2010b). Another possibility is that EI (or at least its self-related facets) relates especially to the energetics of self-relevant processing. This idea might be explored through studies of EI and relevant higher-order cognitive functions, such as constructing and maintaining mental worlds of the self and the surrounding social world (Sedek, Brzezicka, & von Hecker, 2010) and the processing of autobiographical memories performed by a working self-memory (Conway & Pleydell-Pearce, 2000).

The enigma that remains is the nature of stable dispositional traits that predict higher engagement in performance contexts. Standard traits such as conscientiousness are only modestly associated with engagement, and—as we have seen—measures of EI add little to our ability to predict levels of engagement. It may be that engagement is more strongly related to situational cognitive processes (such as appraisal and coping) than to general traits.

REFERENCES

Austin, E. J. (2005). Emotional intelligence and emotional information processing. *Personality and Individual Differences, 39*, 403–414.

Bar-On, R. (1997). *The Emotional Intelligence Inventory (EQ-i): Technical manual.* Toronto: Multi-Health Systems.

Brody, N. (2004). What cognitive intelligence is and what emotional intelligence is not. *Psychological Inquiry, 15*, 234–238.

Chuderski, A., & Nęcka, E. (2010). Intelligence and cognitive control. In A. Gruszka, G. Matthews, & B. Szymura (Eds.), *Handbook of individual differences in cognition: Attention, memory, and executive control* (pp. 263–282). New York: Springer-Verlag.

Conway, M. A., & Pleydell-Pearce, W. (2000). The construction of autobiographical memories in the self-memory system. *Psychological Review, 107*, 261–288.

Corr, P. J. (2008). Reinforcement Sensitivity Theory (RST): Introduction. In P. L. Corr (Ed.), *The Reinforcement Sensitivity Theory of personality* (pp. 1–43). Cambridge, UK: Cambridge University Press.

Ekman, P. (2003). *Emotions revealed: Recognizing faces and feelings to improve communication and emotional life.* New York: Holt.

Eysenck, H. J. (1967) *The biological basis of personality.* Springfield, IL: Charles C. Thomas.

Fellner, A. N., Matthews, G., Funke, G. J., Emo, A. K., Pérez-González, J. C., Zeidner, M., et al. (2007). The effects of emotional intelligence on visual search of emotional stimuli and emotion identification. *Proceedings of the Human Factors and Ergonomics Society, 51*, 845–849.

Fellner, A., Matthews, G., Warm, J. S., Shockley, K., MacCann, C., & Roberts, R. D. (2009, July). Emotional intelligence and teamwork: An experimental study. Paper presented at the Biennial Meeting of the International Society for the Study of Individual Differences, Evanston, IL.

Fellner, A., Matthews, G., Warm, J. S., Zeidner, M., & Roberts, R. D. (2006). Learning to discriminate terrorists: The effects of emotional intelligence and emotive cues. *Proceedings of the Human Factors and Ergonomics Society, 50*, 1619–1623.

Goleman, D. (1995). *Emotional intelligence: Why it can matter more than IQ.* New York: Bantam Books.

Goleman, D (2001). Emotional intelligence: Issues in paradigm building. In C. Cherniss & D. Goleman (Eds.), *The emotionally intelligent workplace* (pp. 13–26). San Francisco: Jossey-Bass.

Goryńska, E. (2005). A three-dimensional model of mood research with the "UWIST" mood adjective check list (UMACL). *Studia Psychologiczne, 43*, 35–46.

Helton, W. S., Matthews, G., & Warm, J. S. (2009). Stress state mediation between environmental variables and performance: The case of noise and vigilance. *Acta Psychologica, 130*, 204–213.

Humphreys, M. S., & Revelle, W. (1984). Personality, motivation, and performance: A theory of the relationship between individual differences and information processing. *Psychological Review, 91*, 153–184.

Jordan, P. J., Ashkanasy, N. M., & Ascough, K. (2007). Emotional intelligence in organizational behavior and industrial-organizational psychology. In G. Matthews, M. Zeidner, & R. D. Roberts (Eds.), *Emotional intelligence: Knowns and unknowns* (pp. 356–375). New York: Oxford University Press.

Lazarus, R. S. (1999). *Stress and emotion: A new synthesis*. New York: Springer Publishing.

Lucas, R. E., & Baird, M. (2004). Extraversion and emotional reactivity. *Journal of Personality and Social Psychology, 86*, 473–485.

Matthews, G. (1985). The effects of extraversion and arousal on intelligence test performance. *British Journal of Psychology, 76*, 479–493.

Matthews, G. (in press). Personality and individual differences in cognitive fatigue. In P. L. Ackerman (Ed.), *Cognitive fatigue: The current status and future for research and applications* (pp. 209–227). Washington, DC: American Psychological Association.

Matthews, G., & Campbell, S. E. (1998). Task-induced stress and individual differences in coping. *Proceedings of the Human Factors and Ergonomics Society, 42*, 821–825.

Matthews, G., & Campbell, S. E. (2009). Sustained performance under overload: Personality and individual differences in stress and coping. *Theoretical Issues in Ergonomics Science, 10*, 417–442.

Matthews, G., Campbell, S. E., Falconer, S. Joyner, L., Huggins, J., Gilliland, K., et al. (2002). Fundamental dimensions of subjective state in performance settings: Task engagement, distress, and worry. *Emotion, 2*, 315–340.

Matthews, G., Davies, D. R., & Lees, J. L. (1990). Arousal, extraversion, and individual differences in resource availability. *Journal of Personality and Social Psychology, 59*, 150–168.

Matthews, G., Deary, I. J., & Whiteman, M. C. (2009) *Personality traits* (3rd ed.). Cambridge, UK: Cambridge University Press.

Matthews, G., Emo, A. K., Funke, G., Zeidner, M., Roberts, R. D., Costa, P. T., Jr., et al. (2006). Emotional intelligence, personality, and task-induced stress. *Journal of Experimental Psychology: Applied, 12*, 96–107.

Matthews, G., & Gilliland, K. (1999.) The personality theories of H. J. Eysenck and J. A. Gray: A comparative review. *Personality and Individual Differences, 26*, 583–626.

Matthews, G., Jones, D. M., & Chamberlain, A. G. (1990). Refining the measurement of mood: The UWIST Mood Adjective Checklist. *British Journal of Psychology, 81*, 17–42.

Matthews, G., Joyner, L., Gilliland, K., Campbell, S. E., Falconer, S., & Huggins, J. (1999). Validation of a comprehensive stress state questionnaire: Towards a state "Big Three." In I. Mervielde, I. J. Dreary, F. DeFruyt, & F. Ostendorf (Eds.), *Personality psychology in Europe* (Vol. 7, pp. 335–350). Tilburg, The Netherlands: Tilburg University Press.

Matthews, G., Warm, J. S., Reinerman, L. E., Langheim, L. K., & Saxby, D. J. (2010a). Task engagement, attention, and executive control. In A. Gruszka, G. Matthews, & B. Szymura (Eds.), *Handbook of individual differences in cognition: Attention, memory, and executive control* (pp. 205–230). New York: Springer-Verlag.

Matthews, G., Warm, J. S., Reinerman, L. E., Langheim, L. K., Washburn, D. A., & Tripp, L. (2010b). Task engagement, cerebral blood flow velocity, and diagnostic monitoring for sustained attention. *Journal of Experimental Psychology: Applied, 16*, 187–203.

Matthews, G., Warm, J. S., Shaw, T. H., & Finomore, V. (2010c). A multivariate test battery for predicting vigilance. *Proceedings of the Human Factors and Ergonomics Society, 54*, 1072–1076.

Matthews, G., Zeidner, M., & Roberts, R. D. (2002). *Emotional intelligence: Science and myth*. Cambridge, MA: MIT Press.

Mayer, J. D., Salovey, P., & Caruso, D. R. (2000). Models of emotional intelligence. In R. J. Sternberg (Ed.), *Handbook of human intelligence* (2nd ed., pp. 396–422). New York: Cambridge University Press.

Mayer, J. D., Salovey, P., Caruso, D. R., & Sitarenios, G. (2003). Measuring emotional intelligence with the MSCEIT v2.0. *Emotion, 3*, 97–105.

Navon, D. (1984). Resources: A theoretical soup stone? *Psychological Review, 91*, 216–234.

Nęcka, E. (1997). Attention, working memory and arousal: Concepts apt to account for "the process of intelligence." In G. Matthews (Ed.), *Cognitive science perspectives on personality and emotion* (pp. 503–554). Amsterdam: Elsevier.

Norman, D. A., & Bobrow, D. B. (1975). On data-limited and resource-limited processes. *Cognitive Psychology, 7*, 44–64.

Petrides, K. V., & Furnham, A. (2003). Trait emotional intelligence: Behavioural validation in two studies of emotion recognition and reactivity to mood induction. *European Journal of Personality, 17*, 39–57.

Petrides, K. V., Furnham, A., & Mavroveli, S. (2007). Trait emotional intelligence: Moving forward in the field of EI. In G. Matthews, M. Zeidner, & R. D. Roberts (Eds.), *The science of emotional intelligence: Knowns and unknowns* (pp. 151–166). New York: Oxford University Press.

Sala, F. (2002). *Emotional Competence Inventory (ECI): Technical manual*. Boston: Hay/McBer Group.

Salovey, P., & Mayer, J. D. (1990). Emotional intelligence. *Imagination, Cognition, and Personality, 9*, 185–211.

Salovey, P., Mayer, J. D, Goldman, S., Turvey, C., & Palfai, T. (1995). Emotional attention, clarity, and repair: Exploring emotional intelligence using the Trait Meta-Mood Scale. In J. W. Pennebaker (Ed.), *Emotion, disclosure, and health* (pp. 125–154). Washington, DC: American Psychological Association.

Saucier, G. (2002). Orthogonal markers for orthogonal factors: The case of the Big Five. *Journal of Research in Personality, 36*, 1–31.

Schutte, N. S., Malouff, J. M., Hall, L. E., Haggerty, D. J., Cooper, J. T., Golden, C. J., et al. (1998). Development and validation of a measure of emotional intelligence. *Personality and Individual Differences, 25*, 167–177.

Schweizer, K. (2010). The relationship of attention and intelligence. In A. Gruszka, G. Matthews, & B. Szymura (Eds.), *Handbook of individual differences in cognition: Attention, memory, and executive control* (pp. 247–262). New York: Springer-Verlag.

Sedek, G., Brzezicka, A., & von Hecker, U. (2010). The unique cognitive limitation in subclinical depression: The impairment of mental model construction. In A. Gruszka, G. Matthews, & B. Szymura (Eds.), *Handbook of individual differences in cognition: Attention, memory, and executive control* (pp. 335–352). New York: Springer-Verlag.

Shaw, T. H., Matthews, G., Warm, J., Finomore, V., Silverman, L., & Costa, P. T., Jr. (2010). Individual differences in vigilance: Personality, ability and states of stress. *Journal of Research in Personality, 44*, 297–308.

Shiffrin, R. M., & Schneider, W. (1977). Controlled and automatic human information processing: II. Perceptual learning, automatic attending, and a general theory. *Psychological Review, 84*, 127–190.

Spearman, C. (1927). *The abilities of man: Their nature and measurement.* London: Macmillan.

Stankov, L. (2000). *Gf/Gc Test Battery.* Sydney, Australia: School of Psychology, University of Sydney.

Szymura, B. (2010). Individual differences in resource allocation policy. In A. Gruszka, G. Matthews, & B. Szymura (Eds.), *Handbook of individual differences in cognition: Attention, memory, and executive control* (pp. 231–246). New York: Springer-Verlag.

Szymura, B., & Nęcka, E. (1998). Visual selective attention and personality: An experimental verification of three models of extraversion. *Personality and Individual Differences, 24*, 713–729.

Tett, R. P., Fox, K. E., & Wang, A. (2005). Development and validation of a self-report measure of emotional intelligence as a multidimensional trait domain. *Personality and Social Psychology Bulletin, 31*, 859–888.

Thayer, R. E. (1978). Toward a psychological theory of multidimensional activation (arousal). *Motivation and Emotion, 2*, 1–34.

Thayer, R. E. (1989). *The biopsychology of mood and arousal.* Oxford, UK: Oxford University Press.

Thayer, R. E. (1996). *The origin of everyday moods.* New York: Oxford University Press.

Warm, J. S., & Dember, W. N. (1998). Tests of a vigilance taxonomy. In R. R. Hoffman, M. F. Sherrick, & J. S. Warm (Eds.), *Viewing psychology as a whole: The integrative science of William N. Dember* (pp. 87–112). Washington, DC: American Psychological Association.

Warwick, J., & Nettelbeck, T. (2004). Emotional intelligence is ... ? *Personality and Individual Differences, 37*, 1091–1100.

Zeidner, M., Matthews, G., & Roberts, R. D. (2009). *What we know about emotional intelligence: How it affects learning, work, relationships, and our mental health.* Cambridge, MA: MIT Press.

Zhuang, X., MacCann, C., Wang, L., Liu, L., & Roberts, R. D. (2008). *Development and validity evidence supporting a teamwork and collaboration assessment for high school students.* Educational Testing Service Research Report #RR–08–50.

CHAPTER 3

The Impact of Aging on Information Integration in Reasoning and Decision Making

Szymon Wichary
Ewa Domaradzka
Grzegorz Sedek

INTRODUCTION

Declines related to chronological age have been documented in a variety of cognitive tasks (e.g., Birren & Schaie, 2006; Craik & Salthouse, 2000; Mayr, Spieler, & Kliegl, 2001; Perfect & Maylor, 2000; Salthouse, 2006). For example, West and Bowry (2005) report that aging has a negative effect on conflict and error processing, goal maintenance, and set switching. Aging is also associated with increased susceptibility to goal neglect, slowed encoding of contextual information, and an inability to maintain this information in order to guide task performance. Verhaeghen, Cerella, Bopp, and Basak (2005), in their review, conclude that processes that are considered markers of selective attention (i.e., resistance to interference and local task switching) do not decline with age when base differences in processing speed are taken into account, whereas processes that are associated with divided attention (i.e., coordination and global task switching) decline with age, beyond the expected effects of general slowing.

Cognitive deficits—as well as some compensation strategies—in older adults (65 years and more) become especially obvious in complex tasks, particularly in tasks that require the integration of piecemeal information into a more coherent

Personality, Cognition, and Emotion edited by Michael W. Eysenck, Małgorzata Fajkowska, and Tomasz Maruszewski. Eliot Werner Publications, Clinton Corners, New York, 2012.

mental representation. For example, performance of older adults on complex impression-formation tasks is more variable and motivation dependent compared with that of younger adults (Hess, Follett, & McGee, 1998). This chapter attempts to compare limitations, biases, and compensations in older and younger adults on decision-making and integrative reasoning tasks that require them to integrate piecemeal information into a more coherent representation. Is integration of piecemeal information really or only seemingly impaired by aging, and if so how is it impaired in older adults? To review such processes in more detail, we deliberately focus on the potential impairments or compensations of older adults in decision making and reasoning—since these processes usually require information integration and, moreover, since most of our studies come from these domains.

AGING AND DECISION MAKING

In decision-making research it was found that older adults, compared with younger adults, prefer decision tasks of lower complexity with fewer choice alternatives (Reed, Mikels, & Simon, 2008). Older adults also use simpler, less cognitively demanding decision-making strategies (Chen & Sun, 2008; Mata, Schooler, & Rieskamp, 2007), process less information prior to making a decision, and take longer to process this information (Mata et al., 2007). Note, however, that older adults—like younger adults—process the predecisional information adaptively, changing their strategies according to the task information structure (Mata et al., 2007). Also, in the study by Dror, Katona, and Mundur (1998), no differences were found between older and younger participants in adaptation to risk levels in a risky decision task. Furthermore, older participants did not exhibit any decrease in speed of processing of the predecisional information, when compared with younger participants.

For a better understanding of the decision processes in aging, it is useful to succinctly review the distinction between two systems of reasoning—System 1 and System 2. Such division of mental processes is not new; in modern psychology it dates back to the early 1900s, when Freud described the unconscious processes taking place in human minds. In more recent times and within a more cognitive and empirical perspective, this topic has also been researched quite extensively and a great number of studies have been conducted. Among others, they deal with stereotypes (Banaji & Greenwald, 1995), learning (Lewicki, Hill, & Czyzewska, 1994), or perception (Boag, 2008).

The terms "System 1" and "System 2" were coined by Stanovich and West (2000), who published a review of the numerous approaches to the topic—including a summary of how the two kinds of processes had been described by other authors. They concluded that although differing in some aspects, the processes described by other researchers can be grouped into two clusters, which they called System 1 and System 2. The idea was further developed by Kahneman (2003), who proposed that there are three kinds of processes taking place in our minds: perception, intuition (System 1), and reasoning (System 2). System 1 consists of processes that are fast, parallel (many processes can take place at the same time, without interfering with one another), automatic, effortless, associative, slow-learning (requiring rehearsal), and emotional; while System 2 consists of processes that are slow, serial, controlled, effortful, rule governed, flexible, and emotionally neutral.

The division into the two systems may be important in the context of aging research. Since generally we observe a decline in cognitive functioning in aging adults (Salthouse, 1996), but at the same time observe that their general everyday functioning often does not deteriorate, we can consider explaining this phenomenon in terms of two distinct systems that cooperate with each other, but in which one can take on the functions of the other if necessary. What we mean here is that when the "explicit" functions of the mental system become less efficient, as happens when people get older, the processes that do not require as much cognitive effort begin to play a more important role. This results in a different pattern of mental processes, which leads to an efficient way of functioning in the absence of usual indexes of high cognitive skills, as measured by psychological tests (working memory capacity, mental speed, etc.).

Now we will concentrate on the affective and unconscious processes of System 1, which play an important role in reasoning and decision making and gain importance with age. In general, affective information can be used in two ways in decision making (Weber & Lindemann, 2008). One possibility is the problem of emotional outcomes, when we ask ourselves, "How will I feel after making this decision?" Second, it can be considered as the immediate feeling. When we are to decide, we may try to answer the question "How do I feel about this person/object/situation now?" In this case it can lead to behaviors of approach or avoidance. This notion is connected to the idea of "somatic marker" proposed by A. R. Damasio (1994). Based on the research by Bechara and associates (Bechara, Damasio, Damasio, & Anderson, 1994; Bechara, Damasio, Tranel, & Damasio, 1997), Damasio suggests the existence of bodily signals that help us decide, thanks to previously gained knowledge of which we are unaware.

For example, Bechara et al. (1994) designed the Iowa Gambling Task, where the participants were supposed to repeatedly draw cards from four decks. Each card meant a certain monetary gain or loss. Choosing cards from two of the decks led to an overall gain ("good decks") and choosing from the other two led to an overall loss ("bad decks"). However, in the beginning of the experimental session, the bad decks were more appealing because the single rewards were higher than the penalties. Drawing from the good decks, on the other hand, gave lower rewards but also lower penalties. The analysis revealed that the participants began to choose from the advantageous decks before they were aware of the pattern of gains and losses. Moreover, it turned out that they developed an anticipatory skin conductance response, which appeared before a card from the bad deck was drawn.

As an explanation for these findings, the authors suggest that our explicit cognitive processes are "supported" by somatic markers—cues from the body that are formed on the basis of existing knowledge and experience. As recently showed by Wood, Busemeyer, Koling, Cox, and Davis (2005), both older and younger adults were successful at solving the Iowa Gambling Task but used quite different strategies and demonstrated different forms of biases. Older adults placed equal emphasis on gains and losses but demonstrated a bias toward experienced outcomes from recently played trials. By contrast, younger adults demonstrated negativity bias (negative information had much stronger impact on making evaluations than positive information); however, during learning they relied more on choices that maximized expected payoff and not so much on outcomes from recently played trials.

Similar research on associative learning showed that the affective system is more efficient than the "reasoning brain" (Frank, O'Reilly, & Curran, 2006). The participants in that study received midazolam, a drug that temporarily deactivates the hippocampus, and were supposed to solve a transitive inferences task. The results suggest that "turning off" the explicit reasoning system promotes processes of learning governed by the basal ganglia, and in consequence leads to a significantly increased performance on probabilistic learning tasks. The affective processes based on previously acquired knowledge and experience have much to do with the concept of intuition. Betsch (2008) proposes a new "emotion-bound" definition of intuition, which underscores the fact that decision making is strongly connected with affect.

> Intuition is a process of thinking. The input to this process is mostly provided by knowledge stored in long-term memory that has been primarily acquired via associative learning. The input is processed automatically and without conscious awareness. The output of the process is a feeling that can serve as a basis for judgments and decisions. (p. 4)

In this vein Watson and Blanchard-Fields (1998) found that for solving interpersonal problems, older adults tend to use strategies that focus on both action and emotions, while younger participants concentrate on problem-focused strategies. This result, as the authors suggest, might mean that older adults approach the problems differently than do younger people. They have more "social" knowledge and experience and they seem to take advantage of this fact by considering the emotional aspects of situations that they encounter. Even though the strength and valence of experienced emotions might be different in older adults, they seem to have as rich an emotional life as younger people (for a review see Carstensen, Mikels, & Mather, 2006).

Peters, Hess, Västfjäll, and Auman (2007) review results showing that older adults perform worse in tasks relying on deliberative processes, and that they show a smaller decline in implicit memory than explicit memory. Apart from that, they also discuss the so-called positivity effect, which is explained as a greater focus on positive than negative emotional information as people age. Connected with this idea is the socioemotional selectivity theory (Carstensen, 2006), which suggests that as people age their emotional goals become more important. Therefore older people should pay more attention to emotional inputs, especially positive ones, in order to balance their emotional experiences. A number of studies have been conducted on this topic, and from their results we can conclude that in fact older people are more attentive to—and have a better memory for—positive information than negative information (there are a few exceptions, however; for a review see Peters et al., 2007). Another explanation of this phenomenon comes from neuropsychology: there is some evidence for the hypothesis that aging causes more changes in the brain areas that are responsible for deliberative processes than in those connected with affect (MacPherson, Phillips, & Della Sala, 2002).

What is more, we have to remember that the intuitive processes are by definition automatic and effortless (Kahneman, 2003). Since affective components are crucial in intuitive processes, older adults may use more of the emotional information simply because doing so requires less cognitive effort than the deliberative strategies using explicit information. This in turn is easier for older people, who are not as cognitively efficient as younger ones. Therefore, as recently shown by Queen and Hess (2010) in decision making, older adults were less efficient than younger adults as far as deliberative processing is concerned, but processing information on an intuitive level or focusing on emotions were relatively preserved.

The paradigm employed in many studies on decision making is a probabilistic inference task, presented to subjects as a computerized information board (e.g., Rieskamp & Hoffrage, 1999). In such a task, individuals make an inference about a criterion on the basis of several cues (e.g., Gigerenzer & Goldstein, 1996). For instance, one could infer which of two patients requires more urgent treatment on the basis of several cues, such as respiration or heart rate. The cues are only probabilistically related to the criterion, so that a positive cue value makes a positive criterion (e.g., a more precarious physical status) only more likely. Probabilistic inferences require a relatively long sequence of cognitive operations that usually result from the application of cognitive strategies (for an overview see Rieskamp & Hoffrage, 1999). The strategies differ in the amount of information that they require to make an inference and the way information is processed.

One very simple lexicographic strategy is take-the-best (TTB), which allows individuals to make a decision based on a single reason without the need to integrate all available information (Gigerenzer & Goldstein, 1996). An alternative strategy called weighted additive (WADD) integrates the available information; it is computationally costly and thus its execution is cognitively demanding. Although there are many other strategies that people could apply to make inferences, taken together TTB and WADD often appropriately describe people's inferences (Bröder, 2000; Rieskamp & Otto, 2006). People seem to select WADD more often when they make inferences in a new environment with which they have no experience and where the costs of applying the strategy are low. By contrast, in cases with increased application costs—for instance, due to high monetary costs associated with information search or time pressure—TTB more suitably predicts people's inferences (Newell & Shanks, 2003; Rieskamp & Otto, 2006).

Mata, von Helversen, and Rieskamp (2010) assessed how aging influenced the learning of TTB and WADD strategies. They designed the learning situations in which either WADD strategy was more optimal (relatively complex, compensatory environment) or TTB strategy was more optimal (relatively simple, noncompensatory environment). Generally, older adults showed much lower performance in decision tasks than younger adults. However, as predicted, older adults were much better at learning to select the simpler TTB strategy than the more cognitively demanding WADD strategy.

These findings are relevant to the interesting "paradox of choice" (Reed et al., 2008) that excessive choice—that is, too many alternatives—undermines satisfaction in decision making among older adults, mostly because of increasing difficulty in processing information about alternatives. As summarized recently by Mata and Nunes (2010) in meta-analysis of age differences in predecisional information search in real-world consumer environments, older adults decrease such search but this leads to only small limitations in decision quality.

PROPORTIONAL SLOWING AS A POWERFUL EXPLANATORY MECHANISM IN COGNITIVE AGING RESEARCH

There are three basic explanations for impaired information processing in older individuals, drawing on (a) cognitive slowing and/or memory retrieval limitations (Light, 1996; Salthouse, 1996); (b) impaired inhibition (Hasher, Zacks, & May, 1999); and (c) reduced efficiency of cognitive strategies (Hess, 2000; Oberauer & Kliegl, 2001).

The processing speed theory developed by Salthouse (1996) accounts for age-related differences in many cognitive tasks. According to this theory, the lower speed of executing cognitive operations in older age impairs performance in more complex tasks because of two mechanisms. The key defining feature of the first mechanism (time-limited mechanism) is that because of time constraints, the processing of initial information is incomplete and defective. This is in contrast to the second mechanism (simultaneity mechanism), in which processing of initial information is complete but becomes unavailable in the later stages of processing because of decay.

One of the basic findings in the field of cognitive aging is that older adults are slower than younger adults even in very simple cognitive tasks with little demands on control processes, such as simple reaction times (RT) or tests of perceptual speed (Verhaeghen et al., 2005). Therefore age-related slowing and memory impairments have become the basic mediators of more complex age-related deficits. The role of such basic cognitive processes is also highly relevant to the findings about the influence of aging on decision making discussed above. For example, Henninger, Madden, and Huettel (2010) elegantly demonstrated in path analyses that the influence of age on the quality of risky decision making was fully mediated by mental speed and memory limitations. In a similar vein, Pachur, Mata, and Schooler (2009) found that the influence of aging on adaptive use of recognition heuristic in decision making was mediated by age differences in mental speed.

The hypothesis of general slowing is also used as simpler explanation of other more complex age-related deficits. There is an interesting tool of quantification of such slowing effects, the so-called Brinley plot (Brinley, 1965). In a Brinley plot, performance of a group or groups of older adults is displayed as a function of average performance of a group or groups of younger adults who completed the same conditions.

Below we present an illustration of using Brinley plots in our aging research (Sedek, 2010) with a modified Oberauer task (Oberauer, 2005). In this task participants were instructed that after a short presentation of two words with different colors, they would be presented with a single word. They were instructed to press the "Yes" key only if this single stimulus was an already presented word with the same color; this was the positive probe. They were instructed to press the "No" key if the single stimulus was a new word; this was the new probe. They were also told to press the "No" key if the single stimulus was an already presented word with a different color; this was the intrusion probe. The intrusion probe is most difficult because correct reaction demands inhibition of fast familiarity memory signal (incorrectly pressing "Yes," this word was just presented) and waiting for slower recollection signal (correctly pressing "No," the color of the word is different).

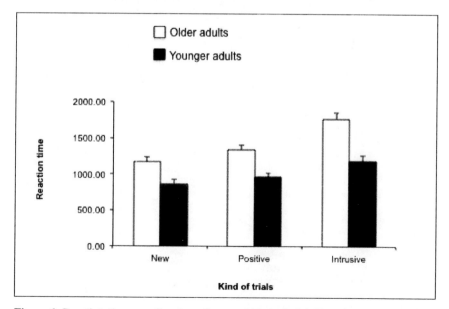

Figure 1. Reaction time as a function of age and kind of trial. Error bars represent standard errors of the mean.

As shown in Figure 1, our study with modified Oberauer task (Sedek, 2010) yielded two significant main effects and a significant interaction effect for reaction time (RT). First, the main effect of probe type: the longest RTs were for intrusion probes, the shortest RTs were for new probes, and RTs for positive probes were in between. Second, the main effect for age was obtained, with much longer response time for older adults compared with younger adults. There was also a significant interaction effect of age and probe type across all kinds of presented material. Subsequent analyses showed that the differences between younger (20–27 years) and older (65–72 years) adults are most reliable for intrusive probes. The results so far seem to support the two models of aging: older adults are substantially slower than younger ones, specifically in probes demanding inhibition (as indicated by significant interaction effect).

However, the same data for RT might be transformed into a Brinley plot (see Figure 2): on the horizontal axis are displayed the RTs for the three kinds of probes (new, positive, intrusive) of younger adults, and on the vertical axis the RTs for the same kinds of probes for older adults. We found a perfectly linear relation between RT of older and younger adults, with slope 2.0 and with small negative intercept, in line with the meta-analyses and the individual studies on Brinley functions (see Cerella, 1990; Verhaghen et al., 2005, for more details). These findings, taken together, indicate that the slope reflects the age-related slowing in central processes (Cerella, 1990; Myerson, Adams, Hale, & Jenkins,

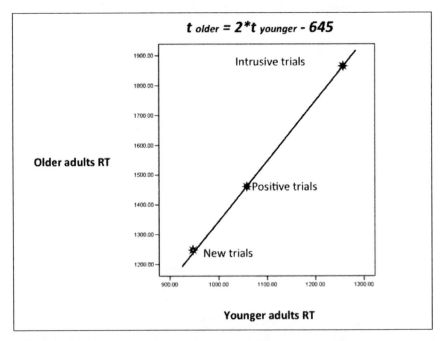

Figure 2. Brinley plot of nearly perfect linear relationship between reaction times of younger adults and older adults across three experimental conditions.

2003). Therefore the general slowing mechanism explains a whole pattern of data, and there is no need to refer to any specific inhibition limitations among older adults. These findings might have implications for other individual differences research using reaction times. Even in the case of significant interaction effects on reaction time data, the Brinley plots should be applied to assess whether the whole pattern of results concerning specific individual differences across all experimental conditions might be explained by a simple rule of proportional slowing.

It should be noted, however, that the interaction effects for the accuracy measures in aging research might tell us somewhat different stories and should not be reduced so easily to the general slowing mechanism. In two conditions of the study with the modified Oberauer task (Sedek, 2010), instead of neutral words there were words frequently used by younger adults for self-description (e.g., *energetic, in love, student*) or words frequently used as self-descriptions by older adults (e.g., *retired, caring, grandfather*). The findings showed the significant interaction effect between age, probe kind, and self-description for the memory accuracy (and also typical main effects of age, with much lower memory accuracy for older adults). The interaction between age and self-description appeared only for the intrusive trials (see Figure 3). For the younger adults, the accuracy in intrusion probes was significantly worse for words with older age self-descriptions, compared with words with younger age self-descriptions. For the older adults, the analyses yielded the opposite pattern. This interesting finding showed that interfering associations with past selves or possible selves (either positive selves or feared selves) might be an important feature of cognitive aging research

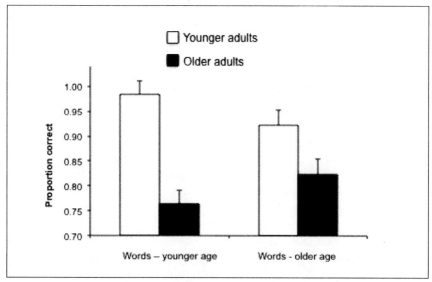

Figure 3. Accuracy of intrusive trials in modified Oberauer task as a function of age and type of word. Error bars represent standard errors of the mean.

(see Cheng, Fung, & Chan, 2009; Hooker, 1999, for the links between aging and possible selves), and that in cognitive functioning across the adult life span—as in the previously reviewed decision-making domain—one should also consider personality, motivational, and emotional mechanisms.

EVIDENCE FOR MEMORY RETRIEVAL LIMITATIONS IN REASONING AMONG OLDER ADULTS

In this section we will review research findings from our laboratory that combine the implications of the general slowing concept with predictions of the cognitive-motivational approach presented above. Salthouse and collaborators (Salthouse, 1992, 2000; Salthouse, Legg, Palmon, & Mitchell, 1990) have examined the effects of aging on integrative reasoning. The replicated findings from Salthouse et al.'s research are that age differences in the ability to integrate information from premises are nearly nonexistent, provided that correct information about the premises is available in memory. In Salthouse's studies there were substantial effects of age on memory of premises; however, increasing the number of premises did not increase the effect of age on reasoning accuracy. Deficiency in premise retrieval attributed by Salthouse (1992) to some basic dysfunctions of working memory in older adults is considered a device for simultaneous maintenance and processing of incoming data. According to this view, the limitations of older adults in integrative reasoning have to do with their problems concerning maintenance of relevant information, rather than with limitations of integrative reasoning per se.

In our series of studies based on a linear order paradigm (Sedek & von Hecker, 2004), we predicted deficits among older adults in terms of maintenance functions in working memory. We reasoned, however, that older adults should not show marked decrements in terms of integrative processing. Linear order construction (linear syllogisms) is a paradigm that may clearly exemplify our perspective on mental models as a process of integrating piecemeal information. The construction of linear orders from pairwise relational information that implies transitivity has received attention since the early days of cognitive psychology, as well as cognitive developmental psychology (Huttenlocher, 1968; Johnson-Laird, 1983; Piaget & Inhelder, 1974; Potts, 1972; Sternberg, 1980).

In this experimental procedure, participants were asked in each trial to study three pairs of relations: A > B, B > C, and C > D, with "A," "B," "C," and "D" standing for first names and ">" standing for a relational signifier such as taller or older, which was transitive by commonsense definition. An integrated mental model representation (Johnson-Laird, 1983) of such a set of pairs would always be a linear order A > B > C > D. Immediately after presentation of the three pairs, participants were tested on all possible pairs within the order—that is, AB, BC, CD (adjacent pairs, which had been learned); AC, BD (two-step relations); and AD (endpoint relation)—by prompting participants with statements in either a correct (e. g., A > D) or false (e. g., D > A) format and asking them for a speed-ed verification. The difficulty of integrating the three pairs was varied by admin-istering sequences in which subsequent pairs always had an element in common by which the two could be linked (e.g., B > C being presented after A > B), ver-sus other sequences in which the pairs were presented in a scrambled way such that there was less overlap of elements between subsequent pairs.

Table 1 illustrates the procedure for the easiest type of linear orders. Study time was self-paced, thus allowing for the assessment of participants' motivation and their time allocation patterns. During the test phase, participants were asked about the just-presented adjacent pair information (one-step relations; this was used as a measure of memory retrieval and did not constitute a reasoning test per se). They were also asked two questions about to-be-inferred but not-yet-present-ed pair relations, which demanded generative reasoning. The questions about two-step relations (e.g., relations between Bruce and Daniel or Edward and Richard) referred to relations between persons that spanned a distance of two steps on the hypothetical mental array and demanded integration of information from two pre-sented pairs. The questions about relations between endpoint persons (e.g., Bruce and Richard) dealt with inferred pairs that spanned the maximum array distance of three steps and demanded integration of information from all three presented pairs.

TABLE 1. Two Phases of Linear Order Paradigm and the Constructed Mental Array

Study phase
(freely paced for participants)
Bruce is faster than Edward
Edward is faster than Daniel
Daniel is faster than Richard

Test phase
(freely paced for participants)
Richard is faster than Daniel: True or False?
(Adjacent relation – memory test)
Edward is faster than Richard: True or False?
(2-step relation – integrating 2 premises)
Bruce is faster than Richard: True or False?
(Endpoint relation – integrating 3 premises)

Mental array
Bruce > Edward > Daniel > Richard

Note. Correct answers in the Test phase are in italics.

In line with the predictions presented above, a series of experiments revealed that differences in memory for adjacent relations almost completely explained the observed group difference in reasoning accuracy concerning endpoint relations. The interesting finding that older participants actually performed better on more difficult orders may reflect greater thinking effort exerted by older adults vis-à-vis the more difficult learning materials, which would appear plausible from an adaptive processing viewpoint. Earlier research has in fact shown that older participants allocate processing resources in a highly selective way. This might be illustrated by older adults engaging in more resource-demanding operations only if cues during learning point to the necessity to engage in such operations (Hess, Bolstad, Woodburn, & Auman, 1999).

In our series of studies (Sedek & von Hecker, 2004), the memory retrieval limitations model received support in the older adult population in three main findings: (a) compared with younger students, older adults had serious limitations in memory retrieval (accuracy on adjacent relations); (b) older adults were clearly able to construct linear orders, in particular responding to endpoint queries, provided that they had correctly preserved the premises; and (c) the effect of age on generative reasoning was nearly completely attenuated in hierarchical regression analyses when we controlled for maintenance of adjacent relations in memory during processing. A clear pattern emerges from this set of findings. Older participants suffered from serious limitations in remembering the premises, whereas their generative reasoning ability was relatively intact.

The interesting predictions for further research might concern the role of processing strategy. Studies on linear orders require either manipulation of propositions concerning relations between objects or forming images of objects and relations between them. The manipulations of propositions, as Allen and Brooks's (1991) review shows, is more demanding for memory than forming images. Therefore we should expect smaller differences between younger and older participants in cases of image-forming strategy, and larger differences in cases of propositional strategy.

PERFORMANCE ON CLASSIC SYLLOGISMS WITH INSTRUCTIONS TO AVOID COGNITIVE CLOSURE

These results, indicating insufficient memory encoding in older adults, were further corroborated in additional correlational analyses (Sedek & von Hecker, 2004, Experiment 2), with an intriguing pattern: the more older participants studied the premises, the better their performance in the reasoning task—resulting in an interaction effect between age and order difficulty. The more difficult the linear order problems, the more time the older adults spent studying and, finally, the better the quality of their integrative reasoning. Therefore we decided to use the explicit instructions in the categorical syllogism tasks to encourage older adult and younger adult participants to spend more time and deliberation in reasoning tasks.

In other words, these instructions were aimed at avoiding premature cognitive closure. The general predictions were that older adults would spend more time on solving such tasks and the typical difference between the accuracy in reasoning would be less pronounced, especially in more difficult tasks (much longer processing time might potentially compensate for working memory and lower-speed limitations).

In this study (Sedek, Oberauer, & von Hecker, 2008), we applied the classic paradigm of categorical syllogisms to examine the relationship between aging and integrative reasoning with the instruction to avoid cognitive closure. A categorical syllogism, in the simpler evaluative form, consists of two premises-which are assumed to be true, independent of the content-and a conclusion that is to be evaluated as valid (when it follows logically from premises) or invalid (when it does not follow from the premises). For example, assuming that all things in the refrigerator can be eaten (premise 1) and some light bulbs are in the refrigerator (premise 2), it logically follows that some light bulbs can be eaten (conclusion).

Johnson-Laird and coworkers developed the most well-known model of syllogistic reasoning, based on mental modeling (Bucciarelli & Johnson-Laird, 1999; Johnson-Laird, 1983). According to this conception, during solving of a categorical syllogism, participants construct a mental model based on the terms and quantifiers in the premises. Such mental models simulate the possible options of relations between terms. The different mental models are compared to contrast different solutions that might be possible, based on the premises. In line with this theory, participants go through three stages when solving syllogisms. In the first stage, an initial model is constructed based on the information from the first premise. In the second stage, information from the second premise is added and participants use this more comprehensive model to draw a conclusion. In the third stage, people examine this initial conclusion by constructing alternative mental models. According to this theory, syllogisms that support the construction of one single model are easier than those supporting two or three different mental models.

Evidence from aging research confirms that working memory maintenance is related to the accuracy of syllogistic reasoning. For example, Copeland and Radvansky (2004) recently demonstrated a reliable relation between operation span (Turner & Engle, 1986) and syllogistic reasoning performance in cognitive aging research.

Another interesting aspect of concrete syllogisms that is relevant for the present research is the possibility of group differences in the so-called belief bias (Gilinsky & Judd, 1994). Belief bias means that people's personal beliefs and factual knowledge may affect their ability to reason logically. Robust research evidence showed that participants, when presented with arguments to evaluate, tended to endorse conclusions that they believed to be true—despite the instructions to base their judgments on logical reasoning alone. Research by Gilinsky and Judd (1994) showed that the relationship between aging and syllogistic reasoning (accuracy and belief bias) is mediated by working memory span (composite of several span measures).

In our research (Sedek et al., 2008), we used both the simplest versions of syllogisms (demanding the construction of only one single mental model) and more complex versions demanding the construction of two or three mental models (Table 2 presents some examples of those syllogisms). To stimulate the emergence of belief bias in the cover story, we informed the participants that they would read about some observations carried out in a normal garden (believable conclusions) versus in a garden with radical genetic transformations (unbelievable conclusions). The observations (premises) themselves were to be taken as valid; however, the task of participants was to decide whether the conclusions from them, made by the gardener, were logically correct (valid) or incorrect (invalid). As shown in the sample cases in Table 2, some syllogisms were valid

TABLE 2. The Structure of Classical Syllogisms Tasks in Sedek, Oberauer, and von Hecker (2008) Study

Validity	Abstract form	Believable (normal garden)	Unbelievable (garden with genetic engineering)
Valid	All A are B	All apple trees have a red mark	All apple trees have a red mark
1 MM	All B are C	All trees with a red mark are leaved	All trees with a red mark are conifers
	→All A are C	→All apple trees are leaved	→All apple trees are conifers
Invalid	All A are B	All fruits are ripe	All fruits are ripe
1 MM	All B are C	All ripe fruits are apples	All ripe fruits are cubic eggs
	→All C are A	→All apples are fruits	→All cubic eggs are fruits
Valid	No A are B	No roots are light	No roots are light
3 MM	All B are C	All light things easily flying	All light things are trees
	→Some C are not A	→Some easily flying things are not roots	Some trees have no roots
Invalid	No A are B	No maples are pine trees	No maples are pine trees
3 MM	All B are C	All pine trees in the park are protected	All pine trees have leaves
	→Some A are not C	→Some maples are not protected	→Some maples do not have leaves

Note. MM = mental models. Exemplary set of eight syllogisms: valid versus invalid; believable versus unbelievable conclusions; simple (1 mental model) versus complex (3 mental models).

and believable, some were valid and unbelievable, some were invalid and believable, and finally some were invalid and unbelievable.

We instructed the participants to think deliberatively before making each judgment, and to refrain from answering until they were completely sure about whether the conclusion of presented syllogisms was true or false. We obtained the typical finding that the operation span among 24 older adults ($M = 16.59$) was less than half that among 21 younger adults ($M = 33.29$). In spite of this disadvantage in working memory span, the results showed intriguing interaction effects between aging and difficulty of syllogism in an atypical direction (see Figure 4). Specifically, older adults were significantly better in solving difficult syllogisms than younger adults and not reliably worse in solving the simple syllogisms. How to explain these paradoxical findings? The cue is studying time: older adults spent more than twice as much time ($M = 16.09$ seconds) analyzing the premises of syllogisms than younger adults ($M = 7.38$ seconds). In this sense they could compensate for the shrinkage in working memory span by spending much more time on deliberative thinking about the reasoning conclusion. These results showed the effectiveness of instruction for avoiding cognitive closure, specifically in older adults. These findings might be also seen as conceptual replication of previous studies on linear order reasoning in the sense that older adults are able to effectively solve even very complex tasks when they devote enough time to finding the solution.

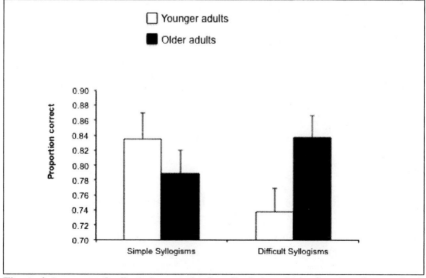

Figure 4. Accuracy of syllogistic reasoning in syllogistic task as a function of age and task difficulty. Error bars represent standard errors of the mean.

CONCLUDING REMARKS

Very often good advice given to youngsters by older people when encountering a difficult problem is "Don't hurry, first think it over, and then decide." Ironically, the results of studies on effectiveness of reasoning show that it is absolutely perfect advice—but only for older adults! Only older adults are able to effectively use the extended deliberation time for improving the reasoning solution. For younger adults the additional inspection time does not improve reasoning accuracy.

In this chapter we showed the evidence for some limitations in effective decision making and reasoning from early adulthood through middle age to old age. However, due to various compensatory mechanisms, a large part of the adult population can cope with increasing limitations in performance on intellectually demanding tasks. The more detailed description of these mechanisms would make it possible to design practical actions for increasing the life quality of elderly people. What is especially valuable for cognitive aging research—as it concerns reasoning and decision making—is the emphasis on age differences not only in purely laboratory tasks, but also in the effectiveness of everyday functioning. Based on literature reviews and our own research, we suggest that at least two compensatory mechanisms play an important role in effective cognitive functioning in older age: (a) decreasing the need for cognitive closure and/or increasing the need to avoid closure, which allows for lengthening of the deliberation process before making a judgment or decision; and (b) deliberative (time-consuming) integration of pieces of information in order to make a correct solution in reasoning task or an optimal decision.

Therefore, both in the experimental laboratory and in social life, we observe that older people can use compensatory strategies (cognitive, motivational, and self-regulatory) more frequently and more efficiently than younger people, and thus may prevent significant impairment in performance on complex cognitive tasks. At the same time, there is evidence suggesting that the mechanisms responsible for affective and nondeliberative processes do not deteriorate with age and allow for efficient functioning of older people.

Acknowledgments

Preparation of this chapter was supported by Swiss Sciex-NMS grant #09–083–1 to Szymon Wichary, and grants #N–N106–219338 to Szymon Wichary and #N–N106–040534 to Grzegorz Sedek from the Polish Ministry of Science and Higher Education.

REFERENCES

Allen, S., & Brooks, L. (1991). Specializing the operation of an explicit rule. *Journal of Experimental Psychology: General, 120*, 3–19.

Banaji, M. R., & Greenwald, A. G. (1995). Implicit gender stereotyping in judgments of fame. *Journal of Personality and Social Psychology, 68*, 181–198.

Bechara, A., Damasio, A. R., Damasio H., & Anderson, S. W. (1994). Insensitivity to future consequences following damage to human prefrontal cortex. *Cognition, 50*, 7–15.

Bechara, A., Damasio H., Tranel D., & Damasio, A. R. (1997). Deciding advantageously before knowing the advantageous strategy. *Science, 275*, 1293–1295.

Betsch, T. (2008). The nature of intuition and its neglect in research on judgment and decision making. In H. Plessner, C. Betsch, & T. Betsch (Eds.), *Intuition in judgment and decision making* (pp. 3–22). New York: Erlbaum.

Birren, J. E., & Schaie, K. W. (Eds.). (2006). *Handbook of the psychology of aging* (6th ed.). Amsterdam: Elsevier Academic Press.

Boag, S. (2008). Making sense of subliminal perception. In A. M. Columbus (Ed.), *Advances in psychology research* (Vol. 54, pp. 117–139). Hauppauge, NY: Nova Science Publishers.

Brinley, J. F. (1965). Cognitive sets, speed, and accuracy of performance in the elderly. In A. T. Welford & J. E. Birren (Eds.), *Behavior, aging, and the nervous system* (pp. 114–149). Springfield, IL: Charles C. Thomas.

Bröder, A. (2000). Assessing the empirical validity of the "take-the-best" heuristic as a model of human probabilistic inference. *Journal of Experimental Psychology: Learning, Memory, and Cognition, 26*, 1332–1346.

Bucciarelli, M., & Johnson-Laird, P. N. (1999). Strategies in syllogistic reasoning. *Cognitive Science, 23*, 247–303.

Carstensen, L. L. (2006). The influence of a sense of time on human development. *Science, 312*, 1913–1915.

Carstensen, L. L., Mikels, J. A., & Mather, M. (2006). Aging and the intersection of cognition, motivation, and emotion. In J. E. Birren & K. W. Schaie (Eds.), *Handbook of the psychology of aging* (6th ed., pp. 343–362). Amsterdam: Elsevier Academic Press.

Cerella, J. (1990). Aging and information processing rate. In J. E. Birren & K. W. Schaie (Eds.), *Handbook of the psychology of aging* (3rd ed., pp. 201–221). San Diego, CA: Academic Press.

Chen, Y., & Sun, Y. (2008) Age differences in financial decision-making: Using simple heuristics. *Educational Gerontology, 27*, 627–635.

Cheng, S., Fung, H., H., & Chan, A. C. M. (2009). Self-perception and psychological well-being: The benefits of foreseeing a worse future. *Psychology and Aging, 24*, 623–633.

Copeland, D. E., & Radvansky, G. E. (2004). Working memory and syllogistic reasoning. *Quarterly Journal of Experimental Psychology, 57A*, 1437–1457.

Craik, F. I. M., & Salthouse, T. A. (Eds.). (2000). *The handbook of aging and cognition* (2nd ed.). Mahwah, NJ: Erlbaum.

Damasio, A. R. (1994). *Descartes' error: Emotion, reason, and the human brain.* New York: G. P. Putnam's Sons.

Dror, I. E., Katona, M., & Mundur, K. (1998). Age differences in decision making: To take a risk or not? *Gerontology, 44*, 67–71.

Frank, M., O'Reilly, R., & Curran, T. (2006). When memory fails, intuition reigns: Midazolam enhances implicit inference in humans. *Psychological Science, 17*, 700–707.

Gigerenzer, G., & Goldstein, D. (1996). Reasoning the fast and frugal way: Models of bounded rationality. *Psychological Review, 103*, 650–669.

Gilinsky, A. S., & Judd, B. B. (1994). Working memory bias in reasoning across the life span. *Psychology and Aging, 9*, 356–371.

Hasher, L., Zacks, R. T., & May, C. P. (1999). Inhibitory control, circadian arousal, and age. In D. Gopher & A. Koriat (Eds.), *Attention and Cognitive Performance XVII. Cognitive regulation of performance: Interaction of theory and application* (pp. 653–675). Cambridge, MA: MIT Press.

Henninger, D. E., Madden, D. J., & Huettel, S. A. (2010). Processing speed and memory mediate age-related differences in decision making. *Psychology and Aging, 25*, 262–270.

Hess, T. (2000). Aging-related constraints and adaptation in social information processing. In U. von Hecker, S. Dutke, & G. Sedek, G. (Eds.), *Generative mental processes and cognitive resources: Integrative research on adaptation and control* (pp. 129–155). Dordrecht, The Netherlands: Kluwer Academic Publishers.

Hess, T. M., Bolstad, C. A., Woodburn, S. M., & Auman, C. (1999). Trait diagnosticity versus behavioral consistency as determinants of impression change in adulthood. *Psychology and Aging, 14*, 77–89.

Hess, T. M., Follett, K. J., & McGee, K. A. (1998). Aging and impression formation: The impact of processing skills and goals. *Journals of Gerontology: Psychological Sciences, 53*, 175–188.

Hooker, K. (1999). Possible selves in adulthood: Incorporating teleonomic relevance into studies of self. In T. M. Hess & F. Blanchard-Fields (Eds.), *Social cognition and aging* (pp. 97–122). San Diego, CA: Academic Press.

Huttenlocher, J. (1968). Constructing spatial images: A strategy in reasoning. *Psychological Review, 75*, 550–560.

Johnson-Laird, P. N. (1983). *Mental models: Towards a cognitive science of language, inference, and consciousness.* Cambridge, MA: Harvard University Press.

Kahneman, D. (2003). A perspective on judgment and choice: Mapping bounded rationality. *American Psychologist, 58*, 697–720.

Lewicki, P., Hill, T., & Czyżewska, M. (1994). Nonconscious indirect inferences in encoding. *Journal of Experimental Psychology: General, 123*, 257–263.

Light, L. L. (1996). Memory and aging. In E. L. Bjork & R. A. Bjork (Eds.), *Handbook of perception and cognition: Memory* (pp. 443–490). San Diego, CA: Academic Press.

MacPherson, S., Phillips, L., & Della Sala, S. (2002). Age, executive function, and social decision making: A dorsolateral prefrontal theory of cognitive aging. *Psychology and Aging, 17*, 598-609.

Mata, R., & Nunes, L. (2010). When less is enough: Cognitive aging, information search, and decision quality in consumer choice. *Psychology and Aging, 25*, 289–298.

Mata, R., Schooler, L. J., & Rieskamp, J. (2007) The aging decision marker: Cognitive aging and the adaptive selection of decision studies. *Psychology and Aging, 22*, 796–810.

Mata, R., von Helversen, B., & Rieskamp, J. (2010). Learning to choose: Cognitive aging and strategy selection learning in decision making. *Psychology and Aging, 25*, 299–309.

Mayr, U., Spieler, D. H., & Kliegl, R. (Eds.) (2001). *Ageing and executive control.* Hove, UK: Psychology Press.

Myerson, J., Adams, D. A., Hale, S., & Jenkins, L. (2003). Analysis of group differences in processing speed: Brinley plots, Q–Q plots, and other conspiracies. *Psychonomic Bulletin and Review, 10*, 224–237.

Newell, B., & Shanks, D. (2003). Take the best or look at the rest? Factors influencing "one-reason" decision making. *Journal of Experimental Psychology: Learning, Memory, and Cognition, 29*, 53–65.

Oberauer, K. (2005). Age differences and individual differences in cognitive functions. In R. W. Engle, G. Sedek, U. von Hecker, & D. N. McIntosh (Eds.), *Cognitive limitations in aging and psychopathology* (pp. 44–72). Cambridge, UK: Cambridge University Press.

Oberauer, K., & Kliegl, R. (2001). Beyond resources: Formal models of complexity effects and age differences in working memory. *European Journal of Cognitive Psychology, 13*, 187–215.

Pachur, T., Mata, R., & Schooler, L. (2009). Cognitive aging and the adaptive use of recognition in decision making. *Psychology and Aging, 24*, 901–915.

Perfect, T. J., & Maylor, E. A. (2000). (Eds.), *Models of cognitive aging*. Oxford, UK: Oxford University Press.

Peters, E., Hess, T., Västfjäll, D., & Auman, C. (2007). Adult age differences in dual information processes: Implications for the role of affective and deliberative processes in older adults' decision making. *Perspectives on Psychological Science, 2*, 1–23.

Piaget, J., & Inhelder, B. (1974). *The child's construction of quantities: Conservation and atomism*. London: Routledge & Kegan Paul.

Potts, G. R. (1972). Information processing strategies used in the encoding of linear orderings. *Journal of Verbal Learning and Verbal Behavior, 11*, 727–740.

Queen, T., & Hess, T. (2010). Age differences in the effects of conscious and unconscious thought in decision making. *Psychology and Aging, 25*, 251–261.

Reed, A. E., Mikels, J. A., & Simon, K. I. (2008) Older adults prefer less choice than young adults. *Psychology and Aging, 23*, 671–675.

Rieskamp, J., & Hoffrage, U. (1999). When do people use simple heuristics and how can we tell? In G. Gigerenzer, P. M. Todd, & ABC Research Group (Eds.), *Simple heuristics that make us smart*. Oxford, UK: Oxford University Press.

Rieskamp, J., & Otto, P. (2006). SSL: A theory of how people learn to select strategies. *Journal of Experimental Psychology: General, 135*, 207–236.

Salthouse, T. A. (1992). Working-memory mediation of adult age differences in integrative reasoning. *Memory and Cognition, 20*, 413–423.

Salthouse, T. A. (1996). The processing speed theory of adult age differences in cognition. *Psychological Review, 103*, 403-428.

Salthouse, T. A. (2000). Item analyses of age relations on reasoning tests. *Psychology and Aging, 15*, 3–8.

Salthouse, T. A. (2006). Mental exercise and mental aging. *Perspectives on Psychological Science, 1*, 68–87.

Salthouse, T. A., Legg, S. Palmon, R., & Mitchell, D. (1990). Memory factors in age-related differences in simple reasoning. *Psychology and Aging, 5*, 9–15.

Sedek, G., (2010). The influence of aging on modified Oberauer task. Unpublished manuscript, Warsaw School of Social Sciences and Humanities, Warsaw.

Sedek, G., Oberauer, K., & von Hecker, U. (2008). Influence of depression and working memory on belief bias and categorical reasoning. Unpublished manuscript, Warsaw School of Social Sciences and Humanities, Warsaw.

Sedek, G., & von Hecker, U. (2004). Effects of subclinical depression and aging on generative reasoning about linear orders: Same or different processing limitations? *Journal of Experimental Psychology: General, 133*, 237–260.

Stanovich K. E., & West, R. F. (2000). Individual diferences in reasoning: Implications for the rationality debate. *Behavioral and Brain Sciences, 23*, 645–665.

Sternberg, R. J. (1980). Representation and process in linear syllogistic reasoning. *Journal of Experimental Psychology: General, 109*, 119–159.

Turner, M. L., & Engle, R. W. (1986). Working memory capacity. *Proceedings of the Human Factors Society, 30*, 1273–1277.

Verhaeghen, P., Cerella, J., Bopp, K. L., & Basak, C. (2005) Aging and varieties of cognitive control: A review of meta-analyses on resistance to interference, coordination, and task switching, and an experimental exploration of age-sensitivity in the newly identified process of focus switching. In R. W. Engle, G. Sedek, U. von Hecker, & D. N. McIntosh (Eds.), *Cognitive limitations in aging and psychopathology* (pp. 160–189). Cambridge, UK: Cambridge University Press.

Watson, T., & Blanchard-Fields, F. (1998). Thinking with your head and your heart: Age differences in everyday problem-solving strategy preferences. *Aging, Neuropsychology, and Cognition, 5*, 225–240.

Weber, E. U., & Lindemann, P. G. (2008). From intuition to analysis: Making decisions with your head, your heart, or by the book. In H. Plessner, C. Betsch, & T. Betsch (Eds.) *Intuition in judgment and decision making* (pp. 191–207). New York: Erlbaum.

West, R., & Bowry, R. (2005) The aging of cognitive control. In R. W. Engle, G. Sedek, U. von Hecker, & D. N. McIntosh (Eds.), *Cognitive limitations in aging and psychopathology* (pp. 197–221). Cambridge, UK: Cambridge University Press.

Wood, S., Busemeyer, J., Koling, A., Cox, C., & Davis, H. (2005). Older adults as adaptive decision makers: Evidence from the Iowa Gambling Task. *Psychology and Aging, 20*, 220–225.

CHAPTER 4

Building Bridges in Psychology as Exemplified by Creative Intuition

Alina Kolańczyk

INTRODUCTION

Recent decades have witnessed the increasing decline of a fragmented understanding of human beings in terms of their emotions, cognition, or personality. Attempts to explain complex mental processes have spurred the natural need for integration. Creative intuition is a particular example of such processes. Twenty years ago I tried to demonstrate that creative intuition depends on the individual's mindset— that is, his or her meta-motivation. Meta-motivation, in turn, evokes an extensive state of attention (Kolańczyk, 1989, 1991a, 1995; see also Nęcka, Grohman, & Słabosz, 2006). Many experimental findings have helped develop these ideas, especially when the time was optimal to study unconscious processes and hence intuition as well. Synthesis of the various research approaches has led to the elaboration of a trifactor model of creative intuition where changes in meta-motivation, attention states, and implicit evaluations are systemically related.

Changes in meta-motivation determine self-control (explicit vs. implicit). According to my understanding of the term, meta-motivation is an individual's general mindset: telic if one is overtly realizing some goal or paratelic if one engages in some activity with no clear intentions (Apter, 1982). A relaxed person—or one who is resting—refrains from goal-oriented behavior, at least consciously. Nevertheless, the behavior in which that person was engaged beforehand may well be further processed by him or her, albeit implicitly. Meta-motivation is also understood as the general approach to achieving goals. It determines the pro-

Personality, Cognition, and Emotion edited by Michael W. Eysenck, Małgorzata Fajkowska, and Tomasz Maruszewski. Eliot Werner Publications, Clinton Corners, New York, 2012.

portion of interest in a task and the concern about making mistakes, as well as the proportion of hoping for success and fearing failure. It is a regulatory focus, described by Higgins (1997) as promotion versus prevention. A shift in meta-motivation to the promotional set and paratelic motivation fosters creative intuition.

The context of meta-motivation affects both our attention states and the way we perceive and think of reality. A preventional mindset focuses one's attention on possible mistakes in his or her reasoning; thus it is a form of conscious self-monitoring. Intensifying attention allows for in-depth and analytical information processing at the cost of narrowing the scope of attention. By contrast, paratelic motivation and a promotional mindset shape more extensive attention. Extensive attention is characterized by a wide scope but shallow, sensual information processing, which is highly valued in theories of creativity since it is viewed as the basis of intuition/insight (Martindale, 1989).

The goal of solving a given problem generates a peculiar state of operational readiness within the structures of cognitive processes. Contents that might be helpful in solving the problem become more readily accessible. For example, in the case of a literary assignment, these are grammatical rules, excerpts of literary pieces, and so forth. Useful contents are also unconsciously favored and valued, much like water is highly valued by a person who is thirsty (Ferguson & Bargh, 2004). By contrast, contents that interfere with attaining the goal are devalued (Brendl, Markman, & Messner, 2003). Automatically assigning value to something or devaluating it is nothing less than temporarily linking positive and negative affect with the nodes of the semantic network, thus creating a kind of "affective map" of meaning within the network. It is affect that determines which contents are processed in the scope of attention. In favorable motivational conditions, contents that are important for solving the problem—positively marked and located in distant places of the semantic network—are simultaneously registered within the scope of attention. It is in the state of extensive attention that we experience so-called "aha" moments by means of synthesizing these meanings.

I shall preface a more complete description of the mechanism of creative intuition by first explaining the concept of intuition itself and by describing the mind of an intuitionist, because dispositional factors (cognitive, motivational, or temperamental) determine the probability of these changes taking place. Therefore the model refers to motivational, cognitive, and affective processes that are activated according to individual dispositions.

WHAT IS CREATIVE INTUITION?

Creative intuition is probably one of the most important ways of transcending the limits of existing knowledge and experience, both individual and cultural. Great creators themselves have described how it works. There is a well-known example of Einstein who decided to rest after a long period of intensive work and let his imagination run free. In this state of uncontrolled "free-wheeling thinking," he saw two beams of light hitting a moving train from two sides at the same instant. The question was whether a bystander standing beside the railway track and a passenger traveling by train would observe these events simultaneously. Einstein's answer was "No," to which he responded with a very emotional "Aha!" Apparently this was how he began to formulate his special theory of relativity (after Knoblich & Oellinger, 2006).

In psychology we devote a lot of effort to the scientific definition of terms borrowed from everyday language. By so doing we end up with dozens of definitions of personality, thinking, or motivation. Intuition is no different. Its recognition is largely based on subjective indicators, on comparing its manifestations with "ordinary" cognition—that is, cognition that is under our control and of whose strategic operations we are aware. This is the case with sequential information processing in the narrow band of attention (analytic processing) that, incidentally, also takes place largely due to automatic operations (including, for example, changing the limits of concepts according to one's mood, activating various memory contents, etc.). It is worth bearing this in mind lest we identify all unconscious processes with intuition.

As far as intuition is concerned, it is largely the direct causes of one's thought or decisions that are unconscious, leading to the feeling that one is losing control of the process. At the subjective level, decisions or solutions "fall from heaven," suddenly and unexpectedly. One is in control of one's thinking, however inattentively and implicitly—at least as far as upholding an initiated activity is concerned.

One feature of intuition that merits special attention is the global approach to the situation (cf. Dane & Pratt, 2007; Nosal, 1992). Several different mechanisms are responsible for this and they also help us to distinguish various types of intuition. The basic type is evaluation and the related emotions. Emotion is a global approach to the situation and a source of information/feelings concerning the nature of an object—that is, how good or bad it is for the subject (Frijda, 2005; Oatley & Jenkins, 1996). If one is with a group of friends and their behavior lacks clarity, this may arouse anxiety and make one feel that one ought to leave the company, although it may be hard to justify the decision rationally. Since women are more emotional than men, I have called such feelings feminine intuition (Kolańczyk, 1991b).

The next global mechanism is statistical intuition (Kolańczyk, 1991b). This form of intuition takes place when an individual utilizes frequency of coincidence of events coded in the process of implicit learning (Czyzewska, 2001; Lewicki, Hill, & Czyzewska, 1992). When negotiating two long queues to the supermarket checkout, for example, we choose the one we think will be quicker. We do this on the basis of our personal experience statistic concerning speed of service, depending on the number of groceries in the carts or other parameters. Linguistic intuition, partly modeled during artificial grammar learning tasks, also probably belongs in this category.

The third mechanism underlying holistic event appraisal is memory schematization and polarization—that is, the self-organization of memory at the level of useful meaning units (not traits or attributes but whole objects or object categories). This mechanism has been known since the time of Frederic Charles Bartlett (if an object is placed in the "eyeglass" category, it is recalled with increasingly clearer inclusion of the prototypic features of eyeglasses) but was only fully appreciated by Dijksterhuis (2004) in the context of "unconscious thinking." This researcher found that during the predecision period filled with "thinking about something else," people utilize the effects of polarization of evaluations of objects from among which they are to choose, because the mind itself calculates their advantages and disadvantages. This is a useful side effect of memory self-organization: schematic intuition.

None of these mechanisms sufficiently accounts for creative intuition, however, although it surely involves encoding event frequency and correlation structure, online evaluation, and memory self-organization. The creative process leads (at least potentially) to new and valuable outcomes, in both the subjective sense and the cultural sense. A global approach to the problem situation may take the form of metaphors or symbolic images (as in the case of Einstein's intuition). More akin to the development of holistic meanings in creativity is certainly intuition understood as perception of coherence (Bauman & Kuhl, 2002). Perception of coherence has been operationalized as premonition of the meaningfulness of unclear perceptual images (Bowers, Regehr, Balthazard, & Parker, 1990) or recognizing conceptual coherence in the Remote Association Test (Bolte, Goschke, & Kuhl, 2003; Mednick, 1963).

It is not easy to verbalize the outcomes of creative intuition; sensations, feelings, and metaphors become the language of communication. Linguistic categories — which are usually archaic with respect to discovered reality — are too analytic and unable to convey the whole meaning, including its sensual-affective aspects.

INSIGHT PROBLEMS AND CREATIVE INTUITION

Ever since Wallas (1926), creative intuition has been identified with insight experienced after a period of incubation. Special "insight problems" have been constructed (Dow & Mayer, 2004). For example, participants are required to join dots with an interrupted line, tie bits of string that cannot be reached without extra help, or move limited numbers of matchsticks encrypting arithmetical operations (in order to maintain arithmetical correctness). The problems are usually of the convergent type, meaning that they have only one correct solution. Insight involves restructuring the problem situation, overcoming so-called functional fixation. For instance, the participant uses pliers as a weight or discovers that not only numbers but also operators (addition or equation signs) can be transformed in an equation. In such cases the search for the solution involves analysis — that is, reformulating the meaning of the various elements of the problem situation such as numbers or arithmetical operators (Knoblich, Ohlsson, Haider, & Rhenius, 1999). No wonder "convergent" insights are facilitated by negative mood, the state that activates analytic thinking (Kaufmann & Vosburg, 1997).

According to Wolfgang Köhler, even monkeys can have insight and construct tools—although other researchers have argued that trial and error is more important (Windholtz & Lamal, 1985). This idea is partly corroborated by Reverberi, Toraldo, D'Agostini, and Skrap (2005), who found that patients with dorsolateral frontal cortex lesions perform better on insight problems than healthy persons. They used the matchstick arithmetic problem, which consists of a false arithmetic statement written with Roman numerals (I, II, III, etc.), arithmetic operations (+, –), and equal signs constructed out of matchsticks. The goal is to move a single stick in such a way that the initial false statement is transformed into a true arithmetic statement. The more difficult the matchstick arithmetic problem, the greater the difference. Patients work without first choosing any strategy and cannot enrich the representation of the problem situation or state of goal realization with former experience (Reverberi et al., 2005). I do not invest much hope in treating this operationalization of insight as an illustration of thinking that leads to important discoveries.

Open-ended problems conducive to divergent thinking have more creative potential. Such problems allow people to grasp completely new structures by freely choosing elements of successively acquired knowledge. In this case freedom of choice involves attributing particular value to certain information because one feels that it may come in handy during further attempts to solve the problem. Attention may be attracted to some observation or thought whose meaning is yet unclear. This emergent sense of coherence with the problem causes the observation or thought to be preferred. Interestingly, intuitive generation of ideas during divergent thinking runs more smoothly when mood is positive rather than negative, as is the case when insight problems are being solved (Baas, de Dreu, & Nijstad, 2008; Isen, 1987; Kolańczyk & Świerzyński, 1995; Vosburg, 1998). Hence research on creative intuition should tend in the direction of moderately divergent problems and should seek to determine the mindset and then the state of motivation, attention, and evaluation (affective processes) during their solution.

PREPARATION FOR CREATIVE INSIGHT: DISPOSITIONAL FACTORS

Creative intuition is an insight leading, at least potentially, to a new and valuable outcome. I suggest that we explain creative intuition in terms of systemic changes in meta-motivation, attention, and implicit evaluations. Some introductory data on the antecedents and dispositional determinants of insight should make this model more comprehensible.

Knowledge

Before the necessary conditions for creative insight are available, important substantive (knowledge acquisition) and motivational preparations are under way.

Bartlett (1955) popularized Edison's maxim that "genius is one percent inspiration and ninety-nine percent perspiration" (p. 735). Great intuitionists worked very hard for many years and acquired expert knowledge before they had their pivotal intuitions. Less significant, private transgressions may involve less deeply elaborated knowledge, although its acquisition also requires effort because it takes place in analytic settings: at school, when reading books, or when gaining experience. Bobłowska (after Kolańczyk, 1991b) found that intuitionists (who typically take in perceptual or problematic wholes and trust their own feelings) organize the material they are to memorize differently and take much longer to do so than rationalists (who typically think analytically and linearly, on the basis of logical premises).[1]

Students in nonbiological academic courses were given biological propositions and schemas and asked to organize them to facilitate memorization. Intuitionists needed more time to organize and memorize the material. They grouped items with similar degrees of generality, but also omitted some items and failed to group them with others. The meaning clusters that they created were based on subjective criteria, yet were memorized more accurately by the intuitionists than the rationalists. Rationalists organized the material in ways that were clearer to the observer, more logical and hierarchical, clustering it around the most informative concepts. The evidence suggests that intuitionists memorize material on the basis of subjective criteria and that their elaboration is stronger and more episodic (and hence more effective; cf. Kahneman & Triesman, 1984). Intuitionists also demonstrated paradoxically superior meta-memory (measured with the Metamemory in Adulthood Questionnaire; Dixon, Hultsh, & Hertzog, 1988). In other words, they were more aware of their own limitations and memory strategies. Perhaps this is how they compensated for their frequent loss of control over thought processes.

Interest and Fulfillment Set

As people learn, information reaches a certain critical mass but this would be useless were it not for the learner's motivation. Creative intuition involves issues that are subjectively significant or even fascinating. Sternberg and Lubart (1995) wrote about set, which facilitates the utilization of the potential of creative intuition. They called this set "buy low and sell high," by which they meant investment of one's commitment to an issue that is not part of the research mainstream at the time, provided that the creator does not view the issue as an important one. The approach itself implies passion and a positive approach to the deliberated issues.

Other research has demonstrated that strong motivation significantly affects memory processing: it keeps the problem representation in an activated state until

---

[1] Bobłowska used the 32-item Intuition–Rationality Questionnaire that has items such as "Before I make a decision I analyze all the pros and cons"; "I often disbelieve rational arguments because I feel that reality looks different"; and "Solutions to my problems usually come to mind quite unexpectedly."

the problem is solved, and therefore increases the mnemonic availability of contents relating to motivation (Kuhl's commitment marker) until motivation has subsided (cf., e.g., Förster, Liberman, & Higgins, 2005; Goschke & Kuhl, 1993). Representation of the problem itself, as well as the functional contents that are necessary to solve it, are even active during sleep (Stickgold & Walker, 2004). They are also reevaluated into more positive ones. Valuation motivates one "toward" (as opposed to "from"); it attracts contents that will be submitted to further elaboration. Devaluation demotivates and reduces one's chances of application (Aarts, Custers, & Holland, 2007; Ferguson & Bargh, 2004; Kolańczyk, 2008; Szymańska & Kolańczyk, 2002).

Creative intuitions are more frequent in individuals set up for fulfillment rather than individuals who try to safeguard themselves against potential errors. Maslow (1958) recognized this long ago but we now have more evidence to help us explain why this is so—not so much with respect to self-actualization as to positivity with respect to goal-directed activity. Fulfillment-oriented (promotion-focused; see Higgins, 1997) individuals seek good enough means to achieve their goal and error monitoring takes place outside of conscious attention. Progress monitoring is largely automatic, as in Wegner's concept of paradoxical control effects (Wegner, 1994). Freed of explicit monitoring (of shortcomings and "lapses"), self-control runs smoothly and changes flexibly depending on the situation; if a mistake is made, attention is also engaged. Information processing in this state is dominated by the search for contents consistent with the task criteria and coherence set, and is therefore an excellent background for intuition and creative achievement (Słabosz, 2000). Immanent motivation, by means of which an individual derives pleasure from simply engaging in the task itself, facilitates the fulfillment set and has also been appreciated in the creative process (Amabile, 1983). The task solving itself becomes a source of reinforcement and the individual no longer takes heed of external circumstances or environmental demands, and no longer wastes energy adapting to external standards. Only this type of set enables the phenomenon that Czíkszentmihály (1996) called flow.

The monitoring set entails concentrating attention on the discrepancies between one's actions and one's goal or task criteria. This may be a trait disposition, as Higgins (1997) in particular emphasizes in his concept of prevention focus. In this case people attentively and to a large extent mindfully control their line of reasoning (Kolańczyk, 2007; Kolańczyk & Pawłowska-Fusiara, 2002). Both error monitoring and the need to optimize solutions use up many cognitive resources. In order to know what not to do, one must negate—one of the most difficult and energy-consuming mental operations to automate (Deutsch, Gawronski, & Strack, 2006). Mostly, the analytic thought mode is triggered. Any difficulty, even difficulty caused by an illegible typeface, switches the thought process from intuitive to analytic (cf. Alter, Oppenheimer, Epley, & Eyre, 2007), probably because attention is highly focused and therefore access to memory resources changes.

When people monitor their actions carefully, they can give up this activity and just relax. In this case too attention will change from intensive to extensive, paving the way for intuitive insight. However, following long periods of "monitoring" thought, contents indicating false ways of thinking and errors will now be more accessible. It is these contents that become particularly significant as the subject pursues his or her goal. Instead of strictly creative insights, we can now expect these signals to enter attention and awareness. Insight is now corrective and may take the form of ruminations that trigger thoughts about how one could behave differently (counterfactual thinking). Negative "background" emotions resulting from the return of negative thoughts will quickly and secondarily intensify attention and shift thinking to the analytic processing track.

THE TRIFACTOR MODEL OF CREATIVE INTUITION

Valuable insight needs much preparation and a favorable mindset. Neither should we ignore temperamental inclinations toward intuitive versus analytic cognitive style. However, the direct determinants (or aspects) of creative intuition—that is, changes in meta-motivation, attention, and implicit evaluations—operate in the "here and now" in a narrower space of time.

Paratelic Meta-Motivation and Implicit Self-Control

The initial prerequisite for loosening the reigns of explicit self-control and instigating creative intuition is change of meta-motivation. If a person—tired of obsessing over a problem for a long time—eventually decides to give himself or herself a break, telic motivation will change into paratelic motivation where no goal orients intentional activity. Apter (1982) described paratelic motivation as motivation born of activity itself, from having too much energy. Momentary resignation from conscious goal pursuit also accompanies individuals who are tired and dreaming, however, and it is they who often have creative insights. In paratelic motivation explicit self-control is unnecessary if we understand it as the control of goal-directed actions and the monitoring of their course. Conscious self-control can only switch on when we violate certain recognized standards of conduct, be they dancing or exploring the environment.

When one stops trying to solve an important problem for a moment, thoughts "think themselves" because the goal-directed activity is still going on, albeit unconsciously. The task representation and the contents positively related to it are still active. Theoretically, Dijksterhuis and Nordgren (2006) postulate, such a process could still continue even during intentional thinking about something else. I suggest, however, that the work of the unconscious mind remains in the service of the conscious solution, and that splitting conscious and unconscious activity into different purposes does not facilitate creative intuition.[2] Unconstrained activity (paratelic motivation) and the related state of extensive attention are more conducive to creative insight.

It is possible to imagine someone who substitutes one goal for another goal and even controls the way he or she rests. Rigid, excessive control is usually defensive at the cost of the opportunity for spontaneous activity and creative intuition (Maslow, 1958). One natural inhibitor of hypercontrol is emotional reactivity, which happens to correlate significantly with intuitiveness (Herzog-Krzywoszańska & Krzywoszański, 2008).

Most laboratory studies of creativity do not include incubation breaks such as relaxation, play, or free exploration. Yet divergent thinking can be more or less flexible and may be either intuitive or analytic. We tested this by means of self-report immediately after subjects completed the Atypical Uses Test (Kolańczyk & Świerzyński, 1995). Some participants declared that ideas ran dizzyingly through their heads and appeared suddenly, they knew not where from. Others analyzed consecutive features of a brick, for example, and this took time and effort. If we assume that the first type of solution was intuitive, then micro-insights took place without the help of incubation. More important, however, was the subject's positive mindset. This was measured in terms of the self-rating of creative thinking—the attitude of hope of success and positive feedback concerning previous outcomes (Kolańczyk & Świerzyński, 1995).

We know that a positive emotional background itself broadens attention span (Derryberry & Tucker, 1994; Fredrickson & Branigan, 2005; Kolańczyk, 2001), More extensive attention span with a weaker filter has been explained in terms of creative productivity (Friedman, Fishbach, Förster, & Werth, 2003; Mendelson & Griswold, 1966), however unrelated to task set. Meanwhile, set may be one of the most important determinants of both mood and attention.[3] Therefore intuitive generation of ideas is not always preceded by incubation, but it always takes place in a relatively extensive state of attention. Thus we decided to further examine the mechanism of extensive attention in a separate set of studies that are described below. Examples of incubation preceding the discoveries of famous scientists suggest that paratelic motivation related to relaxation or some other form of spontaneous activity is extremely effective (Dorfman, Shames, & Kihlstrom, 1996). Creative intuition at the micro level is also possible without a paratelic incubation period in conducive conditions of positive fulfillment set.

---

[2] A rival task may render the mnemonically available concepts/words "untypical." This, however, is a different process from creative intuition. Also, meta-analysis has revealed that if the incubation period is filled with very difficult cognitive tasks, this reduces its effectiveness (Sio & Ormerod, 2009).

[3] On the condition that the subject is really involved; if not, "promotion focus"—evoked, for example, by the sight of cheese in a task where mice seek the way out of a maze—may not remain in any obvious relation to mood even though it facilitates intuitive creativity (Friedman & Förster, 2001).

Meta-motivation		
Paratelic	**Telic**	
	Fulfillment set	**Monitoring set**
Implicit control *of telic processes*	Easy explicit control and implicit control	Effortful explicit control
Extensive attention directed to salient stimuli *sensory-affective and schematic*	**Extensive-intensive** attention directed to objects "good enough" for goal attainment	**Intensive** attention directed to goal-situation discrepancies
Positive mood		Negative mood
INTUITION / CREATIVE INSIGHT; holistic processing	INTUITION; holistic processing or analytical thinking	Analytical thinking
Metaphorical, image-symbolic thinking	Searching for coherence; confirmative strategy	Searching for incoherence; falsifying strategy

Figure 1. Influences of meta-motivation on attention states, modes of information processing, and mood.

The relationship among meta-motivation, mood, and attention states is illustrated in Figure 1. Meta-motivational states and resulting attention states can be presented on the dimension running from complete spontaneity (paratelic) to extremely attentive self-control (monitoring set), from extreme extensiveness to extreme intensity of attention. Attention states are the key to the mode of information processing.

The Extensive Attention State

Due to its significance, I have written about extensive attention elsewhere (Kolańczyk, 1991a, 1999, 2001, 2004). For example, it ensures assimilation of the effects of emotogenic stimuli on the evaluation of other accompanying objects. Positive affect evoked by a smiling face facilitates positive evaluations of a neutral image (a Chinese ideogram) in the visual field. This is because both cues—the affect-generating one and the evaluated one—are approached as one perceptual whole. The relationship between the holistic approach to the situation and extensive attention needs to be explained, however.

The most important features of extensive attention state ensuing from temporary resignation from goal-directed activity is attention span expansion at the expense of depth of processing (as level of information processing is understood by Craik & Lockhart, 1972). Since goals no longer direct attention, it is relatively scattered. It takes in a wider perceptual field and a wider range of concepts is also available to categorize the current situation. Numerous concepts are activated but this activation is less intense and more superficial, just as in Martindale's (1989) model that tried to explain why creative people have a flat association gradient: their associations are weak but distant. Martindale also linked this fact with the attention "scatter" and the broad—although weak—activation of semantic network nodes. The extensive attention concept allows us to elaborate this idea further.

The best instrument with which to describe intensive versus extensive attention states is Posner's (1994) attention theory, which posits three mechanisms: orientation, execution, and arousal. Each of these mechanisms has a different, well-defined function and depends on different brain structures and neurotransmitters. The executive function is phylogenetically the youngest. It is responsible for goal-directed activity and action control. It operates in top-down fashion and processes semantic information from the center of the perceptual field. The orienting mechanism is activated in bottom-up fashion by changes in the perceptual field when the object suddenly moves in our direction or when it is somehow distinctive. The orienting mechanism naturally prevails in children before their executive mechanism is fully mature and sensitive to physical stimulus properties.

During goal-directed activity, the orienting mechanism is largely subordinated to the executive (goal-realization) mechanism. This involves, among other things, directing the gaze or ears in the direction from which the individual expects to receive important information. A state of intensive attention ensues and processing is deep and semantic because the executive mechanism has won the competition for perceptual resources (cf. Figure 2). When a person is in a state of paratelic motivation and extensive attention, the orienting mechanism largely breaks free of executive control. Partial control still remains, however, due to implicit self-control (which is related to the activated goal) and probably also to more important regulative standards, which have a greater readiness to engage attention.

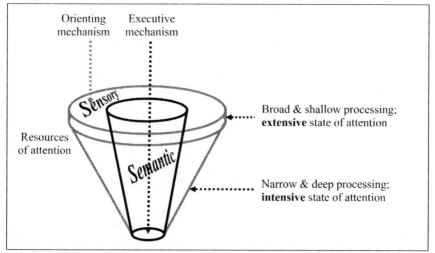

Figure 2. Cost-benefit trade-off between scope and depth of information processing, according to a dominance of the executive over orienting mechanism of attention.

The hypothesis that extensive attention is characterized by shallow, more sensual information processing was initially verified by means of the Stroop task. Participants were asked to name the color of the font in which a given word was printed (Kolańczyk, 1991b). It was assumed that superficial processing would be accompanied by a weaker arousal of the semantic meaning of a given word (e.g., "red"). If the task is to name the color of an ink that is not denoted by the word (e.g., when the word "red" is printed in green ink), weaker interferences should occur; that is, the reaction time ought to be shorter compared with the reaction time in the control group and in the group whose attention is intensified by an additional task. Intensive attention in participants was aroused by asking them to solve syllogisms, whereas extensive attention was aroused in participants by engaging them in casual play accompanied by refreshments. As expected, interference in the Stroop task in the case of paratelic motivation and extensive attention was significantly smaller than in both the control and the group characterized by telic motivation and intensive attention. Based on this result, we inferred that information processing is more shallow in the extensive attention state. However, our conjecture that this shallow information processing is accompanied by a simultaneous widening of the scope of attention is still a theoretical presumption.

The state of "liberating" the orienting mechanism from the total control of the executive mechanism, which is the essence of extensive attention, can be induced through Zen meditation. The basic work that is done during meditation is achieving a state beyond focusing on any goals; this is done through focusing on one's breath or on rhythmically repeated behavior patterns. Paratelic motivation induced through meditation, which is linked with so-called passive attention, probably bears all the characteristics of extensive attention. We used this prediction to check whether Zen meditation would heighten sensitivity to stimuli located on the peripheries of the visual field.

Mikołajczyk (2002) researched the speed of detecting letters in different locations of the visual field by people who had just meditated and their counterparts in a control group. The participants were asked to selectively react only to those letters that were identical to those located in the center of the visual field. As expected, those participants who had meditated before engaging in the task selected information from both the center and the peripheries of the visual field in an equally capable manner, whereas participants from the control group were considerably worse at selecting stimuli from the peripheries of the visual field. The concept of extensive attention was then further verified by means of other forms of manipulation: (a) visualization of paratelic versus telic activity (Różycka, 2003) or (b) broadening detection from a visual field (Szymura, Czarnecka, & Ross, 2005). An optimal indicator of extensiveness versus intensity of attention would naturally combine a measure of both the span and scope of processing. It is a spatial detection task in which words matching and nonmatching in color with the stimulus being detected appear in the center of visual field, as well as on its peripheries (Mikołajczyk, in preparation).

Extensive Attention, Image Representations, and Creative Intuition

In the extensive attention state, processing is more superficial and sensorial but also wider in scope. Individuals remain in closer, more sensorial contact with both the environment and their own bodies. When they stop thinking about a problem to take a rest or do some routine housework, they suddenly begin to feel the discomfort of their posture and the warmth of the lighting, or they begin to hear the quiet music coming from the radio. The more extensive scope of attention is associated with more extensive activation of memory structures (see also Friedman et al., 2003), ready to identify current effects at a more superficial level.

When many categories are superficially activated, their attributes are ignored and their general senses and affective meanings may be used like a puzzle to create the entire situation. No individual category is sufficiently activated to give meaning to the situation; only the contextual whole can do this. The process of memory reorganization described by Bartlett (1932) or Dijkstehuis (2004) applies to this general categorical level, except that in the extensive attention state many categories are similarly available and that is not the end of the process.

Balanced activation of many memory structures means partial "de-freezing," transitory liberation from mindsets concerning their application. There is one exception, however: an unclear, open-ended problem situation (automatic motivation persistence) maintains the process of unconscious search for the solution — that is, valuation of all contents that can help solve the problem. Contents that define the problem area are relatively more intensively activated and therefore more accessible to attention. This lays the groundwork for gaining an understanding of the problem once again in closer sensory contact with the environment. When individuals are in a state of extensive attention, they are very receptive and very sensitive to various sensory modalities (including bodily ones) relating to affective cues. They make greater use of sensory experiences, including imagined ones. The ease with which imagery is activated may be a result of their relative equivalence with respect to visual, auditory, or tactile perception. They involve the same brain structures (Finke, 1980). Imagery—like perception—is a sign of more superficial information processing, but at the same time it may express meaning symbolically, providing an image synthesis of complex abstract meanings.

Image meaning attribution also takes place by creating metaphors. One illustration of this is the spectacular work of Bargh and Williams (2008). Participants held a cup or mat in a lift to help the experimenter, whose hands were occupied with a number of other things. The experience of physical warmth or coldness gleaned from holding a cup of hot or iced coffee (or a warm vs. cold therapeutic mat) affected later person evaluations. Physical warmth invests the evaluated person with metaphorical meaning; he or she is described as warm, meaning more caring and generous.

A similar process of attributing metaphorical meaning via the sensory context can be very easily triggered in conditions of extensive attention when information is processed at a superficial, sensory level. *Nota bene* intuitionists who disperse attention more frequently than rationalists also prefer metaphoric meaning definitions to purely semantic—that is, classic—definitions (Adamska, after Kolańczyk, 1991b).

Reevaluation and Accessibility of Problem-Related Contents in Creative Intuition

Insight essentially involves switching from one experienced reality to another. This happens due to attention and change in mode of information processing. The switch can basically be described in two related terms: semantic network and sensory (image) representations. According to the spreading activation theory, accessibility of semantic memory nodes depends on their direct activation (which is contingent upon their direct activation by means of some external stimulus) and their "network" activation (by means of other associated nodes). In this way the open space of pastures can activate the "space" node; in the semantic network, this node lies near the "time" node and may also be energized when one often ponders the passage of time.

Ordinary node activation in the semantic network—for example, by means of semantic priming (with the word "space")—extinguishes rather quickly (Higgins, Bargh, & Lombardi, 1985). Different rules govern the weakening of accessibility to representations of an important problem and its associated contents. These are affectively marked and motivational activity does not really extinguish until the solution has been closed. Such affective, more permanent activations are partly "drowned out" (in attention space and consciousness) by more powerfully activated nodes that may serve ongoing goal-directed activity. People rarely enjoy the comfort of working only on complex issues and other goals and demands, imposed by the work environment, activate other semantic network nodes. For instance, a microbiologist may perform routine experiments on gene knockout—albeit ones that need his full attention—although these experiments are merely an instrument in his efforts to understand the nature of degenerative bone disease. His attention resources are also partly occupied by his plan to collect his child from nursery school and do some essential shopping. In this situation the strength of activation of different nodes determining current goals and tasks is relatively large. This is a case of intensive attention and attention transfer from task to task, which demands the relatively strong activation of just a few network nodes. The most activated nodes are more accessible to attention and win the processing competition. This is illustrated by time t_1 in Figure 3. Any nodes of the semantic network that may be helpful in solving a given problem and have been marked as positive become accessible to one's attention.

As goal-directed motivation subsides, so do the short-term node activations associated with immediate goals and current tasks. Thanks to extensive attention from relatively weak—although extensive—semantic network activations, an "affective map" of the problem situation emerges just like a submerged town

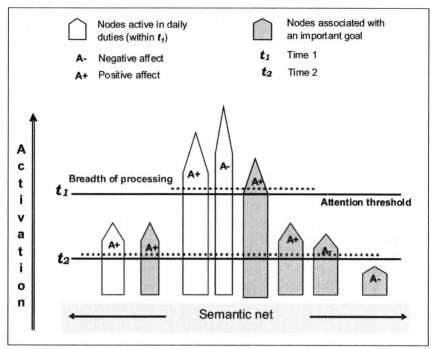

Figure 3. Affective memory and intuition (affective "life" of information coherent with a goal).

from the bottom of the ocean (time t_2 in Figure 3). This can even happen during sleep, in which case shallow, sensory information processing brings out the meaning of these semantic activations—that is, it may represent them symbolically or invest them with a new, metaphorical quality. Of course imagery plays a more important role when one is asleep, whereas perceptual representations are probably more important when one is awake.

In states of both extensive and intensive attention, examination of affect associated with particular nodes of the semantic network is possible thanks to implicit evaluations—for example, with the use of the affective priming paradigm. Similarly, in an experiment designed by Ferguson and Bargh (2004; compare Fazio, 1986, 2001), participants were asked to decide whether given adjectives were positive or negative when they were primed by words associated with the research question. Faster positive than negative associations indicate a positive implicit evaluation.

In conclusion, flexibility of meta-motivation and mindset are the foundation on which creative insight rests. Periods of telic motivation and work on the problem, also in a monitoring mindset, are essential during knowledge acquisition and verification of one's ideas. However, periods of work on the problem in a fulfillment mindset, when states of paratelic motivation and extensive attention are very permeable, are strategic for insight. These periods, in turn, directly determine the conditions of insight. The intuitionist makes distant journeys within the cognitive system—from deep, narrow processing whose purpose is to root semantic meanings in the context of individual values and knowledge-organizing criteria (with great effort and slowly) to superficial, extensive processing saturated with sensory images (effortless and speedy).

EXCEPTIONAL DETERMINANTS OF EXTENSIVE ATTENTION AND CREATIVE INSIGHT

An exceptional negative emotion that evokes the state of extensive attention is anxiety and the arousal associated with it (Eysenck, 1976; Mathews, May, Mogg, & Eysenck, 1990; Szymura & Kolańczyk, 2006). Anxiety is objectless and involves a state of general apprehension and potential focus on the possible, extensive specter of negative events. Due to these qualities, anxiety evokes an extensive attention state with superficial processing. In other words, not only positive emotions but also anxiety and intense arousal broaden attention. According to the affective coherence principle, in a state of anxiety negative contents are more accessible than positive contents. On the other hand, the consequences of defense mechanisms, "hot" denials, and reinterpretations of painful reality also become available. All semantic network nodes corresponding with these contents will be strongly activated. They will take part in the interpretation of the situation and may create the "puzzles" forming holistic, insightful meaning. In the extreme form, when arousals are very intense and long lasting, the insightful meaning may assume the form of delusions—for example, concerning the subject's special mission in a malevolent world or malevolently organized social environment.

The Trifactor Model of Creative Intuition versus Other Explanations

Discriminants of creative intuition cannot be narrowed down to either the cognitive, emotional, motivational, or temperamental domain since all these domains play an important role in the phenomenon of creative intuition. That is probably why it has been so hard to work out a satisfying, comprehensive model of the process. I incorporated many partial explanations in my own approach, trying to put them in perspective and evaluating how they fit into the big picture of determinants. I decided on subject motivation as the axis of the synthesis since it is highly valued in research on creativity, although less so in research on insight. Such an approach not only allows us to understand the functionality of each cognitive operation, but also allows us to consider cognitive processing as part of an individual's overall functioning.

Research on creativity investigates many different processes but researchers seem to agree that creativity is highly correlated with intuitiveness. Policastro (1995) cites studies in which the connection between intuition and creativity was observed in 90–98% of cases. However, was intuition defined in those studies in a similar way as it is defined in this chapter? In those studies creative intuition is seen as some kind of implicit knowledge manifesting itself through a hunch that points an individual in a promising direction and helps him or her determine a preliminary scope of inquiry. This description corresponds to insights experienced by Einstein and other scientists who laboriously translated their early visions into communicative and reasonable words.

Ward, Finke, and Smith (1995) seem to perceive the process in a very similar way as a source of precreative structures. The precreative structures are fragmentary solutions or ideas that point to directions for further investigation. However, these processes are hard to study and therefore researchers relied on the example of a similar process—perceptive coherence—which is experienced before a person is able to see a clear image, and which consists of detecting consistent perceptive patterns or being able to sense their existence (compare Bowers et al., 1990). At this point in our attempt to understand the phenomenon of creative intuition, we are unable to say where such an ability comes from. It has been found that it is closely related to meta-motivation and mood and is facilitated by a positive emotional setting, as well as by the self-fulfillment set (similar inspiration can be found in studies by Friedman & Förster, 2000, 2001). What is more, the strategic structure of the brain by means of which people experience perceptive intuition is the orbitofrontal cortex, which gathers data on the affective state of the organism (Volz & von Cramon, 2006) but which also takes part in learning intuitive strategies of decision making (Bechara, Damasio, Damasio, & Anderson, 1994). Thus, from the perspective of contemporary research, the role of evaluation in the intuitive process can be seen with the naked eye by means of neuroimaging. Combining all these data allows us to establish a synthetic concept of creative intuition that was first developed twenty years ago.

The process of understanding the nature of creative intuition benefited less from the oldest findings and that of examining "convergent" insights. Theories that attempted to explain the essence of creative intuition within the realms of Gestalt psychology trapped researchers in a rut of thinking in terms of incubation and insight in the context of closed-ended tasks. This approach impeded progress in explaining the nature of the phenomenon, but it did trigger interest in the nature of these two subprocesses and a discussion about their inevitability.

To summarize the approach to other theories and studies, it has to be said that the trifactor model of creative intuition includes:

- A type of meta-motivation along with implicit self-control.
- Extensive attention state.
- Changes in information processing (from analytic to holistic) and in evaluations.

The trifactor model, to a small extent, develops existing concepts of insight. To a greater extent, however, it is a synthesis of studies on creativity from the motivational, cognitive, and affective perspectives. Although the theories do not fully explain the nature of creative intuition, they nevertheless were found to be extremely important in providing us with a more complete understanding of the matter, creating a coherent mechanism in place of an index of mental characteristics (such as broad attention and the ability to detect coherence, which are very important).

Does similar modeling of mental processes make sense at all if at this point research methods do not allow them to be verified as a whole? The starting point has to be verifying elementary relationships and then combining them, which will allow us to better explain the process of creative intuition. Dynamically evolving methodology supplies us with increasing possibilities for data synthesis, which in turn gives us hope that one day we will be able to fully encompass such a complex system of variables.

REFERENCES

Aarts, H., Custers. R, & Holland, R. W. (2007). The nonconscious cessation of goal pursuit: When goals and negative affect are coactivated. *Journal of Personality and Social Psychology, 92*, 165–178.

Alter, A. L., Oppenheimer, D. M., Epley, N., & Eyre, R. N. (2007). Overcoming intuition: Metacognitive difficulty activates analytic reasoning. *Journal of Experimental Psychology: General, 136*, 569–576.

Amabile, T. M. (1983). *The social psychology of creativity*. New York: Springer-Verlag.

Apter, M. J. (1982). The possibility of structural phenomenology: The case of reversal theory. *Journal of Phenomenological Psychology, 12*, 173–187.

Baas, M., de Dreu, C. K. W., Nijstad, B. A. (2008). A meta-analysis of 25 years of mood-creativity research: Hedonic tone, activation, or regulatory focus? *Psychological Bulletin, 134*, 779–806.

Bargh, J. A., & Williams, L. E. (2008). Experiencing physical warmth promotes interpersonal warmth. *Science, 322*, 606–607.

Bartlett, F. C. (1932). *Remembering: A study in experimental and social psychology*. Cambridge, UK: Cambridge University Press.

Bartlett, J. (1955). *Familiar quotations*. Boston: Little, Brown.

Bauman, N., & Kuhl, J. (2002). Intuition, affect, and personality: Unconscious coherence judgments and self-regulation of negative affect. *Journal of Personality and Social Psychology, 83*, 1213–1223.

Bechara, A., Damasio, H., Damasio, A, R., & Anderson, S. W. (1994). Insensitivity to future consequences following damage to human prefrontal cortex. *Cognition, 50*, 7–15.

Bolte, A., Goschke, T., & Kuhl, J. (2003). Emotion and intuition: Effects of positive and negative mood on implicit judgments of semantic coherence. *Psychological Science, 14*, 416–421.

Bowers, K. S., Regehr, G., Balthazard, C., & Parker, K. (1990). Intuition in the context of discovery. *Cognitive Psychology, 22*, 72–110.

Brendl, C. M., Markman, A. B., & Messner, C. (2003). The devaluation effect: Activating a need devalues unrelated objects. *Journal of Consumer Research, 29*, 464–473.

Craik, F. I. M., & Lockhart, R. S. (1972). Levels of processing: A framework for memory research. *Journal of Verbal Learning and Verbal Behavior, 11*, 671–684.

Czíkszentmihály, M. (1996). *Creativity: Flow and the psychology of discovery and invention*. New York: Harper Perennial.

Czyżewska, M. (2001). Implicit learning: Theoretical and methodological controversies. *Polish Psychological Bulletin, 32*, 45–52.

Dane, E., & Pratt, M. G. (2007). Exploring intuition and its role in managerial decision making. *Academy of Management Review, 32*, 33–54.

Derryberry, D., & Tucker, D. M. (1994). Motivating the focus of attention. In P. H. Niedenthal & S. Kitayama (Eds.), *The heart's eye: Emotional influences in perception and attention* (pp.170–192). San Diego, CA: Academic Press.

Deutsch, R., Gawronski, B., & Strack, F. (2006.) At the boundaries of automaticity: Negation as reflective operation. *Journal of Personality and Social Psychology, 91*, 385-405.

Dijksterhuis, A. (2004) Think different: The merits of unconscious thought in preference development and decision making. *Journal of Personality and Social Psychology, 87*, 586–598.

Dijksterhuis, A., Nordgren, L. F. (2006). A theory of unconscious thought. *Perspectives on Psychological Science, 1*, 95–109.

Dixon, R. A., Hultsch, D. F., & Hertzog, C. (1988). The Metamemory in Adulthood (MIA) questionnaire. *Psychopharmacology Bulletin, 24*, 671–688.

Dorfman, J., Shames, V. A., & Kihlstrom, J. F. (1996). Intuition, incubation, and insight: Implicit cognition in problem solving. In G. D. M. Underwood (Ed.), *Implicit cognition* (pp. 257–296). New York: Oxford University Press.

Dow, G. T., & Mayer, R. E. (2004). Teaching students to solve insight problems: Evidence for domain specificity in training. *Creativity Research Journal, 16*, 389–402.

Eysenck, M. W. (1976). Arousal, learning, and memory. *Psychological Bulletin, 83*, 389–404.

Fazio, R. H. (1986). How do attitudes guide behavior? In R. M. Sorrentino & E. T. Higgins (Eds.), *Handbook of motivation and cognition: Foundations of social behavior* (pp. 204–243). New York: Guilford Press.

Fazio, R. H. (2001). On the automatic activation of associated evaluations: An overview. *Cognition and Emotion, 15*, 115–141.

Ferguson, M. J., & Bargh, J. A. (2004). Liking is for doing: The effects of goal pursuit on automatic evaluation. *Journal of Personality and Social Psychology, 87*, 557–572.

Finke, R. A. (1980). Levels of equivalence in imagery and perception. *Psychological Review, 87*, 113–132.

Förster, J., Liberman, N., & Higgins, E. T. (2005). Accessibility from active and fulfilled goals. *Journal of Experimental Social Psychology, 41*, 220–239.

Fredrickson, B. L., & Branigan, C. (2005). Positive emotions broaden the scope of attention and thought action repertoires. *Cognition and Emotion, 19*, 313–332.

Friedman, R. S., Fishbach, J., Förster, J., & Werth, L. (2003). Attentional priming effects on creativity. *Creativity Research Journal, 15*, 277–286.

Friedman, R. S., & Förster, J. (2000). The effects of approach and avoidance motor actions on the elements of creative insight. *Journal of Personality and Social Psychology, 79*, 477–492.

Friedman, R. S., & Förster, J. (2001). The effects of promotion and prevention on creativity. *Journal of Personality and Social Psychology, 81*, 1001–1013.

Frijda, N. (2005). Emotion experience. *Cognition and Emotion, 19*, 473–497.

Goschke, T., & Kuhl, J. (1993). Representation of intentions: Persisting activation in memory. *Journal of Experimental Psychology: Learning, Memory, and Cognition, 19*, 1211–1226.

Herzog-Krzywoszańska, R., & Krzywoszański, Ł. (2008). Cechy temperamentu a intuicyjny vs. racjonalny styl myślenia [The temperament trait and intuitive vs. rational thinking style]. *Studia Psychologiczne, 46*, 73–78.

Higgins, E. T. (1997). Beyond pleasure and pain. *American Psychologist, 52*, 1280–1300.

Higgins, E. T., Bargh, J. A., & Lombardi, W. (1985). Nature of priming effects on categorization. *Journal of Experimental Psychology: Learning, Memory, and Cognition, 11*, 59–69.

Isen, A. (1987). Positive affect, cognitive processes, and social behavior. In L. Berkowitz (Ed.), *Advances in experimental social psychology* (Vol. 20, pp. 203–253). New York: Academic Press.

Kahneman, D., & Triesman, A. (1984). Changing views of attention and automaticity. In R. Parasuraman & R. Davis (Eds.), *Varieties of attention* (pp. 29–61). Orlando, FL: Academic Press.

Kaufmann, G., & Vosburg, S. K. (1997). "Paradoxical" mood effects on creative problem solving. *Cognition and Emotion, 11*, 151–170.

Knoblich, G., Ohlsson, S., Haider, H., & Rhenius, D. (1999). Constraint relaxation and chunk decomposition in insight problem solving. *Journal of Experimental Psychology: Learning, Memory, and Cognition, 25*, 1534–1555.

Knoblich, G., & Oellinger, M. (2006, November/December). The eureka moment. *Scientific American Mind, 17*, 38–43.

Kolańczyk, A. (1989). How to study creative intuition? *Polish Psychological Bulletin, 20*, 149–155.

Kolańczyk, A. (1991a) Rola uwagi w procesie intuicji twórczej [The role of attention in creative intuition]. In A. Tokarz (Ed.), *Stymulatory i inhibitory aktywności twórczej człowieka* (pp. 33–48). Poznań, Poland: Nakom.

Kolańczyk, A. (1991b). *Intuicyjność procesów przetwarzania informacji* [The intuitiveness of information processing]. Gdańsk, Poland: Gdańsk University Publishers.

Kolańczyk, A. (1995). Why is intuition creative sometimes? In T. Maruszewski & C. Nosal (Eds.), *Creative information processing: Cognitive models*. Delft, The Netherlands: Eburon Publishers.

Kolańczyk, A. (1999). *Czuję, myślę, jestem. Świadomość i procesy psychiczne w ujęciu poznawczym* [I feel, think, am: Consciousness and mental processes from a cognitive perspective]. Gdańsk, Poland: Gdańskie Wydawnictwo Psychologiczne.

Kolańczyk, A. (2001). The role of affect in preconscious and conscious processing. *Polish Psychological Bulletin, 32*, 27–37.

Kolańczyk, A. (2004). Stany uwagi sprzyjające wpływom afektywnym na ocenianie [States of attention fostering influences of affect on judgments]. *Studia Psychologiczne, 42*, 93–109.

Kolańczyk, A. (2007) Samokontrola i wpływy bodźców afektywnych na ocenianie [Self-control and influences of affective stimuli on judgments]. *Psychologia Społeczna, 2*, 7–22.

Kolańczyk, A. (2008). Wpływ samokontroli na wartościowanie treści zwiazanych z zadaniem [The effect of self-control on evaluations of meanings related to a task]. *Czasopismo Psychologiczne, 14*, 201–214.

Kolańczyk, A., & Pawłowska-Fusiara, M. (2002). Automatic correction or controlled processing of affective priming. *Polish Psychological Bulletin, 33*, 35–44.

Kolańczyk, A., & Świerzyński, R. (1995). Emocjonalne wyznaczniki stylu i plastyczności imyślenia [Emotional determinants of thinking styles and flexibility]. *Przegląd Psychologiczny, 3/4*, 279–304.

Lewicki, P., Hill, T., & Czyzewska, M. (1992). Nonconscious acquisition of information. *American Psychologist, 47*, 796–801.

Martindale, C. (1989). Personality, situation, and creativity. In J. A. Glover & R. R. Ronning (Eds.), *Handbook of creativity* (pp. 211–232). New York: Plenum Press.

Maslow, A. (1958). Emotional blocks to creativity. *Journal of Individual Psychology, 14*, 51–56.

Mathews, A., May, J., Mogg, K., & Eysenck, M. W. (1990). Attentional bias in anxiety: Selective search or defective filtering? *Journal of Abnormal Psychology, 99*, 166–173.

Mednick, M. (1963). Research creativity in psychology graduate students. *Journal of Consulting Psychology, 27*, 265–266.

Mendelsohn, G. A., & Griswold, B. B. (1966). Assessed creative potential, vocabulary level, and sex as predictors of the use of incidental cues in verbal problem solving. *Journal of Personality and Social Psychology, 4*, 423–431.

Mikołajczyk, P. (2002). *Zależność uwagi od medytacji zen* [Attention dependence on Zen meditation]. Unpublished master's thesis, University of Gdańsk, Gdańsk, Poland.

Mikołajczyk, P. (in preparation). *Mechanizmy uwagi ekstensywnej i intensywnej* [Mechanisms of extensive and intensive attention]. Unpublished doctoral dissertation, University of Gdańsk, Gdańsk, Poland.

Nęcka, E., Grohman, M., & Słabosz, A. (2006). Creativity studies in Poland. In J. C. Kaufman and R. J. Sternberg (Eds.), *The international handbook of creativity* (pp. 270–306). New York: Cambridge University Press.

Nosal, C. S. (1992). *Diagnoza typów umysłu. Rozwinięcie i zastosowanie teorii Junga* [Types of mind diagnosis: Development and application of Jung's theory]. Warsaw: Wydawnictwo Naukowe PWN.

Oatley, K., & Jenkins, J. M. (1996). *Understanding emotions*. Malden, MA: Blackwell.

Policastro, E. (1995). Creative intuition: An integrative review. *Creativity Research Journal, 8*, 99–113.

Posner, M. J. (1994). Attention: The mechanisms of consciousness. *Proceedings of the National Academy of Sciences, 91*, 7398–7403.

Reverberi, C., Toraldo, A., D'Agostini, S., & Skrap, M. (2005). Better without (lateral) frontal cortex? Insight problems solved by frontal patients. *Brain, 128*, 2882–2890.

Różycka, J. (2003). Przetwarzanie centralne i peryferyczne w zależności od stanów uwagi [Central and peripheral processing according to states of attention]. Unpublished master's thesis, University of Gdańsk, Gdańsk, Poland.

Sio, U. N., & Ormerod, T. C. (2009). Does incubation enhance problem solving? A meta-analytic review. *Psychological Bulletin, 135*, 94–120.

Słabosz, A, (2000). *Elementarne składniki procesu twórczego. Aktywacja semantyczna i inhibicja poznawcza* [Elementary components of creative process: Semantic activation and cognitive inhibition]. Unpublished doctoral dissertation, Jagiellonian University, Kraków, Poland.

Sternberg, R. J., & Lubart, T. (1995). An investment perspective on creative insight. In R. J. Sternberg & J. E. Davidson (Eds.), *The nature of insight* (pp. 535–588). Cambridge, MA: MIT Press.

Stickgold, R., & Walker, M. (2004). To sleep, perchance to gain creative insight? *Trends in Cognitive Sciences, 8*, 191–192.

Szymańska, B., & Kolańczyk, A. (2002). Zmiana afektywnego znaczenia pojęć w kontekście zadania w przypadku osób twórczych i nietwórczych [Modification of the affective meaning of words in the context of task in cases of high and low levels of creativity]. *Studia Psychologiczne, 40*, 151–160.

Szymura, B., Czarnecka, K., & Ross, M. (2005, November). Uwaga intensywna i ekstensywna a pozytywne i negatywne skutki automatyzacji procesu selekcji informacji [Extensive vs. intensive attention and positive vs. negative effects of automation of information selection]. Paper presented at the annual meeting of the Autonomous Psychology Club, Warsaw.

Szymura B., & Kolańczyk, A. (2006). Wpływ lęku na przeszukiwanie pola uwagi, [Effect of anxiety on the search of attention field]. In M. Marszał-Wiśniewska, G. Sędek, & J. Stanik (Eds.), *Zaburzenia i optymalizacja procesów emocjonalnych i poznawczych. Nowe kierunki badań* (pp. 25–44). Gdańsk, Poland: Gdańskie Wydawnictwo Psychologiczne.

Volz, K. G., & von Cramon, D. Y. (2006). What neuroscience can tell about intuitive processes in the context of perceptual discovery. *Journal of Cognitive Neuroscience 18*, 2077–2087.

Vosburg, S. K. (1998). The effects of positive and negative mood on divergent thinking performance. *Creativity Research Journal, 11*, 165–172.

Wallas, G. (1926). *The art of thought*. New York: Franklin Watts.

Ward, T. B., Finke, R. A., & Smith, S. M. (1995). *Creativity and the mind: Discovering the genius within*. New York: Plenum Press.

Wegner, D. M. (1994). Ironic processes of mental control. *Psychological Review, 101*, 34–52.

Windholz, G., & Lamal, P. A. (1985). Köhler's insight revisited. *Teaching of Psychology, 12*, 165–167.

PART II

Self in Social Behavior and Emotional Expression

CHAPTER 5

How Emotions Work

Nico H. Frijda

INTRODUCTION

How do emotions work? What are the processes and mechanisms that give rise to the phenomena that we call "emotions"? Those are the major questions for a theory of emotions.

Over the past four decades, insight into the phenomena of emotion has vastly expanded. There has been a tremendous rise in research. There has been extensive work on measurement of emotion components, their conditions and interrelations. And there has been the emergence of the domain of affective neuroscience (Panksepp, 1998). But description and analysis of phenomena and what elicits them do not represent the full work of affective science. They not even do after adding their neuroscientific conditions and concomitants. Psychological science in general proceeds along three levels of description: the phenomenological level that describes the phenomena to be explained; the hardware level that describes the neural provisions and processes; and in between, fed by those two, the functional or psychological level of description in terms of information processes, energetic and control processes, and processes of action constitution (Dennett, 1978).

It is the latter that forms the core goal of emotion theory. How do emotions work? Defining and analyzing the basic emotion processes is difficult, because what we call emotions are multicomponential responses consisting of a number of more or less simultaneous components such as feelings, autonomic reactions, action urges, cognitions, and behaviors (Scherer, 1984). The correlations between components are low, even within what are considered instances of a given kind

Personality, Cognition, and Emotion edited by Michael W. Eysenck, Małgorzata Fajkowska, and Tomasz Maruszewski. Eliot Werner Publications, Clinton Corners, New York, 2012.

of emotion such as joy or fear (Lang, 1993; Scherer, 1984). And yet the components are in some fashion intimately related.

Because of this, conceptions of the most prominent or characteristic emotion features have varied considerably over time. What is the most characteristic of these various components? What defines emotions? They have been defined as feeling states (e.g., James, 1884), as states of pleasure or pain (Ortony, Clore, & Collins, 1988; Russell, 2003; Wundt, 1896), as states of autonomic arousal or dearousal (e.g., Duffy, 1962; Prinz, 2004), as states of response disorganization and cognitive confusion (Kant; Hebb, 1949), as innate patterns of behavior (Damasio, 1994), or as judgments (Nussbaum, 2001; Solomon, 1976). But none of these components is always present when one is inclined to consider a response an emotion. People can feel grief without much autonomic arousal, or nasty without feeling angry.

PASSION

Interestingly and surprisingly, none of the components mentioned above catches the most distinctive aspect of emotions: the aspect that presumably formed the main reason for distinguishing emotions from other kinds of response, and that led to the emergence of words like "emotion" in the first place. These aspects are that certain human and animal responses suggest certain functional aspects of those multicomponential phenomena as a whole. They suggest that emotions are passions.

The core of what we call emotions is their being passions. They involve motive states and they do so with what I call control precedence. They claim priority and usurp attention, and with some intensity they clamor for action, impose inaction, or disrupt motivation. Even in weak emotions, signs of control precedence and changes in motivation are present and give the subject or observers reason to call his or her response an emotion.

The phenomena of emotion suggest, first of all, that these responses are intentional in the sense of bearing on the individual's relationship with some object, most commonly some object outside the individual. They suggest, second, that the responses as a whole each manifest some motive state—that is, some strivings to achieve a future state (as in flight or desire) or to retain a present state, such as remaining very close to some other person or staying away from him or her. And they suggest, third, that these motive states assume control over the individual's responses, including his or her thoughts and actions. They suggest that the individual is "being driven" by his or her inclination to react, or is "being carried away." The individual appears as being to some extent "passive" in regard to his or her response. These three aspects transpire very clearly in the words used to denote these responses before the word "emotion" came into use: the words *pathèma* in Greek, *affectio* in Latin, and *passion* in French and English. The responses concerned appear not the result of deliberation and foresight of outcomes to be obtained, and may show disregard for reasons to stop ongoing action or to do otherwise.

The core process that underlies the major phenomena in what we call emotions is a motive state with control precedence. It represents readiness to achieve or modify one's relationship with some object—some person, some event, some issue, some activity, or the world as a whole—or it represents modification of such readiness as such, as in the apathy of sadness, hopelessness, or despair, the disorganized activity of blind excitement, and the frozen inhibition of anxiety.

ACTION READINESS

Focusing on motive states and striving entails an important change in perspective on emotions, in comparison with the views of emotion mentioned earlier.

This perspective places *action* in the foreground when analyzing emotions. It takes emotions outside of the individual, so to speak. They are states that happen *between* an individual and his or her environment, or some person or object in it, or possibly one's representation of oneself. They are about one's *relationship* with that something, even if the relationship is one of indifference or disinclination to relate. Emotions are constitutive of relationships—or of changes in relationships—with some other person, with some event, with the world as a whole, or with oneself.

Emotions emerge first of all as variants of motive states for action. A given emotion represents a given motive state that can end up in very different kinds of actions: "anger" or "hostility" can be manifest in a frown, a shout, or an attack. Moreover, a given emotion may not end up in any action at all. Motive states are not actions, and they may never get that far. One can feel an urge to flee without tensing a muscle. Emotions can remain entirely private events that merely are felt by their subject. They can remain covert, as mere readiness, mere inner state, mere emotional feeling. Still, mode of readiness for action forms their core.

Because of all that, I call the motive states of emotions "states of action readiness." This term refers not to readiness for some particular action, but to being set to achieve a particular aim. It means readiness to establish, maintain, or change one's relationship to the world or some object. And such states of readiness are not cognitions or mere wishes. They are states of being set for action, if only for welcoming the relationship change when it occurs.

There are different kinds of action readiness. Some can be distinguished by the kind of relation that they aim for or seek to maintain; they are called action tendencies. Many emotion categories or labels are modeled around them. Self-report questionnaire research has found appreciable correlations between emotion labels and ratings of action tendencies (Frijda, Kuipers, & Terschure, 1989; Frijda, Markam, Sato, & Wiers, 1995). The various action tendencies that can be distinguished are listed in Figure 1.

Figure 1. Action tendencies.

Action readiness also can vary in mode of activation—that is, in degree and mode of readiness as such, with a particular object or event, or with anything at all. Examples are states of enthusiasm or violent desire, and apathy and total indifference to anything whatever. But modes of activation also vary in complexity, such as in tenseness, where activation is held in check by contrary activation, or inhibition, where activation is blocked as such. Such complexities contrast to constellations in which action readiness is given free rein in behavior and experience. They are manifest in states of hypoactivation or hyperactivation, in apathy and listlessness, or in states of tenseness in which activation is held in check by inhibition. They lead to descriptive terms like *enthusiastic, interested, easygoing, relaxed, listless, tense, strained, excited,* or *driven,* to what Damasio (2000) has called "background emotions" and Stern (1985) has called "vitality affects."

These various manifestations of action readiness suggest the latter's most general content. Action readiness reflects the individual's engagement with the world, including himself or herself (Higgins, 2006). It reflects the degree and kind of that engagement, up to losing oneself in something in the world, or down to the point of absence of engagement, as in certain pathologies such as akinetic mutism. "Emotion" can be viewed as modulation of engagement beyond its total absence. Capacity for emotion as a basic attribute of vertebrates (or nonreptilian vertebrates, or perhaps even a larger range of animals) can be said to be based on this capacity for engagement: the capacity to be sensitive to events and spend time and effort in dealing with them. These capacities are central to the so-called enactive view of perception and experience (Ellis, 2005; Noë, 2004; Varela, Thompson, & Rosch, 1991).

To be sure, there do exist reflex-like emotions, in which motive states do not play a role. They merely are adaptive responses to challenging events. Some emotional responses are rigid and stereotyped. Examples are startle, freezing, vomiting in sensory disgust, and elementary sexual responses. They fit a simpler and older system architecture that does not yet allow for motive states. Insects and reptiles show them. They remain in operation in mammals, where they form an elementary part of the emotional action repertoires.

Analyzing emotions in terms of states of action readiness clarifies certain theoretically baffling complexities of emotion. Different kinds of emotion, as distinguished by emotion labels, cannot be consistently diagnosed by some particular behavior, such as a given facial expression. Even surprise, for instance, leads only occasionally to the famous widely opened eyes (Reisenzein, 2000). Neither do different emotions consist of standard packages of response that are each composed of a specific expression, autonomic response pattern, and feeling—as the basic view of emotions has proposed (Ekman, 1999; Öhman & Mineka, 2001). This has led to the assertion that emotions are not natural kinds (Barrett, 2006). This assertion is not correct, because it does not locate the distinction between different emotions at the right level of analysis: at that of modes of action readiness, the level of the intentional subject-object relationships. That level reflects the main function of emotions: dealing with particular adaptive and interpersonal contingencies.

PROCESSES OF PASSION

Can we get a closer view of the processes that give rise to the phenomena of passion? Yes, we can.

First, action readiness. This is not an a priori notion. It is suggested by the phenomena themselves. Different behaviors induced by given kinds of event— a threat, an insult, the appearance of an attractive person—show equifinality. Examples given have illustrated this. Appearance of a desirable object may induce looking at her, or walking toward her, or winking, or talking: all enhance interaction. Unfriendly and harmful encounters induce many different actions that all can hurt the antagonist or discourage further interference. Many of the actions derive their precise meaning—emotional or merely pragmatic—from their emotional context. One can bite in order to eat, in the raptures of love, or in the frenzy of rage. In the latter context, it is to hurt. In a particular event encounter, all actions share in serving the particular current aim. Presumably, they are generated by that aim; and a process must underlie its operation.

Second, action readiness—rather than emotion—is what one perceives at a glance from someone's facial expression. The person is seen to draw back, open himself or herself up, getting strained and tight, and so forth. Rating facial expressions in terms of modes of action readiness shows almost as much interobserver consistency as does rating in terms of basic emotions (Frijda & Tcherkassof, 1997).

Third, feelings clearly also reflect states of action readiness. They include feelings of intent, urge, impulse, inclination, and desire. They are frequently mentioned in emotion self-reports. They are what distinguish emotion classes in such reports (Davitz, 1969; Frijda et al., 1989, 1995). In fact, action readiness theory is partly designed to account for such self-reported states, and for the behavioral features that correspond to them.

Finally, mention has been made of the prosodic, dynamic, temporal aspects of behavior that appear indicative of strength and structure of engagement.

Still, action readiness may appear a puzzling notion. It refers to orientation toward some future state, even of motivation for unreflective and impulsive action. But the evidence for states of readiness for action to come, and for its parameters, is ample. Central representations of action to come—including its aim, direction, and intended parameters like force—are evident from the contents and neural manifestations of merely imagined actions (Jeannerod, 1997). That action representations can occur in the absence of efferent motor innervation is also evident from canonical neuron activity while viewing objects of manipulation, as well as from mirror neuron activity when viewing the actions of others (Rizzolatti, Fogassi, & Gallese, 2001).

The proximal mechanism of implicit goal orientation has also become clear in the findings that gave rise to the so-called efferent copy model of goal-directed action, developed by von Holst and Mittelstaedt (1950). Efferent copies are representations of the expected feedback from the final stages of the action to come, or sensory settings that prepare for such feedback. They are produced at the very moment that an action is prepared: an efferent copy is formed as expectancy of the sensation of the action involved, such as the sensation of having an object in one's hand when setting out to grasp it. I will come back to the provenance of states of action readiness and their efferent copies. Efferent copies form the germ of expectations. Efferent copies represent the aims of action tendencies. They originate in appraisal of the emotion-eliciting event.

Action readiness, however central, is but one of the components of emotions. The various components, each with its own function, closely interact and mutually respond to each other. Together they form a response by the entire person. The components are "synchronized," as Scherer (2004, 2005) formulates it, referring to these continuous and reciprocal interactions and feedback circuits in which responses and cognitive inputs cannot be separated (Lewis, 2005). This synchrony implies integration of information from all over the brain, as indeed is being shown by extensive neural interactions (Lewis, 2005) and widespread cerebral coordination, evident in EEG synchronization over large brain regions (Edelman & Tononi, 2000; Lewis & Todd, 2007; Varela, Thompson, & Rosch, 1991).

In this integration, action readiness can plausibly be assigned the organizing role. All component processes contribute to the moment's action readiness, and to tuning how the individual relates to and deals with the given event. The state of action readiness not only represents readiness for appropriate relational action; it also sets perceptual sensitivities. In fear, for instance, threat signals are detected more rapidly (Crombez, Eccleston, Bayens, & Eelen, 1998; MacLeod, Mathews, & Tata, 1986) and it restricts attention to those stimuli (Easterbrook,

1959; Eysenck, 1997). It activates the autonomic nervous system in anticipation of coming motor and attentional efforts (Obrist, 1981). It also readies in advance for the possible consequences of forthcoming actions, as is evident from the fact that emotion regulation is prepared even before response appears.

Insight is growing into the mechanisms of such widespread synchrony. They include neurotransmitter and neuropeptide activations that show distinct degrees of emotion specificity. Some neurohumors are carried by the bloodstream; others are secreted by widely branching neurotransmitter systems. Quite recently it has been demonstrated that others again—notably oxytocin—are carried by the extra-neural liquor in the cerebral ventricles and subarachnoidal space (Veening, de Jong, & Barendregt, 2010).

The nature of the dispositions that underlie the different modes of action readiness forms one of the major questions for emotion theory. What is it that allows them to emerge? Where do they come from?

One major hypothesis is that there exist neural, biologically prepared subcortical dispositions that are activated by events as appraised. Elementary emotions—desire, fear, anger, disgust—are retained under decortication as well as under prefrontal cortical damage (Bard, 1934a, 1934b; Damasio 1994). fMRI studies found differential subcortical activations during recall of different emotions (Damasio et al., 2000). The subcortical circuits identified by lesion and stimulation studies to be involved in emotions show considerable cross-species similarity (Panksepp, 1998). They are best considered motivational systems, linked on one hand to sensitivities for particular event contingencies (such as threats), and on the other to relevant action hierarchies and their control by prefrontal networks.

The evidence has so far not been sufficiently compelling to satisfactorily cover the domain of emotions (e.g., Phan, Wager, Taylor, & Liberzon, 2002). Alternative hypotheses remain, such as an organizing role of innate situation-specific action dispositions and neurotransmitters facilitating them, as well as ad hoc organization of modes of action readiness by universal individual-environment contingencies such as reward opportunities, modes of social interaction, infants to care for, and the like—for example, Scherer's (2005) notion of modal emotions.

CONTROL PRECEDENCE

Passion was characterized as action readiness with control precedence, defined by priority shifts for attention and action, persistence of both after interruptions and in the face of obstacles, neglect of risks, costs, distractions, and propriety, the feeling of being overtaken by one's emotion, and the other behavioral phenomena of engagement.

The phenomena of control precedence in fact index the power or intensity of emotions, also subjectively, as appeared from the data obtained in a study by Sonnemans and Frijda (1994). They asked each of a number of subjects to report on six recent emotion experiences and, for each emotion, to rate how intense it was felt to have been. They also had to rate a number of more specific aspects of each emotion: the effects of the emotion on one's thinking and on one's beliefs regarding the objects or people involved, how strong and how drastic their action readiness had been, how frequently the event recurred in their thoughts, the strength of the felt impact of the event on one's daily conduct of life, one's felt bodily arousal, and the emotion's duration. The first five concern control precedence. Most of these ratings correlated significantly with felt emotional intensity. They accounted for about half the variance of felt intensity ratings in a multiple regression analysis. The control precedence variables contributed to felt intensity independent of felt autonomic arousal, Damasio's somatic marker, which generally is the only variable used to measure emotional intensity. Experienced emotional intensity thus largely comes from the felt impact of the event on thought and the conduct of life.

Control precedence, the push of passion, appears to depend upon the operation of a major biological mechanism: the midbrain dopamine system. The midbrain dopamine system is fundamental in emotion. It appears implicated in its most fundamental dimension: interest in or engagement with the world. As I mentioned, severe disturbance of the midbrain dopamine system tends to lead to severe general decrease in interest and spontaneous action (Damasio, 2000; Sacks, 1973). Disturbance of dopamine activity in the prefrontal brain is being held responsible for avolitional syndromes in schizophrenics (Frith, 2003).

The system has been identified by various names: reward system (e.g., Shizgal, 1999); behavioral activation system (Gray, 1982); behavior facilitation system (Depue & Collins, 1999); seeking system (Panksepp, 1998); or wanting system (Berridge, 1999). The last two conceptions appear the most satisfactory, given the empirical evidence (Berridge, 2007). I therefore call it the system-named desire. Phasic bursts in DA dopamine firing accompany attention shifts toward unexpected valued events and signals for their incipient occurrence. Enduring dopamine increases sustained interest in these events (Leyton, 2009). They occur during heroin rushes and when subjects think of the person with whom they are in love (Fisher, 2004). Experiences of craving and urge tend to correlate with activation of part of the system and dopamine release (Panksepp, 2005). When the system is neurochemically blocked, efforts to obtain formerly coveted food disappear while signs of liking the food remain (Berridge, 1999), indicating that desire—not pleasure as such—is involved.

EMOTION ELICITATION: APPRAISAL

Emotions are elicited by events by way of information processing, which is referred to as appraisal. The appraisal processes use information from event context, from previous experiences, or from additional processing dispositions. Through those processes a given event can be appraised in different ways and, thus, generate different emotions—or no emotion. Few if any specific stimuli trigger any specific emotion.

The word "appraisal" is central for understanding emotions. Yet it is ambiguous. First, it does *not* mean conscious evaluation or interpretation. Most appraisal processes are automatic and proceed nonconsciously, as when a picture of a mutilated face is appraised as highly unpleasant and disgusting. As extensive experimental research has shown, even their outcomes can remain nonconscious and still modify subsequent actions—as when a picture of a smiling face, exposed too briefly to have been consciously perceived (the procedure of priming), increases consumption of some drink (Bargh, 1994; Berridge, 2004; Moors & de Hou- wer, 2006).

The word "appraisal," unfortunately, refers to two entirely different things. It can mean conscious awareness of event meaning and affective impact, as when one views a picture of a mutilated face. It is part of the emotional experience. I will refer to this as felt appraisal. But it can also mean to refer to the information processes that intervene between the arrival of a stimulus event and the occurrence of an emotional response, whether experienced or otherwise. One's shivers when viewing such a picture are not caused only by seeing a face with red blotches, but its automatic interpretation as a picture of blood, mutilation, or pain that renders it unpleasant. I will refer to these processes as appraising. Appraising and felt appraisal do not always correspond. When hitting one's head against the kitchen shelf, one gets angry, feeling that the shelf misbehaved; but what caused the anger was the unexpected pain that also caused the misattribution. The example illustrates that conscious appraisal can be a consequence as well as a cause of emotional response, since one's own responses form part of the appraised emotional situation from the moment they are produced.

The processes of appraising can be relatively simple ("elementary appraisal"), as when the sweet taste of sugar is liked, an unexpected loud sound startles, or viewing a baby elicits pleasure. All that happens is that the stimulus innately triggers a disposition in the subject that matches it and in turn triggers like or dislike. But often appraising involves matching or mismatching with more complex information, such as the context of the stimulus or one's expectations. Grief, for instance, is not elicited by a mere absence, but by a loss: an absence appraised as an absence of something of value that one had before. Then one speaks of "cognitive appraisal": more cognitions play a role. Unexpectedness gives a further example: something unexpected clashes with one's expectations, as it does in the kitchen shelf example. Likewise, an event is appraised as frustrating when another person interferes with one's actions or withholds expected satisfactions (Frijda, 2007a; Parkinson, 2007).

Appraisal is one major source of individual differences in emotions, since life experiences, socially transmitted information, and cultural values belong to the major determinants of appraisal processes—and, thus, to which events elicit which emotions. Another source of individual differences resides in the ease with which different appraisals, as well as modes of readiness, are elicited by the same sorts of event. It can be argued that personality differences for an important part consist of appraisal and action readiness propensities: of inclinations to appraised events as pleasant or unpleasant, threatening or friendly, or as inclincations to respond by moving toward, moving away, or moving against.

Appraising usually involves processing a number of different event aspects. It involves elementary appraisals of novelty or familiarity (it is or is not recognized, for instance) and of intrinsic pleasantness or unpleasantness, as with sweet taste. It may include appraisal of what the event might offer or do to the subject (as with conditioned stimuli or more complex knowledge), and of what the subject can or cannot do to cope or deal with it or make use of it, as with recognizing an event as a serious threat (Frijda, 2007b; Scherer, 2005).

The major appraisal process is appraising concern relevance—appraising the event as possibly promoting or obstructing one of one's concerns. The term "concern" refers to major motives, needs, interests, and all other dispositions that cause an individual to care about what happens: affective sensitivities, ongoing goals, and attachments. Emotions thus result from the encounter between an event and one or more of an individual's concerns. This holds even for elementary appraisals. A baby looks sweet because and when one cares for babies, and presumably particularly in expectant mothers. Mutilations look disgusting because they are perceived in terms of one's concern for one's own bodily integrity. No concern relevance, no emotion. Measures of concern strength (measures of the prominence and number of the individual's concerns implicated in the reported events) accounted for one-fourth of the variance ($R^2 = 0.24$) of felt intensity, in the study by Sonnemans and Frijda (1994) mentioned above.

The analysis of appraisal thus provides a major insight into the function of emotions. It provides insight into what emotions are for. By their underlying appraisal and their states of action readiness and actions, they serve to safeguard the individual's concerns.

But there is a major problem here. Not all concern-relevant information is in fact appraised as such. Smoking, for instance, represents a serious health risk; and almost everyone knows this. But nevertheless few smokers tremble when lighting their cigarette. Evidently, information and concerns are insufficient to cause emotions. What else is involved? Power and Dalgleish (2005) have shown that the format of information is essential. I propose that the information has to be *embodied* in some way. It has to be or have been experienced either as actually affecting one's body, or as actually causing pleasure or pain, or as affecting one's actions and action planning. All of which is natural: emotions occur in creatures geared to acting in a variable environment. But in addition the environment can be expanded by the gift of imagination.

CONCLUSIONS

The preceding analysis provides a coherent story of emotions. It allows an integrative view by linking observable phenomena and subjective experiences to inferred processes at the subpersonal level of description, linking these processes among themselves, and providing occasional pointers from these processes to processes at the neuroscientific level of description.

It has done so with the help of several theoretical constructs. The central one of these is that of passion—that is, of motive states called states of action readiness, aiming to achieve or modify person-object relationships. Second to that is the notion of concerns: the latent dispositions that enable sensitivity to events and the aims of action readiness, and that underlie striving as well as events being enabled to have emotional meaning. Third, there is appraisal: the operation of cognitive information processes that link observed events to the concerns, producing matches of mismatches with representations that elicit action readiness and guide action.

The story has led to a functional interpretation of emotions: safeguarding concerns and their satisfaction in an uncertain and importantly social environment by modifying subject-object relationships.

Then there are some not-very-theoretical constructs, notably those of pleasure and displeasure. I have no occasion to enlarge upon them here, but I have done so elsewhere (Frijda, 2007a). Hedonic sensitivity, it would seem, is itself an outgrowth of the more encompassing capabilities for engagement and interest.

And, finally, what are emotions really? My conclusion, implicit in the preceding, may be a bit surprising. Emotion cannot be adequately defined because the set of phenomena to which the term refers is not unitary, but consists of complex sets of components that do not always co-occur.

Scherer (2005) suggested that emotions—as phenomena of experience and behavior—result from streams of processes running on in close but variable reciprocal interactions and irregular sequencing, pretty much as envisaged by Lewis (2005). "Emotion" is not a coherent category. What are, in principle, solid categories are those of basic emotion-constitutive processes: those of motive states of action readiness and of action tendency; those of the various processes caught under the summary term of appraisal processes, of which again I did not say much; and those of affect.

In what we call emotions, sometimes only one process is present—merely affect, as in eating moderately good ice cream while moderately thirsty; or mere action readiness, as in an irritable mood or lively vital affect; or sheer undirected excitement. Making a transverse cut through the stream on occasion gives a pattern that one may want to call an emotion; but it has no sharp or natural boundaries with other patterns in the stream, except when the processes fully embody in an affect burst—the paradigmatic case of an emotion (Scherer, 1994).

Otherwise one does not "have" emotions. One is emoting, sometimes more, sometimes less, by having a somewhat variable set of synchronized processes going on that may include appraisal processes, ongoing action readiness with variable control precedence, feelings stemming from parts of those processes, regulatory interactions coming from expected consequences of some of these processes on other ones. What more should one wish for? It is a beautiful perspective.

REFERENCES

Bard, P. (1934a). On emotional expression after decortication with some remarks on certain theoretical views: Part I. *Psychological Review, 41*, 309–329.

Bard, P. (1934b). On emotional expression after decortication with some remarks on certain theoretical views: Part II. *Psychological Review, 41*, 424–449.

Bargh, J. A. (1994). The four horsemen of automaticity: Awareness, intention, efficiency, and control in social cognition. In R. S. Wyer & T. K. Srull (Eds.), *Handbook of social cognition* (pp. 1–40). Hillsdale, NJ: Erlbaum.

Barrett, L. F. (2006) Emotions as natural kinds? *Perspectives on Psychological Science, 10*, 20–46.

Berridge, K. C. (1999). Pleasure, pain, desire, and dread: Hidden core processes of emotion. In D. Kahneman, E. Diener, & N. Schwarz (Eds.), *Well-being: The foundations of hedonic psychology* (pp. 525–557). New York: Russell Sage Foundation.

Berridge, K. C. (2004). Unfelt affect and irrational desire: A view from the brain. In A. S. R. Manstead, N. H. Frijda, & A. Fischer (Eds.), *Feelings and emotions: The Amsterdam symposium* (pp. 243–262). Cambridge, UK: Cambridge University Press.

Berridge, K. C. (2007). The debate over dopamine's role in reward: The case for incentive salience. *Psychopharmacology, 191*, 391–431.

Crombez, G., Eccleston, C., Bayens, F., & Eelen, P. (1998). Attentional disruption is enhanced by the threat of pain. *Behaviour Research and Therapy, 36*, 195–204.

Damasio, A. (1994) *Descartes' error: Emotion, reason, and the human brain.* New York: Putnam.

Damasio, A. (2000). *The feeling of what happens: Body, emotion, and the making of consciousness.* London: Random House.

Damasio, A. R., Grabowski, T. J., Bechara, A., Damasio, H., Ponto, L. L. B., Parvisi, J., et al. (2000). Subcortical and cortical brain activity during the feeling of self-generated emotions. *Nature Neuroscience, 3*, 1049–1056.

Davitz, J. R. (1969). *The language of emotion.* New York: Academic Press.

Dennett, D. C. (1978). *Brainstorms: Philosophical essays on mind and psychology.* Montgomery, VT: Bradford Books.

Depue, R. A., & Collins, P. F. (1999). Neurobiology of the structure of personality: Dopamine, facilitation of incentive motivation, and extraversion. *Behavioral and Brain Sciences, 22*, 491–569.

Duffy, E. (1962). *Activation and behavior.* New York: Wiley.

Easterbrook, J. A. (1959). The effects of emotion on cue utilization and the organization of behavior. *Psychological Review 66*, 183–201.

Edelman, G. M., & Tononi, G. (2000). *Consciousness: How matter becomes imagination.* London: Penguin.

Ekman, P. (1999). Basic emotions. In T. Dalgleish & M. J. Power (Eds.), *Handbook of cognition and emotion* (pp. 45–60). Chichester, UK: Wiley.

Ellis, R. D. (2005) *Curious emotions.* Amsterdam: Benjamins.

Eysenck, M. W. (1997). *Anxiety and cognition: A unified theory.* Hove, UK: Psychology Press.

Fisher, H. E. (2004). *Why we love: The nature and chemistry of romantic love.* New York: Holt.

Frijda, N. H. (2007a). *The laws of emotion.* Mahwah, NJ: Erlbaum.

Frijda, N. H. (2007b). Klaus Scherer's article on "What are emotions?" Comments. *Social Science Information, 46*, 381–383.

Frijda, N. H., Kuipers, P., & Terschure, E. (1989). Relations between emotion, appraisal, and emotional action readiness. *Journal of Personality and Social Psychology, 57*, 212–228.

Frijda, N. H., Markam, S., Sato, K., & Wiers, R. (1995). Emotion and emotion words. In J. A, Russell, J. M. Fernández-Dols, A. S. R. Manstead, & J. Wellenkamp (Eds.), *Everyday conceptions of emotion* (pp. 121–144). Dordrecht, The Netherlands: Kluwer.

Frijda, N. H., & Tcherkassof, A. (1997). Facial expressions as modes of action readiness. In J. A. Russell & J. M. Fernández-Dols (Eds.), *The psychology of facial expression* (pp. 78–102). Cambridge, UK: Cambridge University Press.

Frith, C. (2003). Interpersonal factors in the disorders of volition associated with schizophrenia. In N. Sebanz & W. Prinz (Eds.), *Disorders of volition* (pp. 233–247). Cambridge, MA: Bradford Books.

Gray, J. A. (1982). *The neuropsychology of anxiety: An enquiry into the functions of the septo-hippocampal system*. Oxford, UK: Oxford University Press.

Hebb, D. O. (1949). *The organization of behavior: A neuropsychological theory*. New York, Wiley.

Higgins, E. T. (2006). Value from hedonic experience *and* engagement. *Psychological Review, 113*, 439–460.

James, W. (1884). What is an emotion? *Mind, 9*, 188–205.

Jeannerod, M. (1997). *The cognitive neuroscience of action*. Oxford, UK: Blackwell.

Lang, P. J. (1993). The three-system approach to emotion. In N. Birbaum & A. Öhman (Eds.), *The structure of emotion* (pp. 18–30). Bern, Switzerland: Hogrefe & Huber.

Lewis, M. D. (2005). Bridging emotion theory and neurobiology through dynamic system modeling. *Behavioral and Brain Sciences, 28*, 105–131.

Lewis, M. R., & Todd, R. M. (2007). The self-regulating brain: Cortical-subcortical feedback and the development of intelligent action. *Cognitive Development, 22*, 406–430.

Leyton, M. (2009). The neurobiology of desire: Dopamine and the regulation of mood and motivational states in humans. In M. L. Kringelbach & K. C. Berridge (Eds.), *Pleasures of the brain* (pp. 222–243). New York: Oxford University Press.

MacLeod, C., Mathews, A., & Tata, P. (1986). Attentional bias in emotional disorders. *Journal of Abnormal Psychology, 95*, 15–20.

Moors, A., & de Houwer, J. (2006). Automaticity: A theoretical and conceptual analysis. *Psychological Bulletin, 132*, 297–326.

Noë, A. (2004). *Action in perception*. Cambridge, MA: MIT Press.

Nussbaum M. C. (2001). *Upheavals of thought: The intelligence of emotions*. New York: Cambridge University Press.

Obrist, P. A. (1981). *Cardiovascular psychophysiology: A perspective*. New York: Plenum Press.

Öhman, A., & Mineka, S. (2001). Fears, phobias, and preparedness: Toward an evolved module of fear and fear learning. *Psychological Review, 108*, 483–522.

Ortony, A., Clore, G., & Collins, A. (1988). *The cognitive structure of emotions*. Cambridge, UK: Cambridge University Press.

Panksepp, J. (1998). *Affective neuroscience: The foundations of human and animal emotions*. Oxford, UK: Oxford University Press.

Panksepp, J. (2005). Affective consciousness: Core emotional feelings in animals and humans. *Consciousness and Cognition, 14*, 81–88.

Parkinson, B. (2007). Getting from situations to emotions: Appraisal and other routes. *Emotion, 7*, 21–25.

Phan, K. L., Wager, T. D., Taylor, S. F., & Liberzon, I. (2002). Functional neuroanatomy of emotion: A meta-analysis of emotion activation studies in PET and fMRI. *NeuroImage, 16*, 331–348.

Power, M. & Dalgleish, T. (2005). *Cognition and emotion: From order to disorder* (2nd ed.). Mawah, NJ: Erlbaum.

Prinz, J. J. (2004). *Gut reactions: A perceptual theory of emotion.* New York: Oxford University Press.

Reisenzein, R. (2000). Exploring the strength of association between the components of emotion syndromes: The case of surprise. *Cognition and Emotion, 14*, 1–38.

Rizzolatti, G., Fogassi, L., & Gallese, V. (2001). Neurophysiological mechanisms underlying the understanding and imitation of action. *Nature Reviews Neuroscience, 2*, 661–670.

Russell, J. A. (2003). Core affect and the psychological construction of emotion. *Psychological Review, 110*, 145–172.

Sacks, O. (1973). *Awakenings.* New York: Dutton.

Scherer, K. R. (1984). Emotion as a multicomponent process: A model and some cross-cultural data. In P. Shaver (Ed.), *Review of personality and social psychology* (Vol. 5, pp. 37–63). Beverley Hills, CA: Sage.

Scherer, K. R. (1994). Affect bursts. In S. H. M. Van Goozen, N. E. Van de Poll, & J. A. Sergeant (Eds.), *Emotions: Essays on emotion theory* (pp. 161–196). Hillsdale, NJ: Erlbaum.

Scherer, K. R. (2004). Feelings integrate the central representation of appraisal-driven response organization in emotion. In A. S. R. Manstead, N. H. Frijda, & A. Fischer (Eds.), *Feelings and emotions: The Amsterdam symposium* (pp. 136–157). Cambridge, UK: Cambridge University Press.

Scherer, K. R. (2005). What are emotions? And how can they be measured? *Social Science Information, 44*, 695–729.

Shizgal, P. (1999). On the neural computation of utility: Implications from studies of brain stimulus reward. In D. Kahneman, E. Diener, & N. Schwarz (Eds.), *Well-being: Foundations of hedonic psychology* (pp. 500–524). New York: Russell Sage Foundation.

Solomon, R. C. (1976). *The passions.* New York: Doubleday/Anchor.

Sonnemans, J., & Frijda, N. H. (1994). The structure of subjective emotional intensity. *Cognition and Emotion, 8*, 329–350.

Stern, D. N. (1985). *The interpersonal world of the infant: A view from psychoanalysis and developmental psychology.* New York: Basic Books.

Varela, F. J., Thompson, E., & Rosch, E. (1991). *The embodied mind: Cognitive science and human experience.* Cambridge, MA: MIT Press.

Veening, J. G., de Jong, T., & Barendregt, H. P. (2010). Oxytocin-messages via the cerebrospinal fluid: Behavioral effects; a review. *Physiology and Behavior, 35*, 193–210.

von Holst, E., & Mittelstaedt, H. (1950). Das Reafferenzprinzip. Wechselwirkung zwischen Zentralnervensystem und Peripherie [The reafference principle: Interactions between the central nervous system and periphery]. *Naturwissenschaften, 37,* 464–476.

Wundt, W. (1896). *Grundriss der Psychologie* [Outline of psychology]. Stuttgart, Germany: Engelmann.

CHAPTER 6

Emotions in the Individual Mind, in Relationships, and in Reading Fiction

Keith Oatley

EMOTIONS IN OURSELVES

Researchers now tend to agree with Aristotle (330 BCE/1954) that emotions are generally caused by evaluations—in modern terms, appraisals—of events that affect people's goals. The communicative theory of emotions (Oatley & Johnson-Laird, 1987, 1996, in press) follows this idea and proposes that emotions are based on two kinds of signal.

One kind of emotion signal is nonpropositional. It arises from monitoring the progress of plans to achieve goals. It configures the system into one of a small number of modes of readiness, each of which has evolved to deal with a distinctive kind of generic event in relation to a goal—such as making progress, suffering a loss, and so on. Oatley and Johnson-Laird (1996) postulate nine emotion modes. Panksepp (1998) has postulated a set of basic emotions, based on dedicated brain systems, that are slightly different from those proposed by Oatley and Johnson-Laird. The differences are less important than the hypothesis that each emotion sets up a distinctive state of readiness. By contrast, other theorists (e.g., Frijda, 2009; Reisenzein, in press) regard emotions as componential, derived from lower-level, nonemotion components rather than from basic emotions.

In Oatley and Johnson-Laird's theory, each emotion mode prompts a person toward a state of readiness appropriate to the generic kind of event that has occurred. Its function is to finesse the impossible problem of having to choose from the infinity of all possible actions to deal with each new situation.

Personality, Cognition, and Emotion edited by Michael W. Eysenck, Małgorzata Fajkowska, and Tomasz Maruszewski. Eliot Werner Publications, Clinton Corners, New York, 2012.

In much of what follows, I discuss four modes—happiness, sadness, anger, and fear—that can have clear causes but can also be free floating. Oatley and Johnson-Laird (1996) propose that there are five further basic emotions that always take specific objects: attachment love of offspring for a parent; caregiving love for offspring; sexual love; and two emotions of rejection, disgust and contempt.

According to Oatley and Johnson-Laird, during the course of evolution—particularly in relation to what Tooby and Cosmides (1990) call our environment of evolutionary adaptedness—a distinct set of generic events has come to be recognized, and distinct emotions have evolved that configure the cognitive system to states of preparedness appropriate to each of them. For happiness the generic event that has recurred during evolution is progress toward a goal. When it occurs the cognitive system is configured to continue what one was doing. This has positive attributes such as enthusiasm, but some drawbacks like confirmation bias. For sadness the event is loss, which promotes disengagement. For anger the event is frustration, which promotes perseverance. For fear the event is threat, which promotes vigilance and avoidance.

These modes are bundles of heuristics. Thus our theory fits well with the conclusion, now widely accepted (Kahneman & Shane, 2005; Stanovich, 2004, in press), that the cognitive system has two different inferential systems. System 1 is fast and based on heuristics (including emotional heuristics). System 2 is slow and capable of sequential reasoning.

To give an instance of a bundle of emotional heuristics, if an external danger occurs, the result is fear and the cognitive system is configured to a mode that makes ready the following: stop the current plan, reevaluate results of all recent actions, freeze, prepare to avoid, escape, flee, or attack, attend vigilantly to the environment for even the slightest sign of danger. When the cognitive system is configured in this way, the next actions tend to be chosen in accord with the new danger-contingent assessment. When the danger passes, a previous plan can be resumed.

Although a nonpropositional signal carries an urge, it has no meaning. It has an emotional tone—the experience of an emotion—so in this sense it is a communication also to the conscious self. Moods are based on these same nonpropositional signals. When a danger occurs, there is a change to the fear mode, and this change is an emotion. Although Öhman (2008) has found some differences in neural embodiment between fear and anxiety, the two states largely overlap. Fear is the emotion. Anxiety is the corresponding mood, which occurs when this mode is sustained and resists change. With nonpropositional signals, our theory explains not only free-floating emotions and moods but responsiveness to mood-altering drugs. Thus we can feel an emotion or mood—say, fear or anxiety—but without knowing why it has occurred or to what it is directed.

The second type of signal in this theory is propositional. It can indicate what caused the emotion and to what it is directed. We postulate that basic emotions can, in different individuals and societies, be elaborated into complex emotions by adding propositional information. For instance, jealousy is anger or fear at being displaced from a close relationship. Such elaborations give rise to a semantics of emotion terms (Johnson-Laird & Oatley, 1989). Empirical evidence that supports this theory has been offered by Reisenzein (1995). Johnson-Laird and Oatley (2000) have given an account of how, by cognitive and social construction, complex emotions are elaborated from basic emotions. The theory has been used to explain how music and literary fiction can induce emotions (Johnson-Laird & Oatley, 2008). It has also provided a basis for understanding different kinds of psychological disorder based on emotion modes (mania, depression, oppositional states, anxiety states; Power & Dalgleish, 2008), and for understanding the kinds of thinking that occur in these disorders (Johnson-Laird, Mancini, & Gangemi, 2006; Oatley & Johnson-Laird, in press).

Elusive Emotions

In a study in which employed people kept emotion diaries, Oatley and Duncan (1994) found that people usually knew what caused their emotions, but on 6% of occasions they did not. We take this as evidence that nonpropositional signals of emotions can occur separately from propositional signals. Oatley and Duncan (1992) found that, for people with psychiatric problems, the proportion of emotions for which they did not know the cause rose to 27%. Our participants also frequently reported emotions that lasted a long time (as found also by Frijda, Mesquita, Sonnemans, & van Goozen, 1991) and some 30% of emotions changed as they progressed, sometimes into new emotions incompatible with earlier ones.

Although emotions are critical to identity, attitudes, and relationships, findings show that people do not always know what caused their emotions, and further that emotions are often mixed with their opposites and that they can transform and/or make for puzzles. Elusive emotions can arise from conflicts between partly understood goals, from repercussions for relationships with others, as well as from emotional memories that have implications for selfhood. In addition, as Lambie (2009) has shown, emotions can be unconscious but nonetheless affect behavior, and thus make the behavior difficult to understand.

Here is an example. An emotion of anger was experienced by a young woman, recorded in an emotion diary, and described further in a follow-up interview (Oatley & Duncan, 1992). The emotion was anger. It started in an argument between the young woman and her boyfriend about preferences for kinds of music. The initial emotion lasted two and a half hours. It recurred over the next three days and made it difficult for her to sleep. She said, "I just couldn't get through to him." Her thoughts included "Is this going too far? If it goes too far, it [the relationship] would end." Memories occurred: the argument "reminded her of an ex-boyfriend" and made her "wonder if it [the relationship] was worth it." Her behavior included sarcasm and cutting remarks, being withdrawn and sulking, followed by attempts at reparation. The emotion became mixed: her anger was accompanied by guilt because she thought that she was pressing her boyfriend too hard. She felt that her anger was inconsistent with her view of herself: she thought of herself as "a person who would not be irritated by someone with a different opinion." She said, "There was a kernel of something that lowered my estimation of myself on some kind of internal scale." She thought that she should step back and calm down, then thought she was partly to blame.

So although emotions are communications to ourselves (Oatley, 2009), they are not always clear communications: their function is primarily configurational. With the possibilities of emotions being vague or elusive, or without obvious causes, mixed with opposites, or changing over time, and even being unconscious, they are frequently difficult to understand, even when—and perhaps particularly when—they are important. So a need arises to understand our emotions better.

EMOTIONS BETWEEN OURSELVES AND OTHERS

Just as the nonpropositional communications of inner emotions configure the individual cognitive system to deal with recurring kinds of contingency (progress, loss, frustration, etc.), corresponding emotions between people configure interpersonal relationships into distinctive modes, which are kinds of interpersonal commitment (Aubé, 2009). If one is happy, an interpersonal mode is set up of commitment to cooperate. If one is in love, a mode of continuing affection is set up, which sometimes becomes a commitment to live together. If one is angry, there is an urge to contend, plus a commitment to see the conflict through to a resolution—typically a readjustment of the relationship. When fearful, one often joins with others in a commitment to avoid a shared danger. This function of emotion-based relating is discussed further by Oatley, Keltner, and Jenkins (2006). In a comparable way, Fischer and Manstead (2008) propose that social emotions function to promote social relationships, and to establish and maintain social position relative to others.

We humans are the most social of primates. Our adaptation includes not just the mammalian attachment system of joining with immature offspring to enable them to thrive, not just that of living social lives of cooperation and conflict like that of the chimpanzees (Goodall, 1986), but of being able to plan explicitly to accomplish things together that we could not do alone. Thus, early in development—around the age of one—human infants are able to recognize others as agents like themselves (Hermann, Call, Hernandez-Lloreda, Hare, & Tomasello, 2007), and by the age of four they are able to mindread—that is, to infer what is going on in other minds (Astington, 1993). Neither of these abilities is possessed by our closest relatives, the chimpanzees.

If we accept that emotions derive from goals, then social emotions relate to social goals. Biologically, as Jenkins and Oatley have argued (see Oatley et al., 2006), three social goals are foremost: assertion, attachment, and affiliation. In evolutionary terms the oldest of these is assertion to achieve and maintain status. When a desired status is achieved, a mood of pride occurs. From striving for status, anger and conflict occur. With the evolution of mammals, attachment emerged with the goal of having a caregiver protect offspring. When this goal is satisfied, a mood of comfort in closeness obtains, but when it is threatened anxiety occurs. Affiliation is the most recently evolved of the major social goals. It enables cooperation with peers. Its positive mood is happy trustfulness and its negative emotion is the sadness of loss. Our success as a species—our families, our societies, our technologies, our cultures—depends on the system of affiliative cooperation (Oatley, 2004). We can say, indeed, that affiliative cooperation is the key to our ultrasocial human adaptation. There are also antisocial goals—most importantly the rejection, exclusion, and even the killing of others when they are seen as unacceptable members of outgroups. Among the emotions of this goal are contempt and destructive anger.

Here is the issue in cognitive terms. When we do something cooperatively, or even sometimes when we compete within a cooperative framework, we promote shared goals to the top of our own goal hierarchy. Then the cognitive systems of the two or more people involved have to be coordinated. This typically involves agreeing on a plan, assigning roles, and accomplishing actions in the service of the overall shared goal or goals. Much of this is done by exchanging verbal messages in the way that Power (1979) has shown. Power did not treat emotions, but they are critical: we can think of relational emotion modes as inverse scripts. For a stage play, an actor learns from a script a set of words that he or she will say. He or she utters the words and must supply the emotions that are implied. In ordinary life it is the other way around. Emotions provide scripts not of words but of modes of relating—for instance, to cooperate happily, to conflict in anger, to disengage in sadness, to take part in shared fear of a danger— and we supply the words appropriate to these emotions.

When we coordinate with someone else, some kinds of joint plans are easy and well rehearsed—for example, buying something at a shop. The shared goal is to conduct the exchange of a general resource (money) for specific goods. Even here the transaction must be conducted with the right emotional tone, and Hochschild's (1983) work with airline cabin staff has explained a great deal about emotions at the customer interface. Customer and provider must understand each other emotionally and trust each other. The emotions are those of cooperation. Economists have told us that exchanges occur because both parties gain an increment of net utility, but this is the wrong way around. Commercial exchange can occur because of the human skill of being able to cooperate with others, and the structure for doing this is set by happy emotions. Exchange is a useful byproduct. Other kinds of social interaction are more complex. In them one needs to know not only one's own emotions but also, using theory of mind (e.g., Nickerson, 1999), the emotions and intentions of the other.

Empathy, Simulation, and Projective Mindreading

For a long time in emotion research, facial expressions of emotion were seen in the rather individual terms of the human ability to make and recognize displays.

But if we take a relational focus, something else is needed: a consideration of the role of such expressions in relation to social goals of interaction. This has started to be provided—for instance, by Keltner and Buswell (1997) who have shown how displays of embarrassment function in mutual adjustments of status.

The discovery of mirror neurons by Rizzolatti, Fadiga, Gallese, and Fogassi (1996) has prompted a further movement toward understanding the role of emotions in sociality. Mirror neurons in monkeys were found to fire either if the monkey saw an intended action, or if it initiated the same action itself. Thus recognition of action seems to involve being able to create the action: analysis by synthesis or, as these authors call it, simulation. For emotions, Wicker et al. (2003) have made a similar finding in an fMRI study of humans, where the brain area involved in recognizing the emotion of disgust was also involved in feeling disgust (see also de Vignemont & Singer, 2006). Although the original work on mirror neurons was on monkeys and the mirroring of action, in humans the most extensive evidence has been on the mirroring of emotions (reviewed, e.g., by Oatley, 2009).

The important implication is that recognizing emotional expressions often involves empathy. We recognize another's emotion in terms of our own comparable feeling. De Vignemont and Singer describe empathy as having an emotion that is (a) similar to that of another person, (b) elicited by observation or imagination of the other's emotion, and (c) involves knowing the other is the source of one's own emotion.

Goldman (in press) argues that the simple case of recognizing an emotional expression involves low-level mindreading, attributing an emotion to another person based on being able to feel (simulate) the same emotion in oneself. For instance, we see a smile: we also feel happy and smile back in a mode of potential cooperation. If we see tears, we also feel sad and are inclined to help. We see a frown and start to feel slightly angry, prepared for some conflict because we sense something antipathetic to our plans. When we hear someone cry out in fear, we feel frightened ourselves. Each kind of empathetic emotion configures a particular mode of relating.

When we cannot directly see or hear another person, a second kind of empathy can occur that, Goldman (in press) says, requires high-level mindreading that involves imagination. Here empathy is cognitively constructed from whatever information is available, including information about a character in a novel.

Although empathy frequently prompts cooperation or helping, we can feel empathy without feeling sympathy for the person whose mind we are trying to read—for example, when we perceive the other to be angry and we are angry ourselves. Even in anger there is engagement with the other person. In his diary studies of anger, Averill (1982) found that the large majority of episodes of anger concerned a person whom the subject knew and liked. The emotions of contempt and disdain, however, involve a lack of empathy: lack of any interest in the other person and his or her emotions. Moreover, Blair, Mitchell, and Blair (2005) have argued that some psychopaths behave in the way they do because of deficits in being able to recognize—or empathize with—emotions of others.

Empathy seems central to social interaction. Adam Smith (1759/1976) thought that emotions of compassion and sympathy (and empathy, which he included as part of sympathy) were the glue that holds society together. But although we humans are good at empathetic recognizing—mindreading—the emotions of others, we are not that good. Nickerson (1999) calls projective mindreading "imputation." In this process we draw on what we know of ourselves and project it while making corrections for things we know about the other person. But mindreading is difficult. Often we project too much and correct too little. In the final part of this chapter, I shall inquire whether engaging with fictional literature and its emotions might enable us to improve our simulative and projective abilities.

EMOTIONS DURING THE READING OF LITERARY FICTION

In the first part of this chapter, I discussed how emotions can be important but often difficult to understand. Collingwood (1938) has proposed that because emotions are frequently problematic, art has become the expression of emotions in languages that are verbal, musical, visual, and so forth—with the purpose of exploring emotions and understanding them when their meanings are elusive (Oatley, 2003). Art can then be seen, perhaps, as an extension of the ways in which people confide their emotions to friends and loved ones (Rimé, 2009).

We can often understand emotions in literary fiction better than in the welter of everyday life. An approach that follows this idea comes from Indian poetics (see Ingalls, Masson, & Patwardhan, 1990). Unlike the tradition of Western poetics, in Eastern poetics (which has a comparable antiquity) emotions are central. Literary emotions are thought of as being special, in some ways similar to but in other ways unlike, the everyday emotions to which they correspond. The Sanskrit term for an everyday emotion is *bhava,* and for a literary emotion *rasa.* The ancient Indian theorists proposed nine fundamental emotions, *bhavas* and *rasas,* as follows:

Bhava	*Rasa*
Sexual delight	The amorous or erotic
Laughter	The comic
Sorrow	The pitiable or tragic
Anger	The furious
Perseverance	The heroic
Fear	The terrible
Disgust or disillusion	The odious or loathsome
Wonder	The marvelous
Serenity	The peaceful

Here again are fundamental categories or basic emotions. What marks out *rasas* is that they are better understood than everyday emotions, because we can experience them at the right aesthetic distance and (as the Indian theorists say) without the thick crust of egotism that can blind us to understanding our emotions in our ordinary lives. The Indian theorists thought that to experience a *rasa* one could draw on the experience of one's past lives. A modern Western equivalent might be to say that we can experience emotions in literature because despite the differences, there is something universal about many of the contexts—of union with others, of loss, of conflict—as well as something universal about human emotions. Also we can say, with Nickerson (1999), that when we try to understand others in everyday life, we often project too much of ourselves and our concerns, even though we do not know ourselves too well. This is less likely to happen in works of art.

Ideas similar to those of the Indian theorists have also been explored in the West. Proust, in *À la recherche du temps perdu*, explores his emotions and seeks to understand their transformations in the course of his life. He does this by depicting, in the first part of the novel, the intense childhood love of his narrator Marcel for his mother and Charles Swann's love for Odette. In the later parts of the novel, this series includes the joys and anguish of Marcel's adult love for Albertine. Here is the point: these explorations enable us, the readers, to understand ourselves and our emotions. Proust's narrator Marcel put it like this:

> [I]t would even be inexact to say that I thought of those who read it, as readers of my book. Because they were not, as I saw it, my readers. More exactly they were readers of themselves, my book being a sort of magnifying glass ... by which I could give them the means to read within themselves. (Proust, 1927/1987a, p. 424, my translation)

The argument, then, is that we can understand literary emotions better than some of our everyday emotions, and we can then transfer our understandings to emotional situations of our everyday lives.

Fiction as Simulation That Involves Mindreading and Emotions

I have argued (Oatley, 1999) that fiction is a kind of simulation that runs not on computers but on minds. We could also call it imagination: of characters, their plans as they interact, and the emotions that occur when their plans meet vicissitudes. There are two aspects of literary simulation. One is the simulation of minds of other individuals, mindreading of the kind discussed in the previous section. The other is understanding what goes on in social groups.

The theory-of-mind kind of mental simulation is like a wristwatch, a small model that simulates the alternation of day and night and the wheeling of sun and stars across the sky. Often we cannot see sun or stars, so a little model, a watch, is better for the coordination of our joint plans with others. It happens also to be more accurate than any device like a sundial that gives a direct readout from the heavens. Similarly, although sometimes we know what other persons are thinking because they have just told us, or know what they are feeling because they have demonstrated it in some expression or action, for the most part we construct a model of those persons to know what they are up to. The method is less accurate than a watch but it can serve quite well, both in the immediacy of an interaction and in constructing a mental model of a person's character over time. As Zunshine (2006) has emphasized, fiction gives enjoyable exercise in building our theory of mind. Indeed, some genres of fiction—for instance, the mystery novel—are entirely about working out what one character is really thinking and feeling when he or she is trying to conceal it.

The second kind of simulation involves processes in interaction. For instance, a simulation based on atmospheric pressure, winds, and humidity generates weather forecasts. We humans are quite good at understanding how winds blow from areas of high pressure to areas of low pressure. But when we have to think of interactions of two or more such processes—for example, how winds will be affected by oceans or mountains—we are not so good and the output of a simulation is what we see in the forecast. In novels there are often depictions of groups of people in interaction. For instance, near the beginning of Jane Austen's (1813/1906) *Pride and Prejudice*, a public dance is held. Whatever are people up to in this strange ritual that is a matter of excitement for some of the characters and a matter of boredom for others? A principal concern of most novels is what is going on in human social gatherings.

If you learn to fly, you might spend time in a flight simulator where you can learn more things—and learn them better—than in actual flying, when much time is spent aloft with little happening. The skills that you learn in the simulator then transfer to flying an actual airplane. Similarly, if you want practice in understanding what goes on in the social world, you can read fiction (Oatley, 2008). Following this argument Mar, Oatley, Hirsh, dela Paz, and Peterson (2006) asked whether people who read a lot of fiction would be better at empathetic theory of mind and other social abilities than those who read mainly nonfiction. We measured how much fiction and how much nonfiction our participants read. Then we measured empathetic theory of mind by means of Baron-Cohen, Wheelwright, Hill, Raste, and Plumb's (2001) Mind in the Eyes Test. A person taking the test looks at pictures of people's eyes, without the rest of the face as if seen through a mailbox, and then says which of four mental states the photographed person is in (e.g., *joking, flustered, desire, convinced*). To measure people's understanding of what goes on in social groups, we used an Interpersonal Perception Test: fifteen brief video clips of people in interaction, each of which requires an answer to a question about what is going on in the group. People who predominantly read fiction were found to be considerably better than those who predominantly read nonfiction at the Mind in the Eyes Test, and somewhat better at the Interpersonal Perception Test.

In a replication Mar, Oatley, and Peterson (2009) measured readers' Big Five personality traits: extraversion, neuroticism, openness, agreeableness, and conscientiousness. Differences in personality between readers of fiction and nonfiction were small and not significant. Individual differences did not explain the effects that we found. Fiction readers still did substantially better than nonfiction readers on the Mind in the Eyes Test when personality differences were controlled for. (We did not use the Interpersonal Perception Test in this study.) In an experimental study, Mar (2007) had people read either a fictional story or a nonfictional piece from *The New Yorker*. Immediately after reading, those who read the fictional story—compared with those who read the nonfictional piece—did better on a test of social reasoning but not on a test of analytical reasoning.

Mar, Djikic, and Oatley (2008) explain these results as due to expertise. Because fiction is mainly about people, their motivations, and what they are up to in the social world, readers of fiction become good at understanding such matters. Nonfiction has many kinds of subject matter—for instance, the history of warfare, climate change, astronomy. People reading these topics become more expert in them. There are, of course, differences between social interaction and engaging in fiction. In fiction there are extra cognitive steps: one has to imagine oneself cognitively into a scene, and one sets aside some of one's own concerns to take up those of a fictional protagonist. Nonetheless, direct interaction and conversation with other persons seem to be the basis for the understanding one has of fictional narrators and characters, and the empathy one feels for them (Bortolussi & Dixon, 2003; Oatley, in press).

Does reading change selfhood? Djikic, Oatley, Zoeterman, and Peterson (2009a) conducted an experiment in which people were assigned randomly to read either a short story ("The Lady With the Little Dog" by Anton Chekhov) about two people who have a holiday affair at the seaside resort of Yalta, or a version of the story written as a report from a divorce court. The courtroom version, in a nonfictional format, contained the same characters and events as Chekhov's original story. It was the same length, the same level of reading difficulty, and it was rated as just as interesting—though not as artistic—as Chekhov's story.

Before and after they read the text, we measured readers' personality traits (extraversion, neuroticism, openness, agreeableness, and conscientiousness) and we also asked subjects to rate the intensity at which they were feeling each of ten emotions. The results were that the personality traits of readers of Chekhov's story changed significantly more than those of the readers of the account in nonfictional form. The changes were mediated by the emotions experienced while they were reading. Different readers' personalities changed in different ways. We explain the result in terms of people who read Chekhov's story first being taken out of themselves by this work of art, and second being taken into the world of the story. In this world they empathized with one or both characters, or perhaps disapproved of them, or perhaps imagined themselves acting in a similar situation. In this new setting and in relation to the characters, small changes occurred in their everyday personality.

We also found (Djikic, Oatley, Zoeterman, & Peterson, 2009b) that readers of the original story who were avoidantly attached—defended against the emotions of relationships—experienced greater changes in emotions than those who were securely attached. The avoidant readers' defenses against emotions were circumvented by art.

In order to interact with others, we need to know ourselves, and this in turn is important for the kind of mindreading that involves projection. We all of us have room for improvement in these areas. Fiction offers us simulated social worlds, far more various than those we can ever encounter in everyday life, and in them we can follow the trajectories of characters and feel with them or for them, by empathy and sympathy. The emotions we feel are our own emotions in the circumstances of the characters in the stories.

Proust thought that if we can properly understand a fault or quirk in a fictional character, it becomes easier to recognize it in ourselves. This then enables us to build a more accurate model of ourselves. Proust was saying that fiction can be regarded as a potentially theory-changing set of thought-experiments by which we can understand both others and ourselves. The theory that changes is our implicit theory of ourselves.

Here is an example from Proust along these lines: a moment in the first part of his novel in which the Princess des Laumes—whose first name is Oriane—is addressed by her cousin Madame de Gallardon, whom she despises.

> Madame Gallardon drew herself up to her full height and made an expression that was even more chilly, yet still concerned about the Prince's condition.
>
> "Oriane," said Madame de Gallardon to her cousin.
>
> Here the Princess des Laumes looked with an expression of astonishment and amusement at an invisible third person to whom she seemed anxious to attest that she had never authorized Madame de Gallardon to call her by her first name.
>
> "I would very much like you to stop by my house for a moment tomorrow evening," continued Madame de Gallardon, "to hear a Mozart clarinet quintet. I would appreciate your opinion."
>
> She seemed not to be making an invitation, but requesting a service.
> (Proust, 1913/1987b, p. 328, my translation)

The next time that we see people competing for status, we might think of the lower-born Madame de Gallardon and her aristocratic cousin Princess Oriane des Laumes. And the next time that we find ourselves thinking of doing something of the kind that the princess does—contriving, by a facial expression, to snub or lower someone from a desired social status—we might recognize this as part of our own repertoire, and reflect on why status is so important to us.

Here is another example in which Proust's narrator Marcel explicitly describes an effect on himself. One of the people whom a reader encounters in *À la recherche du temps perdu* is Monsieur de Charlus, whose mother was a Bavarian countess. Descriptions are given of the pleasure that Monsieur de Charlus took during the First World War, which was raging at the time, in recognizing the illogical nature of many of the arguments offered by French people who were overly optimistic about how things would go for the French. Later Marcel says:

The Germanophilia of Monsieur de Charlus ... had helped me to detach myself for a moment, if not from my Germanophobia, at least from my belief in its pure objectivity, and made me think that perhaps in this way hatred was similar to love. (Proust, 1927/1987a, p. 227, my translation)

By seeing our fellow human beings act in ways that are less credible than they would like to think, we are able to recognize similar attributes in ourselves, and are more able to accept them so that we can form a better implicit model of ourselves. Thus we may become better able to understand and interact with others.

REFERENCES

Aristotle. (1954). *Rhetoric*. In W. R. Roberts (Ed.), *Aristotle: Rhetoric and poetics* (pp. 3–218). New York: Random House (Original work written in circa 330 BCE).

Astington, J. W. (1993). *The child's discovery of the mind.* Cambridge, MA: Harvard University Press.

Aubé, M. (2009). Unfolding commitments management: A systemic view of emotions. In J. Vallverdú & D. Casacuberta (Eds.), *Handbook of research on synthetic emotions and sociable robotics: New applications in affective computing and artificial intelligence* (pp. 198–227). Hershey, PA: Information Science Reference.

Austen, J. (1906). *Pride and prejudice.* London: Dent. (Original work published in 1813)

Averill, J. R. (1982). *Anger and aggression: An essay on emotion.* New York: Springer-Verlag.

Baron-Cohen, S., Wheelwright, S., Hill, J., Raste, Y., & Plumb, I. (2001). The "Reading the Mind in the Eyes" Test revised version: A study with normal adults, and adults with Asperger's syndrome or high-functioning autism. *Journal of Child Psychology and Psychiatry, 42*, 241–251.

Blair, J., Mitchell, D., & Blair, K. (2005). *The psychopath: Emotion and the brain.* Oxford, UK: Blackwell.

Bortolussi, M., & Dixon, P. (2003). *Psychonarratology: Foundations for the empirical study of literary response.* New York: Cambridge University Press.

Collingwood, R. G. (1938). *The principles of art.* Oxford, UK: Oxford University Press.

de Vignemont, F., & Singer, T. (2006). The empathetic brain: How, when, and why. *Trends in Cognitive Sciences, 10*, 435–441.

Djikic, M., Oatley, K., Zoeterman, S., & Peterson, J. (2009a). On being moved by art: How reading fiction transforms the self. *Creativity Research Journal, 21*, 24–29.

Djikic, M., Oatley, K., Zoeterman, S., & Peterson, J. (2009b). Defenseless against art? Impact of reading fiction on emotion in avoidantly attached individuals. *Journal of Research in Personality, 43*, 14–17.

Fischer, A. H., & Manstead, A. S. R (2008). Social functions of emotions. In M. Lewis, J. Haviland-Jones, & L. Feldman Barrett (Eds.), *Handbook of emotions* (3rd ed., pp. 456–468). New York: Guilford Press.

Frijda, N. H. (2009). Not passion's slave. *Emotion Review, 1*, 68–75.

Frijda, N. H., Mesquita, B., Sonnemans, J., & van Goozen, S. (1991). The duration of affective phenomena or emotions, sentiments and passions. In K. T. Strongman (Ed.), *International review of studies on emotion* (Vol. 1, pp. 187–225). Chichester, UK: Wiley.

Goldman, A. (in press). Two routes to empathy: Insights from cognitive neuroscience. In A. Coplan & P. Goldie (Eds.), *Empathy: Philosophical and psychological perspectives*. New York: Oxford University Press.

Goodall, J. (1986). *The chimpanzees of Gombe: Patterns of behavior*. Cambridge, MA: Harvard University Press.

Hermann, E., Call, J., Hernandez-Lloreda, M. V., Hare, B., & Tomasello, M. (2007). Humans have evolved specialized skills of social cognition: The cultural intelligence hypothesis. *Science, 317*, 1360–1366.

Hochschild, A. R. (1983). *The managed heart: Commercialization of human feeling*. Berkeley: University of California Press.

Ingalls, D. H. H., Masson, J. M., & Patwardhan, M. V. (1990). *The Dhvanyaloka of Anandavardana with the Locana of Abhinavagupta*. Cambridge, MA: Harvard University Press.

Johnson-Laird, P. N., Mancini, F., & Gangemi, A. (2006). A hyper-emotion theory of psychological illnesses. *Psychological Review, 113*, 822–841.

Johnson-Laird, P. N., & Oatley, K. (1989). The language of emotions: An analysis of a semantic field. *Cognition and Emotion, 3*, 81–123.

Johnson-Laird, P. N., & Oatley, K. (2000). Cognitive and social construction in emotion. In M. Lewis & J. Haviland (Eds.), *Handbook of emotions* (2nd ed., pp. 458–475). New York: Guilford Press.

Johnson-Laird, P. N. & Oatley, K. (2008). Emotions, music, and literature. In M. Lewis, J. Haviland-Jones, & L. Feldman Barrett (Eds.), *Handbook of emotions* (3rd ed., pp. 102–113). New York: Guilford Press.

Kahneman, D., & Shane, F. (2005). A model of heuristic judgement. In K. J. Holyoak & R. G. Morrison (Eds.), *The Cambridge handbook of thinking and reasoning* (pp. 267–293). New York: Cambridge University Press.

Keltner, D., & Buswell, B. N. (1997). Embarrassment: Its distinct forms and appeasement functions. *Psychological Bulletin, 122*, 250–270.

Lambie, J. (2009). Emotional experience, rational action, and self-knowledge. *Emotion Review, 1*, 272–280.

Mar, R. A. (2007). *Simulation-based theories of narrative comprehension: Evidence and implications*. Unpublished doctoral dissertation, University of Toronto, Toronto.

Mar, R. A., Djikic, M., & Oatley, K. (2008). Effects of reading on knowledge, social abilities, and selfhood. In S. Zyngier, M. Bortolussi, A. Chesnokova, & J. Auracher (Eds.), *Directions in empirical literary studies: In honor of Willie van Peer* (pp. 127–137). Amsterdam: Benjamins.

Mar, R. A., Oatley, K., Hirsh, J., dela Paz, J., & Peterson, J. B. (2006). Bookworms versus nerds: Exposure to fiction versus non-fiction, divergent associations with social ability, and the simulation of fictional social worlds. *Journal of Research in Personality, 40*, 694–712.

Mar, R. A., Oatley, K., & Peterson, J. B. (2009). Exploring the link between reading fiction and empathy: Ruling out individual differences and examining outcomes. *Communications: The European Journal of Communication Research, 34*, 407–428.

Nickerson, R. (1999). How we know—and sometimes misjudge—what others know: Imputing one's own knowledge to others. *Psychological Bulletin, 125*, 737–759.

Oatley, K. (1999). Why fiction may be twice as true as fact: Fiction as cognitive and emotional simulation. *Review of General Psychology, 3*, 101–117.

Oatley, K. (2003). Creative expression and communication of emotion in the visual and narrative arts. In R. J. Davidson, K. R. Scherer, & H. H. Goldsmith (Eds.), *Handbook of affective sciences* (pp. 481–502). New York: Oxford University Press.

Oatley, K. (2004). *Emotions: A brief history.* Oxford, UK: Blackwell.

Oatley, K. (2008). The mind's flight simulator. *The Psychologist, 21,* 1030–1032.

Oatley, K. (2009). Communications to self and others: Emotional experience and its skills. *Emotion Review, 1,* 206–213.

Oatley, K. (in press). *Such stuff as dreams: The psychology of fiction.* Oxford, UK: Wiley-Blackwell.

Oatley, K., & Duncan, E. (1992). Incidents of emotion in daily life. In K. T. Strongman (Ed.), *International review of studies on emotion* (Vol. 2, pp. 250–293). Chichester, UK: Wiley.

Oatley, K., & Duncan, E. (1994). The experience of emotions in everyday life. *Cognition and Emotion, 8,* 369–381.

Oatley, K., & Johnson-Laird, P. N. (1987). Towards a cognitive theory of emotions. *Cognition and Emotion, 1,* 29–50.

Oatley, K., & Johnson-Laird, P. N. (1996). The communicative theory of emotions: Empirical tests, mental models, and implications for social interaction. In L. L. Martin & A. Tesser (Eds.), *Striving and feeling: Interactions among goals, affect, and self-regulation* (pp. 363–393). Mahwah, NJ: Erlbaum.

Oatley, K., & Johnson-Laird, P. N. (in press). Basic emotions in social relationships, reasoning, and psychological illnesses. *Emotion Review.*

Oatley, K., Keltner, D., & Jenkins, J. M. (2006). *Understanding emotions* (2nd ed.). Malden, MA: Blackwell.

Öhman, A. (2008). Fear and anxiety: Overlaps and dissociations. In M. Lewis, J. Haviland-Jones, & L. Feldman Barrett (Eds.), *Handbook of emotions* (3rd ed., pp. 709–729). New York: Guilford Press.

Panksepp, J. (1998). *Affective neuroscience: The foundations of human and animal emotions.* Oxford, UK: Oxford University Press.

Power, M., & Dalgleish, T. (2008). *Cognition and emotion: From order to disorder* (2nd ed.). Hove, UK: Psychology Press.

Power, R. (1979). The organization of purposeful dialogues. *Linguistics, 17,* 107–152.

Proust, M. (1987a). *À la recherche du temps perdu VIII: Le temps retrouvé* [In search of lost time: The past recaptured]. Paris: Gallimard. (Original work published in 1927)

Proust, M. (1987b). *À la recherche du temps perdu I: Du côté de chez Swann* [In search of lost time: Swann's way]. Paris: Gallimard. (Original work published in 1913)

Reisenzein, R. (1995). On Oatley and Johnson-Laird's theory of emotions and hierarchical structures. *Cognition and Emotion, 9,* 383–416.

Reisenzein, R. (in press). Emotional experience in the computational belief-desire theory of emotion. *Emotion Review.*

Rimé, B. (2009). Emotion elicits social sharing of emotion: Theory and empirical review. *Emotion Review, 1,* 60–85.

Rizzolatti, G., Fadiga, L., Gallese, V., & Fogassi, L. (1996). Premotor cortex and the recognition of motor action. *Cognitive Brain Research, 3,* 131–141.

Smith, A. (1976). *The theory of moral sentiments.* Oxford, UK: Oxford University Press. (Original work published in 1759)

Stanovich, K. E. (2004). *The robot's rebellion: Finding meaning in the age of Darwin.* Chicago: University of Chicago Press.

Stanovich, K. E. (in press). *Rationality and the reflective mind.* New York: Oxford University Press.

Tooby, J., & Cosmides, L. (1990). The past explains the present: Emotional adaptations and the structure of ancestral environments. *Ethology and Sociobiology, 11,* 375–424.

Wicker, B., Keysers, C., Plailly, J., Royet, J.-P., Gallese, V., & Rizzolati, G. (2003). Both of us disgusted in my insula: The common neural basis of seeing and feeling disgust. *Neuron, 40,* 655–664.

Zunshine, L. (2006). *Why we read fiction: Theory of mind and the novel.* Columbus: Ohio State University Press.

CHAPTER 7

Agency and Communion as Basic Dimensions of Social Cognition

Bogdan Wojciszke

INTRODUCTION

This chapter presents three ideas. The first is that there are two broad classes of content employed in the perception of self and others—agentic versus communal—which are logically and semantically independent, though they tend to be used as mutually exclusive classes of construal in person perception. Although these two semantic dimensions are known by very different names, both conceptual and empirical analyses suggest substantial overlaps between various conceptual opposites used to capture this duality of social cognition content. The second idea is that cognitive and affective responses to others are dominated by communal content, because communal construal captures the functional significance of others' actions for the perceiver. The third idea is that self-perception and self-evaluation are dominated by agentic content, because agentic construal captures the functional significance of the perceiver's own actions.

DUALITY OF SOCIAL COGNITION CONTENT

Over the last seventy years, researchers in several areas of social and personality psychology have postulated two kinds of content under different names: masculinity versus femininity, instrumentality versus expressiveness, competence versus morality, egoistic versus moralistic bias, individualism versus collec-

Personality, Cognition, and Emotion edited by Michael W. Eysenck, Małgorzata Fajkowska, and Tomasz Maruszewski. Eliot Werner Publications, Clinton Corners, New York, 2012.

tivism, intellectually versus socially good-bad (cf. Fiske, Cuddy, & Glick, 2007; Judd, James-Hawkins, Yzerbyt, & Kashima, 2005). Main variations of this content distinction are listed in Table 1.

Importance of the Two Contents

Several lines of research on person and group perceptions show the paramount role of these two types of content. In an early study, we asked participants for recollections of episodes in which they had come to a clear-cut evaluative conclusion about another person or themselves. Wojciszke's (1994) content analysis of over one thousand episodes showed that in three-quarters of them the evaluative impression was based on considerations related to morality (communion) or competence (agency). In another study we asked participants for global evaluations of twenty well-known persons from their social environment and for the assessment of those persons' agentic and communal traits. On average, these trait ascriptions explained 82% of the variance of global impressions (Wojciszke, Bazinska, & Jaworski, 1998). The same was true for the perception of participants' supervisors in two different organizations (Wojciszke & Abele, 2008).

It is also well known that agency (competence) and communion (caring for coworkers) constitute two separate and basic clusters of traits in the perception of leaders (Chemers, 2001), and that these clusters define the two classical styles of organizational leadership—task and relation oriented. The two trait types appear frequently in voters' open-ended commentaries on political candidates in various countries (e.g., in the United States, Kinder & Sears, 1985; or in Poland, Wojciszke & Klusek, 1996). They constitute two basic clusters in the perception of political leaders (under the labels of competence and integrity) and trait descriptions along these two dimensions are strong predictors of the president's approval.

Another line of support for the two basic content dimensions comes from the Stereotype Content Model (Cuddy, Fiske, & Glick, 2008; Fiske, Cuddy, Glick, & Xu, 2002). Although previous theories assumed prejudice to be a univalent antipathy, numerous studies inspired by this model showed that group stereotypes actually involve two separate dimensions of warmth and competence, predicted (respectively) by the perceived competition and status of stereotyped groups. In effect, there are four kinds of stereotyped groups with distinct beliefs, emotions, and behaviors assigned to each type. First, groups perceived as both warm and competent (friendly and high in status, typically ingroups) are admired and meet with active facilitation (help) and passive facilitation (association). Second, groups perceived as warm but not competent (friendly and low in status, like elderly people) are pitied and meet with ambivalent combination of active help and passive ignorance. Third, groups perceived as cold and not competent (not friendly and low in status, like homeless people) elicit contempt and meet with both active and passive harm (attack and neglect). Fourth, groups perceived as cold and competent (not friendly but high in status, like Asians) elicit envy and ambivalent behaviors such as active harm and passive facilitation.

TABLE 1. Various Conceptualizations of Agentic and Communal Contents

Agentic content	Communal content	Posited status
Masculine	**Feminine**	
Initially traits and activities typical to and desirable in men, then typical for cultural stereotype of this gender (linked by various authors to agency, instrumentality, potency, activity, and competence). E.g., *individualistic, independent, logical, dominant, insensitive, conceited.*	Initially traits and activities typical to and desirable in women, then typical for cultural stereotype of this gender (linked by various authors to communion, expressivity, other-directedness). E.g., *caring, emotional, helpful, irrational, timid, wavering.*	Initially opposite poles of a dispositional dimension (Terman & Miles, 1936), then separate dimensions of gender stereotypes and identities (Bem, 1974).
Agency	**Communion**	
Reflects one's existence as an individual. Strivings to individuate through forming separations, reflected in tendency to self-confidence, self-protection, self-expansion, self-assertion. Focus on self, related to power motivation. E.g., *aggressive, ambitious, dominant, forceful, self-sufficient, independent.*	Reflects the participation of the individual in a larger organism of which the individual is part. Strivings to integrate self in a larger social unit through caring for and cooperating with others. Focus on others, caring for their welfare, related to intimacy motivation. E.g., *affectionate, kind, helpful, interpersonally sensitive, nurturing.*	Separate dimensions of human existence (Bakan, 1966; Helgeson, 1994); descriptive and prescriptive norms constituting gender roles (Eagly & Karau (2002).
Individualism	**Collectivism**	
Focus on individual's rights above duties, concern for oneself and family, emphasis on personal autonomy and self-fulfillment; identity based on own personal accomplishments. Priority given to personal goals, uniqueness, and control. E.g., *independent, unique, self-reliant, original.*	Focus on group membership, sacrifice for the common good, maintaining harmonious relations with ingroups. Priority given to social roles and group obligations. E.g., *loyal, compromising, cooperative, respectful.*	Initially bipolar opposites referring to cultures (Hofstede, 1980), then separate dimensions referring to both cultures and individuals (Schwartz, 1990; Triandis, 1995; descriptors: Sedikides et al., 2003).
Independent self	**Interdependent self**	
Stress on individual's uniqueness, independence, self-sufficiency, ego-focused emotions (e.g., anger), freedom from societal constraints, agency, separateness from others, and personal success.	Stress on relatedness to others, coordination, cooperation, group cohesion, other-focused emotions (shame), emotional self-control, interpersonal harmony, the importance of others, responsibility to the group.	Separate but opposite types of self-construal (Markus & Kitayama, 1991).

Intellectually good-bad	Socially good-bad	
Traits having to do with intellectual activities (deciding whether a person exhibiting the traits would be good or bad in such activities). E.g., *persistent, determined, skillful, foolish, irresponsible, wasteful.*	Traits having to do with social activities (deciding whether a person exhibiting the traits would be good or bad in such activities). E.g., *warm, sociable, good natured, unpopular, unhappy, cold.*	Separate analytical dimensions underlying co-occurrences of traits (Rosenberg & Sedlak, 1972).

Self-profitable	Other-profitable	
Traits that are unconditionally profitable or harmful for the trait holder. E.g., *ambitious, industrious, self-confident, slow, stupid, weak.*	Traits that are profitable or harmful for others who interact with the trait holder. E.g., *conciliatory, tolerant, trustworthy, envious, insensitive, selfish.*	Separate types of traits (Peeters, 1992).

Competence	Moral	
Information on capabilities, skills, and efficiency in goal attainment. E.g., *efficient, competent, foolish, unintelligent.*	Information on how the person's goals relate to well-being (benefits or harms) of other people and moral norms. E.g., *honest, fair, insincere, merciless.*	Separate types of traits and behavioral information (Reeder, 1993; Wojciszke, 1994).

Social utility	Social desirability	
Traits reflecting persons' "market value" (i.e., their chances of success or failure in social life based on how well they meet their society's requirements). E.g., *ambitious, active, intelligent, lazy, stupid, timid.*	Traits reflecting persons' likability or ways in which they can satisfy motivations of others. E.g., *generous, sociable, warm, false, intolerant, selfish.*	Separate dimensions of a person's social value (Dubois & Beauvois, 2004).

Competence of stereotyped groups	Warmth of stereotyped groups	
Stereotypical perception of groups as competent or incompetent follows from their high or low position in the status-power hierarchy. E.g., *capable, efficient, intelligent, skillful.*	Perception of groups as warm results from their deference and benevolence (i.e., their lack of intention to compete against the perceiver's own group). E.g., *friendly, sincere, trustworthy, warm.*	Separate dimensions of the stereotype contents (Fiske et al., 2002).

Dominance	Valence	
Second principal component interpreted as the dominance/power dimension of face evaluations.	First principal component interpreted as the valence/trustworthiness dimension of face evaluations.	Separate dimensions of traits underlying face perception (Todorov, in press).

Note. Examples refer to person descriptors most typical for the concept.

Although the concept pairs listed in Table 1 vary considerably in origin, scope, and level of abstraction, there are some common threads in all of them. One convergence is the assumption of independence between the contents listed in the two columns. Whereas early accounts postulated them to be opposite poles of the same dimension, as was the case with masculinity-femininity (Terman & Miles, 1936), individualism-collectivism (Triandis, 1995), and independent-interdependent self-construal (Markus & Kitayama, 1991), more recent theorizing and data support the view of independence. The data have shown that self-ascriptions of agency are relatively independent of self-ascriptions of communion (e.g., Abele, 2003), that self-ascribed individualism is independent of self-ascribed collectivism (e.g., Singelis, 1994), and that both independent and interdependent self-construals are available to the same individual and each of them may acquire a temporary primacy due to recent activation (Oyserman & Lee, 2008).

A second convergence of the concepts listed in Table 1 is their common core meaning. Whereas each of the left-hand concepts refers to human existence as individuals striving to accomplish their goals by means of competence and skill acquisition, each of the right-hand concepts refers to humans as participants in social life who connect with others and care for or are cared for by them (Bakan, 1966; Ybarra et al., 2008). After Bakan (1966) we choose "agentic" and "communal" as generic terms to name these two types of content because the terms convey the idea that agentic categories are important in the agent perspective, while the communal categories weigh much in the recipient perspective. Additionally, these terms are common in different fields of social psychology like person perception, group perception, self-description, and social motives. Finally, their usefulness has also been demonstrated in other areas of psychology—auto-biographical memory, psychological well-being, occupational development, attachment styles, or motivational influences on information processing, to name just a few (cf. Abele & Wojciszke, 2007). These terms are thus widely acknowledged, and they are conceptualized broadly enough to cover a number of related concepts.

Functional Meaning of the Two Contents

We assume that agentic concepts developed in natural languages to denote interests of the agent (the person who performs the action) and the agent perspective is assumed when perceivers construe their own action or actions of other persons who are close to them (symbolically included in the self; Aron et al., 2005) or who serve as vicarious agents (like my lawyer). The agentic content should dominate perceptions and evaluations made from this perspective (e.g., self-perceptions and self-esteem). On the other hand, communal terms developed to capture interests of the recipient (the person at whom the action is oriented) and this perspective is applied when the observer construes actions of others who do something to her or him. Therefore communal content is expected to dominate the observer's perceptions. If our assumptions are right, the general agency dimension should be composed of individualistic, masculine, and competent content, and it should be related to the extent that a trait serves self-interest (of the agent or trait possessor). The general communion dimension should be made up of collectivist, feminine, and moral content, and it should be related to interests of recipients—persons who are target others and in a negative way by self-interest.

We gave this idea a comprehensive treatment in a normative study of a pool of three hundred adjectival names of traits that were selected to be representative for Table 1 concepts and also for Big Five markers (Abele & Wojciszke, 2007). Every trait was rated for agency and communion, masculinity and femininity, competence and morality, and individualism and collectivism by one group of raters each; that is, the concepts were rated independently. The traits were also rated for self-interest (how much each trait serves the interest of the trait possessor or agent) and other-interest (how much it serves the interest of surrounding others—i.e., recipients of actions underlain by the trait). As can be seen in Table 2, all agent-relevant dimensions of meaning strongly correlated with each other

TABLE 2. Correlations Between Trait Content Dimensions Denoting Agency and Communion

(a) Agentic Dimensions

	AG	MA	IN	CO	SI
AG	–	0.84	0.85	0.93	0.84
MA	0.68	–	0.82	0.90	0.87
IN	0.72	0.60	–	0.84	0.74
CO	0.94	0.64	0.66	–	0.93
SI	0.71	0.49	0.39	0.69	–

(b) Communal Dimensions

	CM	FE	CL	MO	OI
CM	–	0.82	0.92	0.91	0.92
FE	0.42	–	0.74	0.77	0.81
CL	0.83	0.35	–	0.78	0.82
MO	0.62	0.27	0.42	–	0.88
OI	0.65	0.23	0.66	0.38	–

Note. AG = agency; MA = masculinity; IN = individualism; CO = competence; SI = self-interest; CM = community; FE = femininity; CL = collectivism; MO = morality; OI = other-interest. Zero-order correlations are above the diagonal; partial correlations controlled for trait valence are below the diagonal. All correlations are significant at $p < 0.001$.

and with self-interest (the mean correlation was 0.86). Similar correlations were found among all recipient relevant dimensions, which also correlated with other-interest (the mean correlation was 0.84).

When these ratings were subjected to factor analysis, only two factors emerged that accounted for 90% of the variance (and the communal factor emerged as a much stronger one, accounting for 71% of the variance). Moreover, when the two resulting factor scores were entered into a simultaneous linear regression analysis as predictors of trait favorability (rated independently by another group of participants), they accounted for nearly all the variance in favorability (adjusted $R^2 = 0.97$). These results suggest a high redundancy across the variously named agentic and communal dimensions, and that these two content dimensions are practically sole predictors of content-free favorability (i.e., whether a trait is positive or negative)—additional evidence for the exclusive prominence of these two contents in person cognition.

Because both agency and communion are positively evaluated dimensions, valence may obscure relations between the two (Suitner & Maass, 2008); hence partial correlations controlling for trait valence are presented below the diagonal of Table 2. Understandably, the partial correlations appeared somewhat lower, but the pattern remained the same. Interestingly, controlling for valence has an entirely different influence on between-dimensions correlations. As can be seen in Table 3, the zero-order correlations between the two dimensions are positive, but when valence is controlled for (either by means of partial correlations or by ana-

TABLE 3. Correlations Between the Same Content (Paired) Dimensions for Positive, Negative, and All Traits

	Positive traits (N = 175)	Negative traits (N = 125)	All traits (N = 300)
Agency vs. communion	-0.41*** (-0.68***)	-0.53*** (-0.58***)	0.38*** (-0.63***)
Masculinity vs. femininity	-0.36*** (-0.62***)	-0.16* (-0.38***)	0.50*** (-0.54***)
Individualism vs. collectivism	-0.60*** (-0.76***)	-0.58*** (-0.43***)	0.15** (-0.76***)
Competence vs. morality	-0.24*** (-0.58***)	-0.41*** (-0.72***)	0.55*** (-0.69***)
Self- vs. other-interest	0.43*** (-0.27***)	-0.11 (-0.23*)	0.86*** (-0.10)

Note. *$p < 0.05$; **$p < 0.01$; ***$p < 0.001$. Partial correlations controlled for trait valence are in parentheses. Based on data of Abele and Wojciszke (2007).

lyzing positive and negative traits separately), the relation becomes negative. So the more a trait is agentic (or competence related, or individualistic, etc.), the less it is communal (or morality related, or collectivistic, etc.).

This invariably negative relation holds, however, only on the level of trait descriptors where the purely semantic phenomena are studied. On the level of person and group perception, additional psychological processes may intervene: evaluative consistency pressures or halo effect, leading to positive correlation; or compensatory processes (such as a group perceived as relatively low on one dimension is compensated for on the other dimension), leading to negative correlation between the two dimensions (Judd et al., 2005; Kervyn, Yzerbyt, Demoulin, & Judd, 2008). The results of Tables 2 and 3 were originally obtained for Polish speakers, but subsequent research showed that they hold for other natural languages as well (English, French, German, and Italian) and that the large majority of traits retain their communal-agentic meaning in these languages (Abele, Uchronski, Suitner, & Wojciszke, 2008).

The studies reviewed so far suggest that agentic versus communal content is related differently to self-interest than other-interest. If agency is more relevant for the self and communion is more relevant for another person, then agentic skills should be more desirable from the perspective of the self and communal skills should be more desirable from the perspective of another person. To test these predictions, we presented our participants with descriptions of psychological trainings that focused on the improvement of either agentic skills (*time management* or *persuading an audience*) or communal skills (*giving social support* or *moral self-development*). We asked them either how much they would like to par-

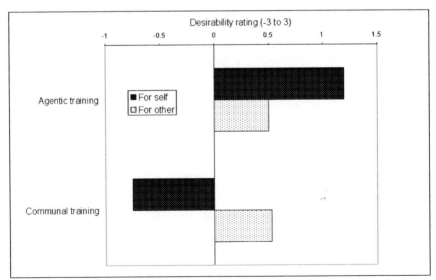

Figure 1. Desirability of agentic and communal trainings from the perspective of self versus another person. Based on data of Abele and Wojciszke (2007, Study 3).

ticipate in each of these trainings or how much they would like another person (a specific peer, not a close friend) to participate in these trainings (Abele & Wojciszke, 2007, Study 3). As can be seen in Figure 1, we found the predicted interaction between the perspective (self vs. other) and training type (agentic vs. communal). Whereas trainings in agentic skills were preferred for the self, trainings in communal skills were preferred for the other. Actually, our participants refused to take part in communal trainings; we suspect that this is because improving such skills would be beneficial not to the participants, but to those who surround them.

DIFFERENCES IN BEHAVIOR CONSTRUAL

We assume that behavioral acts vary along a continuum according to the relative strength of their agentic and communal meaning. There is a small minority of acts that have only agentic but no communal meaning or, rather, that are amenable to construal only in agentic terms but cannot be construed in communal ones. Getting a promotion, losing a chess competition, or failing a driving test have clear agentic meaning, but these acts can be hardly construed in communion categories without additional information. There is also a small minority of acts construable in communal but not agentic terms (visiting a friend in the hospital or robbing a fragile elderly person). The majority of acts, however, are amenable to both interpretations and are more or less ambiguous, like helping a friend in math (it is prosocial to help others, but helping in math shows competence as well) or publicly criticizing a math lecturer (criticizing others is nasty but in this case it also shows courage and knowledge). My theory posits the agent-recipient perspective to function as a strong disambiguating factor: whereas own behavior (and that of symbiotic others) tends to be construed in an agentic way, behavior of nonsymbiotic others tends to be read in communal terms. This is because the self-interest is differently implicated under the agent versus recipient perspective.

In the recipient perspective (when responding to others' behavior), people either are directly involved as actual recipients of the action or automatically assume the position of an action recipient even if they are not personally involved (Vonk, 1999; Wojciszke, 1994, 2005). Communality becomes more pertinent to their self-interests than agency because the acting person's communal behavior is beneficial to other people (the perceiver included), while his or her lack of communion is usually harmful to them. It is pleasant and rewarding to interact with others who are caring, fair, or helpful, just as it is unpleasant and punishing to interact with persons who are cold, inconsiderate, or disloyal. Others' agency is of secondary importance and its bearing on the observer's interests is contingent on the agent's goals. When he or she strives for something beneficial, efficiency and competence will maximize the observer's interests, but efficiency may be also detrimental to those interests when the agent's goals are vicious.

In the agent perspective (when one's own or symbiotic others' behavior or qualities are at stake), agency is more pertinent to self-interest because own competence, efficiency, or resourcefulness is unconditionally important for the acting person. Intentionally self-harmful behavior—such as suicide—is extremely rare (Baumeister, 1998) and a majority of people's actions serve their own interests (which does not mean that they are directed against the interest of others). Practically speaking, whatever a person does, it is beneficial to him or her to do it in an efficient way. To achieve any goal, actors have to monitor how they are doing (i.e., whether their behavior is moving them closer to the goal). Therefore actors focus to a much greater extent on their agency than on communion, at least at the phase of action execution.

The hypotheses that agentic categories are used to a greater extent by agents, and that communal categories are used to a greater extent by recipients, received clear empirical support in several studies. In one of them (Wojciszke, 1994, Study 1), participants interpreted identical actions construable both in competence (agentic) and moral (communal) terms and were instructed to take either the agent or the recipient perspective when reading them. For example, they received a description of an employee who ingratiated herself to her supervisor in such a blatant way that it infuriated the supervisor. The participants were to evaluate this action from the perspective of the employee or the supervisor and to write down the rationale of their evaluation. The rationale was rated by a pair of judges for the degree to which it referred to competence (i.e., that the employee's behavior was clumsy, transparent, and socially unskilled) and another pair rated the rationale for its relatedness to morality (i.e., that the employee's behavior was a dishonest and insincere act of ingratiation). These ratings of the

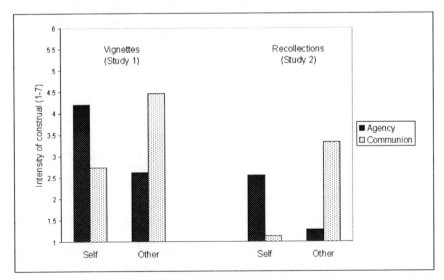

Figure 2. Construal of own and others' actions in terms of agency and communion. Based on data of Wojciszke (1994, Studies 1 and 2).

rationale served as an index of behavior construal. As can be seen in Figure 2, a strong crossover interaction between the perspective and construal content was found. Within the agent perspective (self), the rationale referred more strongly to competence than morality, but within the recipient perspective (other) the opposite was true. Moreover, when another sample of participants took the perspective of an uninvolved observer (neither the employee nor the supervisor), their interpretations closely paralleled those of the recipient. This is consistent with my argument that when observing actions of (nonsymbiotic) others, people spontaneously assume a recipient—not an agent—perspective.

A weakness of this study was that participants only imagined their responses in hypothetical situations. Therefore we also conducted a correlational study where participants recollected and interpreted real-life episodes that had led them to strong evaluations of themselves or others (Wojciszke, 1994, Study 2). As can be seen in the right panel of Figure 2, the analysis of rationales for these evaluations showed a pattern similar to that already discussed (independently of whether the recollected episode had led to a positive or negative evaluation). Finally, in another experiment the perspective was induced indirectly by a seemingly unrelated priming task (Wojciszke, 1997). All three studies showed that the agent perspective resulted in a preference for agentic over communal construal, but that the opposite was true for the construal of identical or similar actions from the recipient (or uninvolved observer) perspective. Moreover, global evaluations accompanying this difference in construal were also perspective-dependent: whereas in the agent perspective evaluations depended to a greater degree on competence than on moral considerations, the opposite was true in the recipient perspective.

In those early studies, moral versus competence-related construal was studied, although very similar results were obtained in recent studies where the more abstract, communal versus agentic construal was examined. In one of those studies, participants recalled important events that had changed their self-evaluation or evaluation of another person who was either unrelated (a distant peer) or interdependent (a close friend). Participants described the behavior and the rationale for their evaluations, which were rated afterward for the degree to which they referred to agency and communion (Wojciszke & Abele, 2008, Study 1). We hypothesized that behavior of an unrelated peer would be construed in communal rather than agentic terms (the usual communion over agency effect), but that the opposite would be true in the construal of both own and close friend's behavior (a reversal of the usual communion over agency effect). Figure 3 shows the data that confirmed these expectations. Interestingly, when construing behavior of a close friend, participants heavily employed agentic categories (like in the self-construal). Still, they retained much sensitivity to the communal meaning of that behavior, presumably because they were frequently on the receiving end of those behavioral acts.

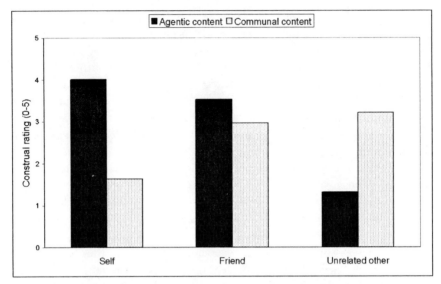

Figure 3. Construal of own versus a friend's versus unrelated others' actions in terms of agency and communion. From "The Primacy of Communion Over Agency and Its Reversals in Evaluations" by B. Wojciszke and A. E. Abele, 2008, *European Journal of Social Psychology, 38*, p. 1143. Copyright 2008 by John Wiley & Sons. Reprinted with permission.

DIFFERENCES IN EVALUATIVE RESPONSES

The present theorizing leads to the prediction that global evaluative impressions of others are more heavily influenced by information on their communion than their agency, while evaluations of self (self-esteem) are more dependent on agentic than communal information. In an initial test of these hypotheses, participants were asked to describe several persons from their social milieu with several communal and agentic traits carefully balanced in favorability, and were asked to show their global evaluations of these persons (Wojciszke et al., 1998, Study 3). Global impressions of those real persons were significantly better predicted from the communal than agentic trait ascription, and these two contents of trait-ascription accounted for 53% and 29% of the variance of global evaluations, respectively.

In a subsequent study, we manipulated communal (moral-immoral) and agentic (competent-incompetent) information on behaviors of fictitious target persons, asking perceivers for their global evaluations of the targets. As can be seen in Figure 4, both types of information influenced global evaluations, but communal information exerted a much stronger effect ($\eta^2 = 0.95$) than the agentic one ($\eta^2 = 0.41$). Moreover, when the former was negative (immoral condition), the global impressions were always negative—even when the agentic input information was positive. But when the communal information was positive (moral condition), the impressions were always positive. Interestingly, when the target's behavioral acts were immoral, high competence led to a more negative impression than incompe-

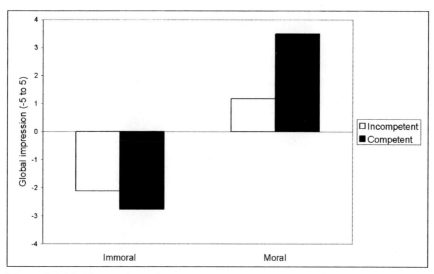

Figure 4. Global impressions of persons who acted in a moral or immoral way, showing competence or incompetence in these actions. Based on data of Wojciszke et al. (1998, Study 4).

tence, because the former meant a higher efficiency in wrongdoing (as in the case of a thief or a con man: such a person is more harmful when competent rather than incompetent). Communal meaning of another person's act, then, can radically change evaluative implications of accompanying agentic information, but not the other way around (cf. Peeters, 1992, for a related discussion).

Though impressions of others are more strongly influenced by communal than agentic information, this regularity is context-sensitive—as predicted by the present theorizing. It ceases to be true when the target is symbiotically related to the perceiver; that is, the target's agency contributes as much to the perceivers' well-being as their own abilities, as in the case of "my supervisor's competence." We found that employees based global evaluations of their supervisors more on the latter's agency than community (Wojciszke & Abele, 2008, Study 2). This was true, however, only in efficiency-oriented organizations (e.g., competitive businesses) where employees' outcomes increase with competence of their supervisor. It did not hold in bureaucratic organizations (e.g., state administration) where competence of the supervisor does not contribute to employees' outcomes (in Poland salaries in such organizations depend on bureaucratic criteria rather than efficiency, so the competence of a supervisor is not a source of benefits for his or her subordinates). In those organizations employees' attitudes toward their supervisor were based to a greater extent on communal than agentic traits of the latter.

In the area of self-perception, the closest parallel of global evaluations of others is self-esteem (which is understood here as an affective response toward the self, whereas perceived self-agency and self-communion are understood as important but more specific parts of self-concept). To complete the argument that agency dominates self-attitudes (just like communion dominates interpersonal evaluations), it should be shown that self-esteem depends on agentic rather than communal information. To test this hypothesis, several samples were asked for self-ascription of seven communal traits (*fair, good, honest, loyal, selfless, sincere, truthful*) and seven agentic traits (*clever, competent, efficient, energetic, intelligent, knowledgeable, logical*) that were carefully balanced for favorability. In addition, participants filled various measures of self-esteem (as a trait, as a state, narcissism, and an implicit measure consisting of preferences for letters

TABLE 4. Mean Self-Evaluations of Communal and Agentic Traits and Their β Values as Predictors of Various Indices of Self-Esteem in Six Samples

	Mean	SD	β	Adj. R^2
Polish students (*N* = 153), dependent: Trait self-esteem				0.27***
Communal traits	5.39	0.71	0.05	
Agentic traits	4.84	0.90	0.53***	
Polish students (*N* = 88), dependent: Implicit self-esteem				0.13***
Communal traits	48.45	22.10	−0.05	
Agentic traits	36.18	19.68	0.38***	
Polish employees (*N* = 162), dependent: Narcissism				0.18***
Communal traits	5.52	0.82	−0.06	
Agentic traits	5.12	0.76	0.45***	
Polish employees (*N* = 89), dependent: State self-esteem				0.30***
Communal traits	5.76	0.82	−0.13	
Agentic traits	5.48	0.73	0.36***	
Dutch students (*N* = 120), dependent: Trait self-esteem				0.25***
Communal traits	5.59	0.59	0.03	
Agentic traits	5.23	0.60	0.50***	
American Internet users (*N* = 92), dependent: Trait self-esteem				0.20***
Communal traits	5.64	0.68	0.17	
Agentic traits	5.49	0.81	0.39***	
Colombian students (*N* = 60), dependent: Trait self-esteem				0.42***
Communal traits	5.63	0.75	−0.07	
Agentic traits	5.51	0.75	0.67***	
Japanese Internet users (*N* = 103), dependent: Trait self-esteem				0.24***
Communal traits	4.96	1.03	0.09	
Agentic traits	4.54	1.06	0.47***	

Note. *$p < 0.05$; **$p < 0.01$; ***$p < 0.001$. Self-ratings on a scale ranging from 1 to 7 with 4 being the midpoint (with the exception of the Implicit self-esteem sample, where ratings were made on 100-mm-long graphic scales). Based on data of Wojciszke et al. (in press).

constituting the participant's own initials). For each sample a linear regression analysis was performed on self-esteem as a dependent measure, while self-ascribed agency and communion served as predictors (Wojciszke, Baryla, Parzuchowski, Szymków, & Abele, in press).

As can be seen in Table 4, self-esteem was more strongly predicted by agentic than communal self-ascription. Although in absolute terms participants ascribed to themselves significantly more communion than agency, the former was a much stronger predictor of self-esteem. This was found for all measures of self-esteem and in all samples (student vs. nonstudent, younger vs. older, men vs. women). In addition to Poland (which is intermediate on the individualism-collectivism dimension), the samples came from highly individualistic cultures (the United States, the Netherlands), as well as highly collectivistic ones (Colombia, Japan). Still, the dominance of agency over communion in predicting self-esteem appeared universal. People ascribe themselves communal qualities to a great extent, but this has no effect on their self-esteem. They ascribe themselves agentic qualities to a lesser degree, but these self-ascriptions have much to do with their self-esteem.

CONCLUDING REMARKS

A quarter-century ago Rothbart and Park (1986) noticed and showed empirically that not all traits are created equal, meaning that not all sorts of content are uniform or processed in the same way. By and large, however, the social cognition field has tended to ignore content as a variable of serious interest. For example, classical theorists of information integration (Anderson, 1981) assumed that all sorts of information are combined in an evaluative impression according to the same algebraic rules. Similarly, more recent theorizing on social cognition assumes that any cognitive structure (category, script, or episodic representation) can underlie and dominate the process of a stimulus construal and encoding, if it only has happened to be activated due to its recent or frequent use in the past, or due to its semantic similarity to the target stimulus or co-occurring stimuli (cf. Higgins, 1996). Actually, the independence of any rule from the specific content on which the rule is tested proves its scientific reality, as evidenced by countless experiments using replications over the content of stimuli and/or dependent measures (i.e., behavioral descriptions, traits, judgments, attitudes, attributions — whichever is used as an independent or dependent variable). This is understandable in psychology, which is a scientific endeavor that attempts to reveal general rules governing human cognition and behavior. The problem, however, is that treating the processed content merely as a source of random error may endanger the very quest for valid rules that underlie social cognition.

It seems that differences between agentic and communal content (which are known by different names but overlap substantially) should not be averaged away, because these two types of content differ in theoretically meaningful ways. Early works of Reeder (1993; Reeder & Brewer, 1979) showed that these two types of traits (identified more narrowly as ability vs. morality) are inferred in different ways: whereas ability attributions are more heavily influenced by positive than negative behaviors, moral attributions are based on negative rather than positive behaviors (Wojciszke, Brycz, & Borkenau, 1993). This chapter goes beyond these regularities by showing that the same behaviors are construable in both agentic and communal categories. Which of these construals will be actually applied to behavior interpretation is heavily influenced by whether the behavior is seen from the perspective of the agent or the recipient of the behavioral act. When behavior is perceived from the agent perspective (like one's own behavior or that of close others), the agentic interpretation dominates the communal one and evaluative responses follow this pattern. When behavior is perceived from the recipient perspective (e.g., when the observer is a recipient of the behavioral act in question), communal interpretation dominates the agentic one and evaluative responses follow this pattern.

It is well known that people perceive themselves differently from how they see others. This is usually explained by self-serving motivations and the fact that self-perceptions are based on subjective experience and cognitions, while perceptions of others are mainly based on observable behavior (Pronin, 2008). My work suggests that even when self-perceptions are based on behavior, its construal may be completely different from an interpretation of the same behavior performed by others. Undoubtedly, the perspective is not the only factor deciding on the preference of agentic versus communal content. This preference is also a matter of individual differences, such as the strength of the achievement and affiliation motives (Woike, Lavezzary, & Barsky, 2001), and may be a matter of independent versus interdependent self-priming. Like the question of possible subdimensions within the general agentic or communal domains (cf. Leach, Ellemers, & Barreto, 2007), this is a subject of possible future research.

REFERENCES

Abele, A. E. (2003). The dynamics of masculine-agentic and feminine-communal traits: Findings from a prospective study. *Journal of Personality and Social Psychology, 85*, 768–776.

Abele, A. E., Uchronski, M., Suitner, C., & Wojciszke, B. (2008). Towards an operationalization of the fundamental dimensions of agency and communion: Trait content ratings in five countries considering valence and frequency of word occurrence. *European Journal of Social Psychology, 38*, 1202–1217.

Abele, A. E., & Wojciszke, B. (2007). Agency and communion from the perspective of self versus others. *Journal of Personality and Social Psychology, 93*, 751–763.

Anderson, N. H. (1981). *Foundations of information integration theory*. New York: Academic Press.

Aron, A., Mashek, D., McLaughlin-Volpe, T., Wright, S., Lewandowski, G., & Aron, E. N. (2005). Including close others in the cognitive structure of the self. In M. W. Baldwin (Ed.), *Interpersonal cognition* (pp. 206–232). New York: Guilford Press.

Bakan, D. (1966). *The duality of human existence: An essay on psychology and religion*. Reading, PA: Addison-Wesley.

Baumeister, R. F. (1998). The self. In D. T. Gilbert, S. T. Fiske, & G. Lindzey (Eds.), *The handbook of social psychology: Vol. 2* (4th ed., pp. 680–740). New York: McGraw-Hill.

Bem, S. L. (1974). The measurement of psychological androgyny. *Journal of Clinical and Consulting Psychology, 42,* 155–162.

Chemers, M. M. (2001). Leadership effectiveness: An integrative review. In A. M. Hogg & R. S. Tindale (Eds.), *Blackwell handbook of social psychology: Group processes* (pp. 376–399). Oxford, UK: Blackwell.

Cuddy, A. J. C., Fiske, S. T., & Glick, P. (2008). Warmth and competence as universal dimensions of social perception: The Stereotype Content Model and the BIAS map. In M. P. Zanna (Ed.), *Advances in experimental social psychology* (Vol. 40, pp. 61–149). San Diego, CA: Academic Press.

Dubois, N., & Beauvois, J.-L. (2004). Normativeness and individualism. *European Journal of Social Psychology, 35,* 123–146.

Eagly, A. H., & Karau, S. J. (2002). Role congruity theory of prejudice toward female leaders. *Psychological Review, 109,* 573-598.

Fiske, S. T., Cuddy, A. J. C., & Glick, P. (2007). Universal dimensions of social cognition: Warmth and competence. *Trends in Cognitive Sciences, 11,* 77–83.

Fiske, S. T., Cuddy, A. J. C., Glick, P., & Xu, J. (2002). A model of (often mixed) stereotype content: Competence and warmth respectively follow from the perceived status and competition. *Journal of Personality and Social Psychology, 82,* 878–902.

Helgeson, V. S. (1994). Relation of agency and communion to well-being: Evidence and potential explanations. *Psychological Bulletin, 116,* 412–428.

Higgins, E. T. (1996). Knowledge activation: Accessibility, applicability, and salience. In E. T. Higgins & A. W. Kruglanski (Eds.), *Social psychology: Handbook of basic principles* (pp. 133–168). New York: Guilford Press.

Judd, C. M., James-Hawkins, L., Yzerbyt, V., & Kashima, Y. (2005). Fundamental dimensions of social judgment: Understanding the relations between judgments of competence and warmth. *Journal of Personality and Social Psychology, 89,* 899–913.

Kervyn, N., Yzerbyt, V. Y., Demoulin, S., & Judd, C. M. (2008). Competence and warmth in context: The compensatory nature of stereotypic views of national groups. *European Journal of Social Psychology, 38,* 1175–1183.

Kinder, D. R., & Sears, D. O. (1985). Public opinion and political action. In G. Lindzey & E. Aronson (Eds.), *The handbook of social psychology: Vol. 3* (3rd ed., pp. 659–741). New York: Random House.

Leach, C. W., Ellemers, N., & Barreto, M. (2007). Group virtue: The importance of morality (vs. competence and sociability) in the positive evaluations of in-groups. *Journal of Personality and Social Psychology, 93,* 234–249.

Markus, H. R., & Kitayama, S. (1991). Culture and the self: Implications for cognition, emotion, and motivation. *Psychological Review, 98,* 224–253.

Oyserman, D., & Lee, S. W. S. (2008). Does culture influence what and how we think? Effects of priming individualism and collectivism. *Psychological Bulletin, 134,* 311–342.

Peeters, G. (1992). Evaluative meanings of adjectives in vitro and in context: Some theoretical implications and practical consequences of positive negative asymmetry and behavioural-adaptive concepts of evaluation. *Psychologia Belgica, 32,* 211–231.

Pronin, E. (2008). How we see ourselves and how we see others. *Science, 320,* 1177–1180.

Reeder, G. D. (1993). Trait-behavior relations and dispositional inference. *Personality and Social Psychology Bulletin, 19,* 586–593.

Reeder, G. D., & Brewer, M. B. (1979). A schematic model of dispositional attribution in interpersonal perception. *Psychological Review, 86*, 61–79.

Rosenberg, S., & Sedlak, A. (1972). Structural representations of implicit personality theory. In L. Berkowitz (Ed.), *Advances in experimental social psychology* (Vol. 6, pp. 235–297). New York: Academic Press.

Rothbart, M., & Park, B. (1986). On the confirmability and disconfirmability of trait concepts. *Journal of Personality and Social Psychology, 50*, 131–142.

Schwartz, S. H. (1990). Individualism-collectivism: Critique and proposed refinements. *Journal of Cross-Cultural Psychology, 21*, 139-157.

Sedikides, C., Gaertner, L., & Toguchi, Y. (2003). Pancultural self-enhancement. *Journal of Personality and Social Psychology, 84*, 60–79.

Singelis, T. M. (1994). The measurement of independent and interdependent self-construals. *Personality and Social Psychology Bulletin, 20*, 580–591.

Suitner C., & Maass, A. (2008). The role of valence in the perception of agency and communion. *European Journal of Social Psychology, 38*, 1073–1082.

Terman, L. M., & Miles, C. C. (1936). *Sex and personality: Studies in masculinity and femininity*. New York: McGraw-Hill.

Triandis, H. C. (1995). *Individualism and collectivism*. Boulder, CO: Westview Press.

Todorov, A. (in press). Evaluating faces on social dimensions. In A. Todorov, S. T. Fiske, & D. Prentice (Eds.), *Social neuroscience: Toward understanding the underpinnings of the social mind*. New York: Oxford University Press.

Vonk, R. (1999). Effects of other-profitability and self-profitability on evaluative judgements of behaviours. *European Journal of Social Psychology, 29*, 833–842.

Woike, B., Lavezzary, E., & Barsky, J. (2001). The influence of implicit motives on memory processes. *Journal of Personality and Social Psychology, 81*, 935–945.

Wojciszke, B. (1994). Multiple meanings of behavior: Construing actions in terms of competence or morality. *Journal of Personality and Social Psychology, 67*, 222–232.

Wojciszke, B. (1997). Parallels between competence- versus morality-related traits and individualistic versus collectivistic values. *European Journal of Social Psychology, 27*, 245–256.

Wojciszke, B. (2005). Morality and competence in person and self-perception. *European Review of Social Psychology, 16*, 155–188.

Wojciszke, B., & Abele, A. E. (2008). The primacy of communion over agency and its reversals in evaluations. *European Journal of Social Psychology, 38*, 1139–1147.

Wojciszke, B., Baryla, W., Parzuchowski, M., Szymków, A., & Abele, A. E. (in press). Self-esteem is dominated by agency over communion. *European Journal of Social Psychology*.

Wojciszke, B., Bazinska, R., & Jaworski, M. (1998). On the dominance of moral categories in impression formation. *Personality and Social Psychology Bulletin, 24*, 1245–1257.

Wojciszke, B., Brycz, H., & Borkenau, P. (1993). Effects of information content and evaluative extremity on positivity and negativity biases. *Journal of Personality and Social Psychology, 64*, 327–336.

Wojciszke, B., & Klusek, B. (1996). Moral and competence-related traits in political perception. *Polish Psychological Bulletin, 27*, 319–325.

Ybarra, O., Chan, E., Park, H., Burnstein, E., Monin, B., & Stanik, C. (2008). Life's recurring challenges and the fundamental dimensions: An integration and its implications for cultural differences and similarities. *European Journal of Social Psychology, 38*, 1083–1092.

CHAPTER 8

Emotions and Morality
You Don't Have to Feel Really Bad to be Good

June Price Tangney
Elizabeth Malouf
Jeff Stuewig
Debra Mashek

"Conscience doesn't always keep you from doing wrong, but it does keep you from enjoying it." H. L. Mencken

The attempt to adapt behavior to moral standards is a uniquely human endeavor. While the behavior of other living creatures is dictated by impulses and drives, humans have the capacity to overcome these in order to act according to higher moral standards. According to social wisdom, human beings are aided in this difficult quest by a "conscience." The conscience guides moral behavior by punishing moral transgression with emotional torment, so-called pangs of conscience. In many religious traditions, feeling bad for moral transgressions is believed to strengthen moral character. "Good" people suffer for their moral wrongdoings, whereas "bad" people ignore the voice of conscience. In short, conventional wisdom suggests that emotional suffering is good, providing an essential mechanism of the conscience.

There are different ways to feel bad after violating one's moral standards. An individual may focus on—and feel bad about—the *self*, or an individual may focus on and feel bad about the *behavior*. This distinction between self and behavior is supported by clinical theory (Lewis, 1971), clinical observation (Lewis, 1971, 1987;

Personality, Cognition, and Emotion edited by Michael W. Eysenck, Małgorzata Fajkowska, and Tomasz Maruszewski. Eliot Werner Publications, Clinton Corners, New York, 2012.

Lindsay-Hartz, 1984), and psychological studies drawing on multiple research methods (for reviews, see Tangney, Stuewig, & Mashek, 2007; Tracy & Robins, 2006). Contemporary psychologists refer to the former self-focused negative emotion as shame and the latter behavior-focused negative emotion as guilt. Guilt and shame are regarded as the primary "moral emotions." They are thought to inhibit immoral, socially undesirable behavior and foster altruistic, prosocial behavior.

DIFFERENCES BETWEEN SHAME AND GUILT

Although often used interchangeably in common language, guilt and shame are distinct emotional experiences. Both emotions are associated with "feeling bad" but the focus, intensity, and behavioral, psychological, and social ramifications of guilt and shame differ—as indicated by a range of phenomenological studies (Lewis, 1971; Lindsay-Hartz 1984; Tangney, 1993; Tangney, Miller, Flicker, & Barlow, 1996; Wallbott & Scherer, 1995; Wicker, Payne, & Morgan, 1983).

Shame is an intensely painful, emotional experience. At the heart of shame is a shift in the relationship with the self. Self-worth diminishes and people may feel inferior, unworthy, and even despicable. Since shamed people judge themselves negatively, they become more intensely aware of social evaluation, fearing that others will share their negative judgments. Recent research has identified a physiological component of the experience of shame. Elevations in proinflammatory cytokines accompany episodes of shame, prompting muscles to contract into an archetypal posture of submission (Dickerson, Gruenwald, & Kemeny, 2004). All in all, shame results in an individual feeling psychologically, socially, and even physically diminished.

Although guilt is an unpleasant emotion, it is generally less painful than shame. People experiencing guilt judge their behavior as "bad" or "immoral" without condemning themselves. In this way self-worth is preserved and sense of identity and integrity is retained. Because the self remains strong, it is more likely that people experiencing guilt will perceive the task of righting the wrong to be achievable.

Although both shame and guilt signal a moral transgression or failure, one must question whether they encourage moral behavior. Clinical theory, observation, and qualitative and quantitative empirical studies indicate that shame and guilt—both as emotional states and dispositional tendencies—have different relationships with other morally relevant emotions, action tendencies, and actual behavior.

RELATION OF SHAME AND GUILT TO ACTION TENDENCIES, EMPATHY, ANGER, AND AGGRESSION

The experience of guilt and guilt-proneness appear to be more beneficial than shame and shame-proneness to both individuals and their relationships with others (Baumeister, Stillwell, & Heatherton, 1994; Tangney, 1991; Tangney & Dearing, 2002). Three lines of research illustrate that guilt is the more moral and adaptive emotion (see Tangney et al., 2007). In each case studies span examinations of both states of moral emotions and dispositions (the propensity to experience shame and guilt across a range of situations). Some studies focus on relatively low levels of guilt or shame in response to common everyday events, whereas other research deals with high levels of these emotions triggered by major life events and decisions. Regardless, the findings generally converge across studies and operationalizations, yielding results that appear to generalize across very different situations.

Hiding versus Amending

In the aftermath of a moral transgression or failure, people are often presented with a second moral dilemma: should they (a) own up to their action and attempt to repair the damage or (b) deny responsibility and attempt to escape the situation? In this regard research consistently shows that shame and guilt lead to contrasting motivations or "action tendencies" (Ferguson, Stegge, & Damhuis, 1991; Lewis, 1971; Lindsay-Hartz, 1984; Tangney, 1993; Tangney, Miller et al., 1996; Wallbott & Scherer, 1995; Wicker et al., 1983).

Shame motivates attempts to deny, hide, or escape the shame-inducing situation, whereas guilt motivates reparative action—confessing, apologizing, undoing. For example, when people are asked to anonymously describe and rate personal shame and guilt experiences (Tangney, 1993; Tangney, Miller et al., 1996), their ratings indicate that they feel more compelled to hide from others and less inclined to admit what they had done when feeling shame as opposed to guilt. When feeling guilt, people are more inclined to apologize and/or repair the harm that was done. Taken together, findings across studies suggest that guilt motivates people in a constructive, proactive, future-oriented direction, whereas shame motivates people toward separation, distance, and defense.

Other-Oriented Empathy

Empathy, awareness, and understanding of another's emotional experience are generally considered important hallmarks of moral interpersonal behavior. Empathy motivates prosocial, altruistic behavior and inhibits antisocial behavior and aggression (Eisenberg, 1986; Eisenberg & Miller, 1987; Feshbach, 1978, 1984, 1987; Feshbach & Feshbach, 1969, 1982, 1986). Research suggests that shame and guilt have different relationships with empathy: whereas shame may disrupt the ability to make an empathic connection, guilt and empathy go hand in hand. This differential relationship of shame and guilt with empathy has been observed at the level of both emotion traits (dispositions) and emotion states.

Across methods and studies, shame-proneness and guilt-proneness are differentially related to the ability to empathize (Leith & Baumeister, 1998;

Tangney, 1991, 1994, 1995; Tangney & Dearing, 2002). This finding is remarkably consistent across individuals of all ages and walks of life. In general, guilt-prone individuals tend to show high levels of empathy. Proneness to guilt consistently correlates with measures of perspective taking and empathic concern. By contrast, shame-proneness has been associated with an impaired capacity for other-oriented empathy and a propensity for problematic, self-oriented personal distress responses.

Similar findings are obtained when considering the emotional states of shame and guilt. Regardless of individual differences in shame-proneness and guilt-proneness, when people describe personal shame experiences, they convey less empathy for others compared with their descriptions of personal guilt experiences (Leith & Baumeister, 1998; Tangney, Marschall, Rosenberg, Barlow, & Wagner, 1994). Moreover, people who were experimentally induced to feel shame subsequently reported less empathy for a disabled student, an effect that was most pronounced among low shame-prone individuals (Marschall, 1996). Consistent with dispositional findings (Tangney, 1991, 1995), shame-prone participants were fairly unempathic across experimental conditions. But among low shame-prone participants—who have a higher capacity for empathy in general—the shame induction had an effect, apparently interfering with an empathic response. In short, the shame induction rendered low shame-prone people relatively unempathic—that is, more like their shame-prone peers.

Anger and Aggression

Whereas empathy is an emotional experience that promotes altruistic, prosocial behavior, anger is an emotional experience associated with aggressive and antisocial behavior. Both shame-proneness and the experience of shame in the moment are associated with anger. Clinicians have long observed a link between shame and anger, a link first described by Helen Block Lewis (1971), who noted that clients' feelings of shame often precede expressions of anger and hostility. Over time empirical research has confirmed this observation. Studies of children, adolescents, college students, and adults consistently show that proneness to shame correlates positively with feelings of anger and hostility and an inclination to externalize blame (Tangney, 1994, 1995; Tangney, Wagner, Fletcher, & Gramzow, 1992).

Not only are shame-prone individuals more likely to experience anger than non-shame-prone individuals, they are also less likely to effectively manage their anger. Research shows that, once angered, shame-prone individuals are more apt to express their anger in a destructive fashion. For example, across children, adolescents, college students, and adults (Tangney, Wagner, Hill-Barlow, Marschall, & Gramzow, 1996), proneness to shame was consistently associated with malicious intentions; propensity to engage in direct physical, verbal, and symbolic aggression; indirect aggression (e.g., harming something important to the target, talking behind the target's back); all manner of displaced aggression; self-directed aggression; and anger held in (a ruminative, unexpressed anger). Likely as a consequence of their maladaptive responses when angry, shame-prone individuals reported that their anger typically results in negative long-term consequences—for themselves and their relationships with others.

By contrast, guilt-proneness is generally associated with more constructive means of handling anger. Proneness to "shame-free" guilt (that is, the unique variance in guilt, independent of shame) was positively correlated with constructive intentions and negatively correlated with direct, indirect, and displaced aggression. Instead, relative to non-guilt-prone persons, guilt-prone individuals are inclined to engage in constructive behavior—such as nonhostile discussion with the target of their anger and direct corrective action. Moreover, guilt-prone individuals reported that their anger typically results in positive long-term consequences. The relationships of shame and guilt with these anger-related dimensions are remarkably robust, holding across demographically diverse samples, and when controlling for the influence of social desirability.

The link between shame and anger has also been observed for event-specific experiences of shame. For example, in an analysis of college students' personal shame and guilt experiences, Wicker et al. (1983) found that college students reported a greater desire to punish others when experiencing shame versus guilt. Tangney, Miller et al. (1996) found a similar trend among college students. When providing narrative accounts of personal shame experiences, these young adults reported more feelings of anger than in connection with narrative accounts of guilt experiences.

Even stronger evidence comes from a study of real-life episodes of anger among romantically involved couples (Tangney, 1995). Shamed partners were significantly more angry, more likely to engage in aggressive behavior, and less likely to elicit conciliatory behavior from their perpetrating significant other than angry, nonshamed partners. Not only were shamed partners more aggressive, but when they confronted their partners, the latter in turn responded with anger, resentment, defiance, and denial—leading to increasingly hostile situations. Reflecting a "shame-rage spiral" (Lewis, 1971; Scheff, 1987), couples reported more negative long-term consequences for anger episodes involving partner shame compared with those not involving shame. Taken together, the data portrayed a painful vicious cycle in which partner shame led to feelings of anger (sometimes rage) and destructive retaliation, which then set into motion anger and resentment in the perpetrator as well as expressions of blame and retaliation in kind, which were then likely to further shame the initially shamed partner.

In short, research consistently shows a robust link between shame and anger—observed in a broad range of studies using multiple methods, diverse samples, and multiple contexts. Clinicians readily recognize the dynamics of shame and anger suggested by these data (Dearing & Tangney, 2011). Desperate to escape painful feelings of shame, shamed individuals may be inclined to defensively "turn the tables," externalizing blame and anger outward onto aspects of the situation or unwitting bystanders. Why do people engage in such defensive maneuvers that are likely to be costly in their interpersonal relationships? There are short-term gains in blaming someone else and feeling indignant anger, if only because such anger can serve to reactivate the self and help the self regain some sense of control and superiority. But unfortunately the long-term costs are often steep. Friends, acquaintances, and loved ones are apt to be truly puzzled and hurt by what appear to be irrational bursts of anger, coming seemingly out of the blue. And typically the initially shamed and irrationally angry partner has little insight into the pain of shame that initiated what is often a mutually painful and bewildering interpersonal exchange.

RELATION OF SHAME AND GUILT TO THE BIG FIVE

Surprisingly few studies have been conducted linking individual differences in proneness to shame and guilt to the Big Five factors of personality. Using multiple measures of shame- and guilt-proneness, Einstein and Lanning (1998) found that a resulting shame factor was positively associated with neuroticism, negatively associated with openness to experience, and (surprisingly) positively associated with agreeableness. The guilt factor based on scenario-based measures, which we argue is the more conceptually congruent operationalization of shame (Tangney, 1996; Tangney & Dearing 2002), was positively associated with agreeableness, but not neuroticism.

MORAL BEHAVIOR: THE BOTTOM LINE

The research reviewed thus far demonstrates that shame and guilt are associated with different motivations and emotions, but are they differentially associated with criminal or otherwise immoral behavior? Empirical evidence indicates that moderately unpleasant guilt, not intensely painful shame, is associated with moral behavior. In a study of college undergraduates, self-reported moral behaviors were substantially positively correlated with proneness to guilt but unrelated to proneness to shame (Tangney, 1994). For example, guilt-prone individuals were more likely than their less guilt-prone peers to endorse such items as "I would not steal something I needed, even if I were sure I could get away with it," "I will not take advantage of other people, even when it's clear that they are trying to take advantage of me," and "Morality and ethics don't really concern me" (reversed). Shame bore no relation to this measure of conventional morality. In short, results from this study suggest that guilt *but not shame* is associated with choosing the "moral paths" in life.

Research on drug and alcohol abuse, aggression, and delinquency similarly demonstrate a differential relationship of shame and guilt with antisocial behavior. In samples of children, adolescents, college students, and adults, shame-proneness (but not guilt-proneness) has been positively related to aggression and delinquency (Ferguson, Stegge, Miller, & Olsen, 1999; Tangney, Wagner et al., 1996; Tibbetts, 1997). In a longitudinal study, Stuewig and McCloskey (2002) found that those high in delinquency and shame-proneness at age 15 were more likely to be later arrested for a violent act—according to juvenile court records—compared with those who were high in delinquency and low in shame. Similarly, proneness to problematic feelings of shame has been linked to substance use and abuse (Dearing, Stuewig, & Tangney, 2005; Meehan et al., 1996; O'Connor, Berry, Inaba, Weiss, & Morrison, 1994).

On the other hand, proneness to shame-free guilt does not show the same positive link to aggression, delinquency, and substance abuse. In fact, guilt-proneness has been negatively related to alcohol and drug problems (Dearing et al., 2005), and negatively related (Merisca & Bybee, 1994; Stuewig & McCloskey, 2002; Tangney, Wagner et al., 1996) or inconsistently related (Ferguson et al., 1999) to aggression and delinquency.

Our longitudinal family study of moral emotions provided further evidence for the link between moral emotions and moral behavior. A sample of 380 fifth grade children, recruited from public schools in an ethnically and socioeconomically diverse suburb of Washington, were enrolled in the study along with their parents and grandparents. Eight years later the index children participated in an in-depth social and clinical history interview when they were 18–19 years old. Analyses of these interviews showed that shame-proneness in the fifth grade predicted critical behaviors in young adulthood, including substance use, risky sexual behavior, involvement with the criminal justice system, and suicide attempts.

The reverse was true for guilt. Guilt-proneness in the fifth grade *negatively* predicted suicide attempts, drug use, driving under the influence, risky sex, and arrests and convictions. These links between early moral emotional style and subsequent behavioral adjustment held when controlling for family income and mothers' education. Therefore this is not simply an effect of socioeconomic status. Equally important, the effects largely remained even when controlling for children's anger at fifth grade. Thus these findings do not simply reflect the fact that badly behaved children are inclined to become badly behaved adults.

Taken together, the evidence reviewed above suggests that the capacity for guilt is associated with a life-long pattern of moral behavior, motivating individuals to accept responsibility and take reparative action in the wake of the inevitable—if only occasional—failures or transgressions. By contrast, there is virtually no direct evidence supporting the presumed inhibitory function of shame vis-à-vis risky, illegal, or otherwise immoral behavior. Feeling really bad, as in the case of shame, does not lead to *being* good.

MORAL EMOTIONS: PAST, PRESENT, AND FUTURE

Conceptually, how do shame and guilt influence moral behavior? Figure 1 provides a framework for thinking about the influence of moral emotions on moral behavior at three different levels: as anticipatory emotions, as consequential emotions, and as emotional dispositions. As depicted in Figure 1, when confronted with a moral dilemma, people often anticipate their likely emotional reactions as they consider behavioral alternatives. For example, a person who is considering shoplifting may be able to "forecast" feeling shame, guilt, or both if he or she were to actually steal a coveted item from a store. Of course anticipatory shame and guilt are less likely in the case of impulsive acts, engaged in with minimal reflection. After action has been taken, moral emotions may occur as a consequence of the behavior, evaluated vis-à-vis moral standards. For instance, having actually stolen an item from a store, an individual may consequently feel shame, guilt, or both.

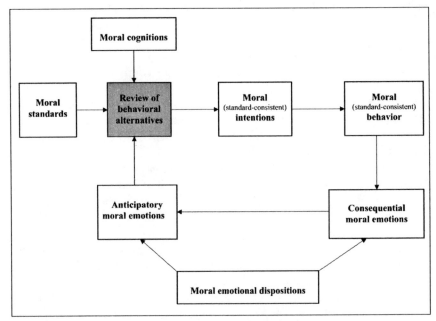

Figure 1. A model of moral emotions, cognitions, and behavior.

As shown in Figure 1, both anticipatory and consequential shame and guilt experiences are intimately related to dispositional tendencies to experience shame and guilt. A guilt-prone person is, by definition, more inclined to anticipate guilt when contemplating a moral transgression. By the same token, that guilt-prone person is more apt to actually experience guilt following the transgression.

Although studies of correlates of shame and guilt as emotional dispositions and emotional states converge, much of the research reviewed so far has focused on moral emotional dispositions—the propensity to experience shame and/or guilt across a range of relevant situations (Tangney, 1990). To assess proneness to shame and proneness to guilt, we use a scenario-based method in which respondents are presented with a series of situations often encountered in daily life. Each scenario is followed by responses that capture phenomenological

aspects of shame, guilt, and other theoretically relevant experiences (e.g., exter-
nalization, pride). For example, in the adult version of our Test of Self-
Conscious Affect (TOSCA; Tangney, Wagner, & Gramzow, 1989), participants
are asked to imagine "You make a big mistake on an important project at work.
People were depending on you and your boss criticizes you." People then rate
their likelihood of reacting with a shame response ("You would feel like you
wanted to hide"), a guilt response ("You would think 'I should have recognized
the problem and done a better job'"), and so forth. Responses across the scenar-
ios capture affective, cognitive, and motivational features associated with shame
and guilt (respectively), as described in the theoretical, phenomenological, and
empirical literature.[1]

As noted above, the likelihood that moral emotions will arise as either anticipatory or consequential emotions depends to a considerable extent on the individual's emotional dispositions. Most of the psychological research reviewed
above on emotion states (feelings of shame and guilt in the moment) focused on
consequential shame and guilt—that is, emotional reactions to a behavior com-
mitted or omitted. Surprisingly few psychologists have examined the nature and
implications of *anticipatory* shame and guilt. The distinction between anticipatory and consequential moral emotions is highlighted when considering self-regulatory functions (and dysfunctions) associated with moral emotions at different
points in the behavioral decision-making process.

A SELF-REGULATORY PERSPECTIVE ON MORAL EMOTIONS

In order to engage in moral behavior, human beings must overcome the tempta-
tions of the moment and conform their behavior to moral standards. In this way
moral behavior involves self-regulation—the ability to intentionally alter one's
responding. Do shame and guilt aid us in this difficult self-regulatory endeavor?
We may draw on the long line of theory and research on the relationship between
emotion and self-regulation to help clarify the conditions under which shame and
guilt may help or hinder moral behavior.

In general, anticipatory emotions are associated with adaptive decision making (Baumeister, DeWall, & Zhang, 2007). Anticipatory emotions are thought to
provide a "common currency" when evaluating the respective costs and benefits

---

[1] See Tangney (1996) and Tangney and Dearing (2002) for a summary of research supporting the reliability and validity of the TOSCA and the more recent TOSCA-3. Importantly,
the TOSCA is not a forced-choice measure; respondents can endorse the guilt response
only, the shame response only, or both in varying degrees. This allows for the possibility
that some respondents may experience both shame and guilt in connection with a given situation. Theoretically, the adaptive features of guilt should be most evident when unaccom-
panied by the painful feelings of shame (Tangney & Dearing, 2002). And this is what is
found empirically: proneness to shame-free guilt is most clearly adaptive. The propensity
to experience "shame-fused" guilt is nearly as problematic as the propensity to experience
shame, per se.

of diverse behavioral options (Baumeister, et al., 2007). Similar to the common conception of the "voice of conscience," the anticipation of "feeling bad" following a moral failure may motivate the individual to adapt his or her behavior to conform to moral norms and standards. In this way the anticipation of shame or guilt may steer individuals away from moral transgressions. Here the capacity for self-control may be critical. To fully process the likely outcomes of a contemplated action, including a consideration of potential shame and guilt resulting from the deed, some delay for reflection is required. Individuals high in self-control may be especially likely to benefit from anticipatory moral emotions because they are less likely to act impulsively without reflection.

Especially among individuals high in self-control, it is likely that anticipatory guilt relates to both guilt-proneness and past guilt experiences. As noted above, people with guilt-prone dispositions should be more likely to anticipate feeling guilt when contemplating guilt-relevant situations. Additionally, it is likely that anticipatory emotional reactions are influenced by previous emotional reactions to similar behaviors. People who have felt guilty for lying to a friend in the past are likely to anticipate feeling guilt when contemplating a future lie.

Anticipatory shame, however, is likely to have a more complicated relationship with shame-proneness and past "consequential" shame experiences. First, shame is inversely related to self-control (Tangney, Baumeister, & Boone, 2004). Second, shame often prompts defensiveness and denial, which would serve to obscure the insight necessary for the anticipation of future shame. People, especially shame-prone people, may have relatively less insight into the causes and consequences of shameful feelings. Indeed, relative to other emotions, people when shamed may have less insight—less explicit, readily retrievable knowledge—to identify the nature of the emotional experience itself. Shame may be a difficult emotion to identify, as Lewis (1971) suggested forty years ago. Empirical research has yet to directly evaluate this possibility, but a range of empirical studies indicates that shame reactions are likely to prompt defensiveness (e.g., denial, blaming others) rather than being owned. As a result, the link between consequential shame and anticipated shame may be attenuated.

This is not to suggest that people do not anticipate feelings of shame and that such anticipated shame feelings do not exert an inhibitory influence on behavior. Rather, the issue is that people are less likely to learn from their shame experiences than their guilt experiences and to carry lessons forward to new situations in the future. In other words, the past may be less informative in the case of shame relative to guilt.

Whereas anticipated negative emotions may fruitfully guide moral decision making, *current* negative emotions appear to have a different effect. Conventional wisdom and scientific research suggest that the experience of intense emotions in the moment is associated with self-regulatory failure (see Muraven & Baumeister, 2000, for a review). The ego depletion theory (Baumeister, Bratslavsky, Muraven, & Tice, 1998) suggests that all types of regulation draw upon a single limited resource. Because different self-control activities are domain-independent, attempts to regulate emotions lead to diminished capacity to regulate other areas. As an example, research shows that momentary emotional distress interferes with ability to delay gratification (Knapp & Clark, 1991).

Compared with guilt, shame is (a) more painful, (b) more difficult to resolve (repair of the self is much more difficult than repair of a behavior), and therefore (c) more difficult to regulate. Because of the difficulty associated with regulating shame, such feelings may be more likely to deplete self-regulatory resources, leaving shamed individuals less able to conform their behavior to moral standards. Self-regulatory depletion during shame is consistent with descriptions of the shame experience provided by Lewis (1971), in which shamed people report experiencing the self as diminished, ineffective, or impaired.

CONCLUSION

Must we feel really bad to be good? Research and theory suggest that emotional pain may encourage moral behavior; however, this is likely to be true only for moderately intense emotional pain experienced in certain contexts. When the pain is overwhelming and/or includes harsh negative evaluations about the self, such pain is likely to interfere with self-regulation in service of moral behavior. In this context it is likely that "a little can go a long way" when it comes to pain (Peeters & Czapinski, 1990). This idea is supported by research by Baumeister, Bratslavsky, Finkenauer, and Vohs (2001) who conclude that "bad is stronger than good," that negative events have a relatively powerful and lasting influence on behavior when compared with positive events. This suggests that a little "bad" may be sufficient to keep us on the straight and narrow, whereas too much "bad" may be counterproductive.

The potency of "bad" experiences on behavior shapes our understanding of the influence of shame and guilt. Research shows that experiences of shame about the self are much more painful than experiences of guilt about a specific behavior (Lewis, 1971; Tangney, 1992; Tangney, Miller et al., 1996; Wicker et al., 1983). In most instances the relatively less painful nature of guilt is sufficient to steer us in a moral direction. By the same token, it is not surprising that the much more painful experience of shame often overwhelms the self—leading to denial, distancing, and sometimes overtly aggressive behavior.

In sum, more is not necessarily better when it comes to moral emotions. This is consistent with research that moderately painful feelings of guilt about specific behaviors motivate people to behave in a moral, caring, socially responsible manner. By contrast, intensely painful feelings of shame do not appear to steer people in a constructive, moral direction. In fact, shame often motivates denial, defensiveness, anger, and aggression. Taken together, theory and research seriously challenge the notion that feeling *really* bad is central to doing good. Some guilt now and then is appropriate and useful to help keep us on the moral path, and more importantly to motivate us to correct and repair following a moral failure. But rather than becoming mired in the agony and self-flagellation of shame, people need to be able to get on with the business of life, taking care of one another rather than condemning the self.

Acknowledgments

This research was supported by Grant #R01–DA14694 from the National Institute on Drug Abuse to June P. Tangney.

REFERENCES

Baumeister, R. F., Bratslavsky, E., Finkenauer, C., & Vohs, K. D. (2001). Bad is stronger than good. *Review of General Psychology, 5,* 323–370.

Baumeister, R. F., Bratslavsky, E., Muraven, M., & Tice, D. M. (1998). Ego depletion: Is the active self a limited resource? *Journal of Personality and Social Psychology, 74,* 1252–1265.

Baumeister, R. F., DeWall, C. N., & Zhang, L. (2007). Do emotions hinder or facilitate the decision-making process? In K. D. Vohs, R. F. Baumeister, & G. Loewenstein (Eds.), *Do emotions help or hurt decision making? A Hedgefoxian perspective* (pp. 11–31). New York: Russell Sage Foundation Press.

Baumeister, R. F., Stillwell, A. M., & Heatherton, T. F. (1994). Guilt: An interpersonal approach. *Psychological Bulletin, 115,* 243–267.

Dearing, R. L., Stuewig, J., & Tangney, J. P. (2005). On the importance of distinguishing shame from guilt: Relations to problematic alcohol and drug use. *Addictive Behaviors, 30,* 1392–1404.

Dearing, R. L., & Tangney, J. P. (Eds.). (2011). *Shame in the therapy hour.* Washington, DC: American Psychological Association.

Dickerson, S. S., Gruenaewald, T. L., & Kemeny M. E. (2004). When the social self is threatened: Shame, physiology, and health. *Journal of Personality, 72,* 1191–1216.

Einstein, D., & Lanning, K. (1998). Shame, guilt, ego development, and the Five-Factor model of personality. *Journal of Personality, 66,* 555–582.

Eisenberg, N. (1986). *Altruistic cognition, emotion, and behavior.* Hillsdale, NJ: Erlbaum.

Eisenberg, N., & Miller, P. A. (1987). Empathy, sympathy, and altruism: Empirical and conceptual links. In N. Eisenberg & J. Strayer (Eds.), *Empathy and its development* (pp. 292–316). New York: Cambridge University Press.

Ferguson, T. J., Stegge, H., & Damhuis, I. (1991). Children's understanding of guilt and shame. *Child Development, 62,* 827–839.

Ferguson, T. J., Stegge, H., Miller, E. R., & Olsen, M. E. (1999). Guilt, shame, and symptoms in children. *Developmental Psychology, 35,* 347–357.

Feshbach, N. D. (1978). Studies of empathic behavior in children. In B. A. Maher (Ed.), *Progress in experimental personality research* (Vol. 8, pp. 1–47). New York: Academic Press.

Feshbach, N. D. (1984). Empathy, empathy training, and the regulation of aggression in elementary school children. In R. M. Kaplan, V. J. Konenci, & R. Novoco (Eds.),

Aggression in children and youth. The Hague, The Netherlands: Martinus Nijhoff Publishers.

Feshbach, N. D. (1987). Parental empathy and child adjustment/maladjustment. In N. Eisenberg & J. Strayer (Eds.), *Empathy and its development* (pp. 271–291). New York: Cambridge University Press.

Feshbach, N. D., & Feshbach, S. (1969). The relationship between empathy and aggression in two age groups. *Developmental Psychology, 1,* 102–107.

Feshbach, N. D., & Feshbach, S. (1982). Empathy training and the regulation of aggression: Potentialities and limitations. *Academic Psychology Bulletin, 4,* 399–413.

Feshbach, N. D., & Feshbach, S. (1986). Aggression and altruism: A personality perspective. In C. Zahn-Waxler, E. M. Cummings, & R. Iannotti (Eds.), *Altruism and aggression: Biological and social origins* (pp. 189–217). Cambridge, UK: Cambridge University Press.

Knapp, A., & Clark, M. S. (1991). Some detrimental effects of negative mood on individuals' ability to solve resource dilemmas. *Personality and Social Psychology Bulletin, 17,* 678–688.

Leith, K. P., & Baumeister, R. F. (1998). Empathy, shame, guilt, and narratives of interpersonal conflicts: Guilt-prone people are better at perspective taking. *Journal of Personality, 66,* 1–37.

Lewis, H. B. (1971). *Shame and guilt in neurosis.* New York: International Universities Press.

Lewis, H. B. (1987). The role of shame in depression over the life span. In H. B. Lewis (Ed.), *The role of shame in symptom formation* (pp. 29–50). Hillsdale, NJ: Erlbaum.

Lindsay-Hartz, J. (1984). Contrasting experiences of shame and guilt. *American Behavioral Scientist, 27,* 689–704.

Marschall, D. E. (1996). *Effects of induced shame on subsequent empathy and altruistic behavior.* Unpublished master's thesis, George Mason University, Fairfax, VA.

Meehan, M. A., O'Connor, L. E., Berry, J. W., Weiss, J., Morrison, A., & Acampora, A. (1996). Guilt, shame, and depression in clients in recovery from addiction. *Journal of Psychoactive Drugs, 28,* 125–134.

Merisca, R., & Bybee, J. S., (1994, April). Guilt, not moral reasoning, relates to volunteerism, prosocial behavior, lowered aggressiveness, and eschewal of racism. Poster presented at the annual meeting of the Eastern Psychological Association, Providence, RI.

Muraven, M., & Baumeister, R. F., (2000). Self-regulation and depletion of limited resources: Does self-control resemble a muscle? *Psychological Bulletin, 126,* 247–259.

O'Connor, L. E., Berry, J. W., Inaba, D., Weiss, J., & Morrison, A. (1994). Shame, guilt, and depression in men and women in recovery from addiction. *Journal of Substance Abuse Treatment, 11,* 503–510.

Peeters, G., & Czapinski, J. (1990). Positive-negative asymmetry in evaluations: The distinction between affective and information negativity effects. In W. Stroebe & M. Hewstone (Eds.), *European review of social psychology* (pp. 33–60). Hillsdale, NJ: Erlbaum.

Scheff, T. J. (1987). The shame-rage spiral: A case study of an interminable quarrel. In H. B. Lewis (Ed.), *The role of shame in symptom formation* (pp. 109–149). Hillsdale, NJ: Erlbaum.

Stuewig, J., & McCloskey, L. (2002, November). Do shame and guilt predict antisocial behavior in late adolescence? Findings from a prospective study. Paper presented at the annual meeting of the American Society of Criminology, Chicago.

Tangney, J. P. (1990). Assessing individual differences in proneness to shame and guilt: Development of the Self-Conscious Affect and Attribution Inventory. *Journal of Personality and Social Psychology, 59,* 102–111.

Tangney, J. P. (1991). Moral affect: The good, the bad, and the ugly. *Journal of Personality and Social Psychology, 61,* 598–607.

Tangney, J. P. (1992). Situational determinants of shame and guilt in young adulthood. *Personality and Social Psychology Bulletin, 18,* 199–206.

Tangney, J. P. (1993). Shame and guilt. In C. G. Costello (Ed.), *Symptoms of depression* (pp. 161–180). New York: Wiley.

Tangney, J. P. (1994). The mixed legacy of the super-ego: Adaptive and maladaptive aspects of shame and guilt. In J. M. Masling & R. F. Bornstein, (Eds.), *Empirical perspectives on object relations theory* (pp. 1–28). Washington, DC: American Psychological Association.

Tangney, J. P. (1995, September). Tales from the dark side of shame: Further implications for interpersonal behavior and adjustment. Paper presented at the annual meeting of the Society for Experimental Social Psychology, Washington, DC.

Tangney, J. P. (1996). Conceptual and methodological issues in the assessment of shame and guilt. *Behaviour Research and Therapy, 34,* 741–754.

Tangney, J. P., Baumeister, R. F., & Boone, A. (2004). High self-control predicts good adjustment, less pathology, better grades, and interpersonal success. *Journal of Personality, 72,* 271–324.

Tangney, J. P., & Dearing, R. L. (2002). *Shame and guilt.* New York: Guilford Press.

Tangney, J. P., Marschall, D. E., Rosenberg, K., Barlow, D. H., & Wagner, P. E. (1994). Children's and adults' autobiographical accounts of shame, guilt, and pride experiences: An analysis of situational determinants and interpersonal concerns. Unpublished manuscript.

Tangney, J. P., Miller, R. S., Flicker, L., & Barlow, D. H. (1996). Are shame, guilt, and embarrassment distinct emotions? *Journal of Personality and Social Psychology, 70,* 1256–1269.

Tangney, J. P., Stuewig, J., & Mashek, D. J. (2007). Moral emotions and moral behavior. *Annual Review of Psychology, 58,* 345–372.

Tangney, J. P., Wagner, P. E., Fletcher, C., & Gramzow, R. (1992). Shamed into anger? The relation of shame and guilt to anger and self-reported aggression. *Journal of Personality and Social Psychology, 62,* 669–675.

Tangney, J. P., Wagner, P., & Gramzow, R. (1989). *The Test of Self-Conscious Affect (TOSCA).* Fairfax, VA: George Mason University.

Tangney, J. P., Wagner, P. E., Hill-Barlow, D., Marschall, D. E., & Gramzow, R. (1996). Relation of shame and guilt to constructive versus destructive responses to anger across the lifespan. *Journal of Personality and Social Psychology, 70,* 797–809.

Tibbetts, S. G. (1997). Shame and rational choice in offending decisions. *Criminal Justice and Behavior, 24,* 234–255.

Tracy, J. L., & Robins, R. W. (2006). Appraisal antecedents of shame and guilt: Support for a theoretical model. *Personality and Social Psychology Bulletin, 32,* 1339–1351.

Wallbott, H. G., & Scherer, K. R. (1995). Cultural determinants in experiencing shame and guilt. In J. P. Tangney & K. W. Fischer (Eds.), *Self-conscious emotions: The psychology of shame, guilt, embarrassment, and pride* (pp. 465–487). New York: Guilford Press.

Wicker, F. W., Payne, G. C., & Morgan, R. D. (1983). Participant descriptions of guilt and shame. *Motivation and Emotion, 7,* 25–39.

PART III

Epilogue
Toward a Common Paradigm

CHAPTER 9

Integrating Personality, Cognition, and Emotion
Seeing More Than the Dots

William Revelle

INTRODUCTION

The process of science is sometimes reminiscent of a pointillistic painting. We all work in our individual laboratories studying how to best color a few dots so they fit together. But when we come together in a well-edited book, we can—if the editors do their job—see a beautiful canvas such as Seurat's *Sunday on La Grand Jatte*. The second volume of the Warsaw Lectures in Personality and Social Psychology is just such a book: the chapters make substantive contributions to the integration of the seemingly disparate fields of personality, cognition, and emotion.

In the original call to the authors, the editors emphasized the need for "a forum for the cross-disciplinary discussion of the important issues concerning human brain and mind." Although an ambitious call, it has been met by the chapters in this volume. For indeed the book

> provide[s] an opportunity to exchange ideas and to work out an integrative and interdisciplinary approach to the considered processes and phenomena within the following study fields: foundations of personality, cognition, and emotion; intraindividual dimensions and unconscious processes in cognition and emotion; the role of self in cognition and emotion; individual differences, atten-

Personality, Cognition, and Emotion edited by Michael W. Eysenck, Małgorzata Fajkowska, and Tomasz Maruszewski. Eliot Werner Publications, Clinton Corners, New York, 2012.

tional processes, and emotion; individual differences, memory, and emotion; individual and social perspectives on emotional disorders; and therapy of emotional disorders.

Some of us who study personality and individual differences tend to focus on the big picture at the cost of blurring over important details in emotion, cognition, and biology. For us this volume is an opportunity to consider the details and also a chance to consider how they relate to each other in the broad-brush picture we call personality. For personality is the study of the coherent patterning over time and space of affect, cognition, and desires as they lead to behavior. That is, personality is the study of patterns over time of how what we do is the consequence of how we feel, what we think, and what we want.

Most psychologists would argue that what they study is at the core of psychology and the understanding they bring to the field is essential. At least for the second point, they are of course correct. But those of us who study personality and individual differences tend to be generalists and are faced with the additional challenge of integrating findings from social psychology, cognitive psychology, neuropsychology, and behavior genetics by using experimental and correlational methodologies combined with recent developments in modeling and psychometrics (Revelle, Wilt, & Condon, 2011). As a result, we face the tradeoff of focusing on the details of each study in each domain at the cost of seeing consistencies across domains, or we can examine the big picture at the cost of throwing away important details. But as we know from the examples of Chuck Close (Pelli, 1999; Storr, Close, Varnedoe, & Wye, 1998) or Georges Seurat (Herbert, Seurat, & Art Institute of Chicago, 2004), confusing details when examined too closely can produce amazing coherence when viewed at a greater distance.

THE ABCDs OF PERSONALITY

This volume discusses the interrelationships of personality, emotion, and cognition. It is useful, then, to consider what we mean by these terms. Unfortunately, these are fuzzy concepts with different meanings to different scholars. The solution that my colleagues and I have attempted is to combine Plato's original tripartite organization of the soul into reason, passion, and desire (*The Republic*) with a levels-of-processing model partially derived from computer science (Ortony, Norman, & Revelle, 2005), as well as from cognitive (e.g., Broadbent, 1971) and biological (MacLean, 1990; MacLean & Kral, 1973) perspectives. That is, in more modern terms we consider how cognition, affect, and desire function at reactive, routine, and reflective levels of processing as they lead to the observable outcome of behavior. We agree with Hilgard (1980), Matthews, Campbell et al. (2002), Mayer (2001), and Scherer (1995) that Plato's trilogy of the mind still has utility in today's thinking. We represent behavior and the trilogy of the mind in terms of a tetrahedron with the four corners denoting the aspects or elements of affect, behavior, cognition, and desire. This then allows us to categorize research into those four aspects as well as six edges (e.g., affect x behavior, affect x cognition, behavior x cognition, etc.), four facets (e.g., affect x behavior x cognition, affect x behavior x desire, etc.), and finally the complete space defined by the tetrahedron. My colleagues and I have used this taxonomy before (Wilt, Oehlberg, & Revelle, 2011; Wilt & Revelle, 2009) and I use this taxonomy when considering the chapters in this volume.

Although we first introduced the affect, behavior, cognition, and desire (ABCD) analysis in the context of studying emotion (Ortony et al., 2005), we have since generalized the analysis over the temporal dimension to define personality. For personality is to emotion as climate is to weather ("Personality is what you expect; emotion is what you get"). That is, personality may be understood as the coherence over time and space of affect, behavior, cognition, and desire. The crucial term here is coherence rather than merely an average. For applying our analogy, although the average temperatures in Warsaw and San Francisco are very similar, the variance and the patterning of the seasons is very different. Personality is thus not just the average ABCD over situations, but rather reflects an individual's unique temporal signature over situations (Fleeson, 2001, 2007; Funder, 2006).

My analysis will be similar to those in which we have considered several dimensions of personality in terms of the relative contributions of the ABCDs. Extraversion may be considered in terms of positive affect, approach behavior, broad versus narrow cognitive processing, and desires for leadership and dominance (Wilt & Revelle, 2009). Similarly, anxiety may be considered in terms of negative affect, avoidance behavior, biased cognitive processing, and prevention goals (Wilt, Oehlberg, & Revelle, 2011).

The Basic Elements

If personality is the coherent patterning over time and space of affect, behavior, cognition, and desire, we need to first consider what these four terms represent. Are they in fact separable? Do they have any defining characteristics? That is, we need to clarify what we mean by affect, behavior, cognition, and desire. Unfortunately, this is not as easy as one would like, for these also are fuzzy concepts with a great deal of conceptual overlap.

Those who study how affective mechanisms can influence executive control process in intelligence and creativity (e.g., Chuderski & Nęcka, 2010; Nęcka, 2000) tend to agree with Zeelenberg, Nelissen, Breugelmans, and Pieters (2008):

> Affect is a generic term that refers to many experiential concepts including moods, emotions, attitudes, evaluations and preferences. The defining feature is the valence dimension.... It refers to the extent that an experience is positive or negative, good or bad, or pleasant or unpleasant. Thus, any experiential concept that is positive or negative can be considered affective. (p 19)

Although we agree with Zeelenberg et al. (2008) when they argue that emotion is more than affect, and that affect includes mood states, we disagree that all affect is necessarily valenced. We rather think in terms of core affect as a feeling state that typically—but not necessarily—includes both valence and arousal. This is a different position from those who conceive of core affect as always representing a mixture of affective valence and arousal (Barrett & Russell, 1998), or those who think solely in terms positive and negative affect (Tellegen, 1985; Tellegen, Watson, & Clark, 1999). We prefer to focus on energetic and tense arousal, which are associated with but do not include valence (Thayer, 1989, 2000), and how the two covary with—but are not synonymous with—positive and negative affect. This issue is discussed in detail in Matthews and Fellner (this volume). Nor do we equate emotion with just affect, for to us a full-fledged emotion represents an integration at one time of all the ABCDs (Ortony et al., 2005). In lay terms, affect is how we feel.

Cognition reflects how we know and make sense of the world; cognitive processes involve perceiving, encoding, storing, and retrieving representations of the world. Cognition reflects one's thoughts, knowledge, and beliefs and ways of thinking and problem solving. However, cognitive processes are not always (in fact, are probably rarely) conscious and available to reflection. Most of our perceptual, encoding, storage, and representation is done automatically and without access to direct control. Nonetheless, whether with or without awareness, cognition is how we think.

Desires are goals, wants, and strivings and are grouped under the rubric of motivations. They may be as mundane as hunger for a pizza or as broad as wanting to help mankind avoid existential threats such as global climate change or nuclear war, but our desires and goals are organizing principles for our actions and inactions. Desires answer the question of why we choose to do something and not something else.

Finally, behavior is what we do. Behavior may be directly observable (walking, talking, fighting, fleeing) or unobservable (increase in heart rate or blood flow in a specific region of the brain). Knowing or wanting to do something is not enough, it is by what we do that we are judged.

Clearly these four aspects are ideal cases and most of what we do involves thinking, feeling, and wanting. But by examining behavior in terms of these aspects, as well as levels of processing and temporal coherence, we find that seeming inconsistencies are resolved (Ortony et al., 2005).

Except for the overemphasis upon stimulus-response (S-R) behaviorism of the early and mid-twentieth century, the use of affect, cognition, and desire as unobservable latent variables characteristic of the organism has had a long and fruitful history. Indeed, a common thread in the thinking of Plato to Thomas Aquinas to Wundt and James has been the distinction between thoughts, feelings, and desires. This distinction continues to this day. We do not want to reject the importance of behavior, for that is the ultimate criterion, but we use these organismic variables of thoughts, feelings, and desires as explanatory devices for the different behaviors that result from a particular set of situational cues. In traditional terms, we want to examine the organism (O) in the S-O-R model (Woodworth & Schlosberg, 1954). In more contemporary terms, we view affect, cognition, and desires as latent mediators between environmental inputs and behavioral outputs (MacKinnon, 2008).

What was missing from the early S-O-R models was the realization that the entire process is a continuous loop, with responses affecting the environment, which in turns leads to different stimuli (Wachtel, 1973). Thus the model could be seen as S-O-R-S-O-R-S-O-R-S-O-R. It is perhaps arbitrary to focus on the response side when we could potentially focus on the latent mediators. For except for rats running mazes, or for undergraduate students in psychology experiments, choices have consequences and yesterday's behaviors affect today's environment and tomorrow's thoughts and feelings.

THE BASIC ASPECTS

Although none of the chapters in this volume can be categorized as pure exemplars of any one aspect, several of them focus more heavily on affect while others focus more heavily on cognition. The rest tend to be integrative studies of edges (e.g., affect and cognition, affect and desire).

Affect

Matthews and Fellner (this volume) consider the energetic components of affect and question how energetics and emotional intelligence affect various performance tasks. Their review of prior work emphasizes the importance of Robert Thayer's distinction between energetic and tense arousal (Thayer, 1989, 2000) and stresses the importance of the energetic arousal component of affect.

This is important work for it shows that one dimension of momentary affective state—energetic arousal, as assessed by either Thayer's scales or Matthews's Dundee Stress State Questionnaire (Matthews, Campbell et al., 2002)—is only slightly related to affective valence but strongly related to various performance measures. Although some describe affective space in terms of a circumplex with no fundamental axes (Russell, 1980; Russell, Lewicka, & Niit, 1989), or in terms of valence and arousal (Barrett & Russell, 1998) or positive and negative affect (Tellegen, 1985; Tellegen et al., 1999), Thayer's energetic arousal dimension relates more to diurnal variation and performance on cognitive tasks. Tense arousal, on the other hand, reflects environmental threats to the organism. That energetic arousal is not just a mixture of valence and arousal has been clearly shown by Schimmack and Reisenzein (2002), and that the affects of sadness and happiness are not bipolar opposites by Rafaeli and Revelle (2006).

Matthews's three dimensions of affect (energetic arousal, tense arousal, and hedonic tone) are reminiscent of the prior work of Wundt (1904), who discussed dimensions of pleasure-displeasure, excitement-inhibition, and tension-relaxation (see also Reisenzein, 1992; Schimmack & Reisenzein, 2002). Emphasizing these three dimensions of affect and their unique pattern of correlations is important: it pushes beyond a premature consensus of a two-dimensional affective structure. By extending the simple analysis of the correlational structure of affective terms, and examining the behavioral correlates or the differential responses to stress manipulations, Matthews and his colleagues have provided strong evidence for a three-dimensional model. My colleagues and I have reported similar demonstrations of the structure of affect when considering differential patterning of tense arousal and negative affect in response to affect-inducing films (Rafaeli & Revelle, 2006).

When the level of analysis changes from between subjects to within subjects, the structure of affect is somewhat more complicated, in that people systematically differ in the correlation between either energetic arousal (EA) and tense arousal (TA) or positive affect and negative affect (Rafaeli, Rogers, & Revelle, 2007; Wilt, Funkhouser, & Revelle, 2011). That is, while the majority of people find EA and TA as independent dimensions, for some they are synchrononous and covary positively while for others they are desynchronous and covary negatively. It seems as if variations in this correlation reflect how the situation is appraised, whether it is seen as a threat leading to desynchrony or a challenge leading to synchronony (Wilt, Funkhouser, & Revelle, 2011).

Matthews and Fellner consider the relationship between energetic engagement and emotional intelligence (EI). That this relationship is less than many would have expected is consistent with prior findings from Matthews and his colleagues (Matthews, Zeidner, & Roberts, 2002). In the first study reported by Matthews and Fellner, they find that perhaps the best measure of emotional intelligence as an ability—the Mayer-Salovey-Caruso Emotional Intelligence Test (MSCEIT; Mayer, Salovey, & Caruso, 2002; Mayer, Salovey, Caruso, & Sitarenios, 2003)—did not support their EI-as-energization hypothesis. This is not completely surprising, because it is not clear that the MSCEIT is actually a measure of emotional affect. If it measures anything, the MSCEIT measures crystalized knowledge about emotion, not fluid emotional experience. For it is conceptually possible to write a computer program that would pass a Turing test if given the MSCEIT (Ortony, Revelle, & Zinbarg, 2007). The three subsequent studies examine EI as a personality trait rather than as an ability (what one normally does versus what one can do). Once again the relationships with important performance measures are not impressive.

The important conclusion from the Matthews and Fellner chapter is that we should pay more attention to task engagement and energetic arousal as indices of attentional resources. State affect does indeed predict state cognition, but mainly through the mechanism of resource availability associated with energetic arousal.

Cognition

As would be expected in a volume emphasizing the integration of personality, affect, and cognition, there are no chapters emphasizing isolated cognitive processes. Some, however, did make cognition their primary focus. Thus the chapter by Szymon Wichary and his colleagues considers the effects of cognitive aging as it moderates reasoning and decision making. When considering such cognitive effects, it is also necessary to examine affect as a source of information—both prospectively when choosing behaviors, as well as in terms of feedback on performance after executing a behavior. Concepts of executive control as modulated by affect need to be considered (Chuderski & Nęcka, 2010). Executive control modulates goal-directed behavior, particularly in the case of choosing between multiple goals and multiple motivations. Attention can be both focused too broadly or too tightly upon stimulus cues (cf., Easterbrook, 1959) and the broadness of the "attentional spotlight" can be modified by individual differences, caffeine-induced arousal, and task demands (Anderson & Revelle, 1982).

AFFECT AND COGNITION

That how we feel influences how we think is a basic assumption of clinical psychology, but one that is unfortunately much ignored by cognitive scientists and their theories of rational decision making so popular in economics. Although early research demonstrated that emotional states affect learning (Yerkes & Dodson, 1908) and motivational states affect performance (Blodgett, 1929; Tolman & Honzik, 1930), the cognitive revolution that began in the mid-1960s and influences theories to this day has tended to ignore the competence-performance distinction. Theories of the effect of anxiety on performance were developed primarily by personality, clinical, and (more recently) sport psychologists. Few cognitive psychologists focused on the problem. A major exception to this generalization is the work of Michael Eysenck and his collaborators (Eysenck, 2000; Eysenck & Derakshan, 2011; Eysenck, Derakshan, Santos, & Calvo, 2007; Eysenck, Lister, & Weingartner, 1991) as well as Gerald Matthews (Matthews, Panganiban, & Hudlicka, 2011), all of whom have consistently argued for an integrative model of affect and cognitive performance. Eysenck's chapter in this volume is a thorough review of his work on the effects of anxiety on cognitive performance.

That high test anxiety is related to poor cognitive performance is well known (Stöber & Pekrun, 2004). However, a recurring problem in the study of the anxiety-performance link is one of causality. That is, do people perform badly because they are anxious, or are they anxious because they perform badly? This cannot be addressed by correlational studies, but can be answered by experimentally manipulating anxiety (either increasing it by threats or decreasing it by clinical interventions) and then observing the effect on performance.

But what performance to measure? Eysenck and his colleagues have followed the cognitive tradition of trying to use "process pure" tasks. The logic is
that the complex tasks associated with anxiety effects are composed of simpler
tasks and it should be possible to find the systematic affects of anxiety on one of
these purer (or at least simpler) tasks. We had a similar desire when trying to
decompose complex tasks into components of working memory and sustained
attention (Humphreys & Revelle, 1984), and argued that the working memory
component was hindered—while the attention component was facilitated—by
arousal. Unfortunately, our experience is that the anxiety effects tend to slip away
as one gets purer and purer measures of process. Yes, they are sometimes there,
but the effects are subtle and hard to replicate (Wilt, Oehlberg, & Revelle, 2011).
The analogy of aggregating many unreliable items to form reliable item compos-
ites (scales) comes to mind. Anxiety might have a small effect upon many pure
cognitive measures, but it is only when we aggregate tasks that require multiple
cognitive processes that the anxiety effects are robust.

Other examples of the difficulty of showing anxiety effects upon pure tasks
include the inconsistent effects of anxiety on visual attention in a cueing paradigm (Cooper, Rowe, Penton-Voak, & Ludwig, 2009). Further complicating the
anxiety-cognition link is the importance of the interstimulus interval (ISI;
Derakshan & Eysenck, 2009). Anxiety effects that show positive cognitive biases at short ISIs are sometimes negative at longer ISIs (Oehlberg, Revelle, &
Mineka, in press).

That anxiety seems more associated with deficits in processing efficiency
related to the central executive is important (Eysenck, this volume). But we need
to make sure that this is more than diversion of central executive resources from
the experimental task due to worry. In an examination of multiple theoretical
explanations for the effect of anxiety upon cognitive performance (Leon &
Revelle, 1985), we found stronger support for the proposal that anxiety is a dis-
tractor (Wine, 1971) that hinders overall availability of cognitive resources than
that it is related to a deficit in specific resources associated with memory
(Eysenck, 1979) or cue utilization (Easterbrook, 1959). We also found strategic
differences in speed-accuracy tradeoffs as a function of level of state anxiety,
which made some of the results very hard to interpret.

When examining the effects of anxiety in a task-switching paradigm, we
should also remember that some of the most robust anxiety-performance findings
(e.g., Spence, Farber, & McFann, 1956) disappear when the subjects' interpretation of their own performance is considered. That is, when given simple or complex tasks without explicit feedback, anxious participants tend to interpret their
performance on difficult or complex tasks as a failure experience and reduce their
effort and task engagement. But when explicitly given success feedback, the anx-
iety-by-task-difficulty interaction effect reverses and the anxious participants do
better on harder tasks (Weiner & Schneider, 1971). This result is an example of
the importance of considering not just the participants' cognitive performance,
but their cognitive framing of their performance.

The continuing importance of anxiety studies in personality is seen in the special issue of *Personality and Individual Differences* dedicated to the memory of Błazej Szymura and edited by Philip Corr and Małgorzata Fajkowska (2011). Important articles in that issue include those by Eysenck and Derakshan (2011) and Matthews et al. (2011).

Going beyond anxiety, Edward Nęcka has examined the affective mechanisms of cognitive control (Chuderski & Nęcka, 2010). For Nęcka emotion controls cognition and acts as a guiding factor in problem solving, and as a moderator in memory retrieval. As do many others, his analysis of affect quickly broadens to full-fledged emotions that involve cognition, desires, and affects (see also Frijda, this volume). He recognizes the bidirectional effects of emotions on behavior as well as behavior on emotions (one runs when afraid, but can take a brisk walk to elevate affect). What is missing from his analysis is a consideration that current and immediately prior affect seem to change the cognitive resources available. Thus people are more likely to stereotype others when their own cognitive resources are diminished. "Morning people" are more likely to stereotype others in the evening, whereas "evening people" are more likely to stereotype in the morning (Bodenhausen, 1990). Resources can be depleted by social interaction with minorities and—although not affecting the immediate task—hinder subsequent performance (Richeson & Shelton, 2003). Affect can also change to breadth of cue utilization: while positive affect leads to a focusing on the broader aspects of a stimulus, negative affect leads to a focusing on the details (Gasper & Clore, 2002). Indeed, as Dalgleish and his colleagues have shown, resources to recall specific autobiographical memories may be reduced by ego depletion induced by doing a Stroop task (Neshat-Doost, Dalgleish, & Golden, 2008).

It is not just the negative affects that can impair performance. Positive affect can impair performance on tasks that involve careful and deliberative processing of stimuli. It seems as if positive affect may induce a more heuristic problem-solving approach and impair set switching (Mitchell & Phillips, 2007).

While Eysenck analyzes how affect changes our cognitions, Keith Oatley (this volume) considers how what we think about changes the way we feel. In particular, after reading emotionally laden fiction, people are more able to process their own and others' emotions than after reading nonfiction. To understand the emotions of others is a skill that may be enhanced by training; one form of such training is the reading of fiction. For Oatley (2009) reading fiction is a simulation of the real world and prepares us for interaction in the world, just as a flight simulator can prepare a pilot for an emergency landing. That this is not just a stable individual difference (people who like to read fiction are different in many ways from those who read the history of the Punic wars) can be shown by experimentally comparing reading short stories with reading factual accounts matched in content but not emotional tone to the stories. Why should this be? Careful readers of fiction are not just reading about the emotions of others, but are experiencing those emotions themselves. We read and watch books, plays, and movies that move us. This provides us with opportunities to simulate the experience of emotion in others and to make us more sensitive to our own and others' emotional states.

Oatley reminds us how important our thoughts are in guiding our interactions. Just as a good narrative can provide training in experiencing emotions, so can one's own narrative allow one to understand and modify his or her emotional reactions. "The stories people fashion to make meaning ouf of their lives serve to situate them within the complex social ecology of modern adulthood" (McAdams, 2008, p. 242).

DESIRE AND BEHAVIOR

At the same time as Hans Eysenck (1952, 1967), Jeffrey Gray (1981, 1982, 1991), and Jan Strelau (1987, 1998) and their colleagues were describing two broad dimensions of affect and behavior that have become associated with positive affect and approach behavior (extraversion) and negative affect and avoidance behavior (neuroticism), others were describing two dimensions of interpersonal behavior. How people interact with others was described by Leary (1957) and Wiggins (1996) in terms of a circumplex that could be construed as having dimensions of agency (dominance/ambition) and socialization/communion. To blend these two models required the addition of a third dimension (agreeableness to the Eysenck two space, neuroticism to the Leary two space).

Circumplex structures are just two-dimensional structures where the items do not show simple structure, but rather have loadings on both dimensions (Gurtman, 1994, 1997). As already discussed, adjectives describing affect typically have this characteristic (Russell, 1980; Russell et al., 1989), but may be equally well represented in terms of the dimensions of tense and energetic arousal (Thayer, 2000) when expressed in polar rather than Cartesian coordinates (Rafaeli & Revelle, 2006). Circumplex theorists tend to reject any fundamental rotation of axes, but when describing the interpersonal circumplex prefer to use dominance (agency) and love (communion). These circumplex models may be generalized by projecting higher-dimensional models into sets of two-dimensional circumplexes. For instance, many of the items describing the Big Five may be represented in circumplexes of pairs of dimensions (Hofstee, de Raad, & Goldberg, 1992).

Subsequent blending of affective, behavioral, and interpersonal descriptions of individual differences led to descriptive taxonomies using such colloquial terms of power and leadership, affection, productivity in work, sensitivity to emotion, and interest in intellectual ideas, or to the more technical dimensions of extraversion, agreeableness, conscientiousness, neuroticism, and openness discussed by Big Five theorists. The Big Five are said to have become consensual descriptions of the important domains of behavior (Digman, 1990; Goldberg, 1990). But saying that there are five orthogonal factors does not make it so. These domains are neither independent (DeYoung, 2010; Digman, 1997) nor universally accepted (Block, 1995, 2010; McAdams & Pals, 2006; McAdams & Walden, 2010; Revelle, 1995).

Two higher-order factors of the Big Five were introduced by Digman (1997), who suggested that the first (α) dimension was associated with good socialization (higher levels of agreeableness, conscientiousness, and emotional stability), while the second (β) dimension was associated with personal growth (extraversion/surgency and intellect/openness to experience). More recently, DeYoung (2010) has proposed that Digman's α and β dimensions have biological bases associated with serotonin and dopamine and are better labeled as stability and plasticity.

Bogdan Wojciszke and his colleagues (Abele & Wojciszke, 2007; Wojciszke, this volume) study the interpersonal dimensions of agency and communion dimensions in their analysis of social information processing. They consider the higher-order structure of the Big Five proposed by Digman (1997) and suggest that α and β dimensions should be interpreted as agency and communion. For them agency is goal pursuit for the self, communion is a desire for integrating with others. Differences in goals naturally lead to different behavioral outcomes.

By adding social goals to the personality agenda, Wojciszke has made a very important contribution. For too much of personality description and theory is at the intrapersonal level, considering how people react to cues for punishment and rewards, how they seek stimulation, how they inhibit behavior in the face of threats. But humans are social animals and it is the complex interplay of people with each other that leads to group cohesion and ultimately to survival. Extraversion, for instance, is partly enjoying being with people, but it is also a desire for social dominance. Positive aspects of agreeableness are associated with positive affect when dealing with others, while the disagreeable end of the spectrum is more associated with desires to impress others, achieve more power, and use flattery to get ahead. Whether the most useful level of analysis is at the two dimensions of agency and communion is not the question, but Wojciszke makes clear that the addition of considering peoples' interpersonal goals is vital for our understanding of how people deal with others.

COGNITION AND DESIRE

Our goals and desires affect not just our actions but also the way we think and feel. The effect of goal direction on creative processes in thinking and emotion is examined by Alina Kolańczyk (this volume), who uses the meta-motivational concepts of Apter (1984, 2001) to examine how playful (paratelic) versus focused (telic) goals affect intuition and creative problem solving. Kolańczyk considers how motivational state affects the allocation and breadth of attention. Compared to a telic motivational state, attentional processes are broader and shallower than when in a paratelic motivational state. With the proper background knowledge and experience, this broader attention can lead to more intuitive and creative problem solving than when attention is more focused on narrower and deeper specific problems. The telic and paratelic states are thought of as meta-motivational in that they are not immediately goal directed, but rather determine the manner in which the goal is achieved. Although originally conceived as motivational states (Apter, 1984) individual differences in the frequency of being in these states has taken on a more trait-like perspective (Apter, 2001).

Other meta-motivational constructs include promotion and prevention focus (Higgins, 1998; Liberman, Molden, Idson, & Higgins, 2001), which can either be seen as state specific or as more trait like. It is intriguing that although these meta-motivations (e.g., telic vs. paratelic, promotion and prevention focus) were introduced as state variables, much of the analysis has been done upon them as more trait like.

AFFECT AND DESIRE

Basic theories of reinforcement learning emphasize the affective reaction to rewards and punishments, as well as differential sensitivities to cues for these rewards and punishments (Corr, 2008; Gray & McNaughton, 2000). But affects do not occur just in response to situational reinforcers; they also are responses to our rates of approach to our goals (Carver & Scheier, 1990). Typically studied goals are as simple as food and sex, or somewhat more complicated such as achievement and accomplishment. But humans also have goals and aspirations to behave in good and moral ways. Unfortunately, these goals are frequently not met. When we behave in ways that violate our basic ethical or moral standards, we feel shame and guilt. Although frequently confused, these two emotions are very different—not just in the eliciting situations, but also in their consequences (Tangney, Malouf, Stuewig, & Mashek, this volume). The experience of shame is associated with higher levels of neuroticism and reflects bad feelings about one's self. Feelings of guilt, on the other hand, are more associated with agreeableness and reflect a focus on one's behavior.

Reacting with shame or guilt is not just a consequence of a focus on self or behavior, for these two emotions also change one's immediate desires and motivations. "Shame motivates attempts to deny, hide, or escape ... whereas guilt motivates reparative action—confessing, apologizing, undoing" (Tangney et al., this volume). People who are more susceptible to feelings of shame are also more susceptible to anger. This is true across but also within subjects; that is, when feeling shame one also feels anger, but less so when feeling guilt (Tangney, Miller, Flicker, & Barlow, 1996). These different emotions also have implications for future desires. Those who are guilt prone are more likely to anticipate future pangs of guilt and set themselves goals to avoid acting in a way that will induce the emotion. Shame-prone people, on the other hand, seem less able to set appropriate future goals.

AFFECT AND BEHAVIOR

How one feels affects what one does. That behavior is a cue to internal emotional and cognitive states can have serious negative repercussions. Consider the work of Book, Wheeler, and their colleagues showing that the way a person walks is a cue of vulnerability to being a victim. Psychopaths can be shown to be particularly sensitive to these cues (Book, Quinsey, & Langford, 2007; Wheeler, Book, & Costello, 2009). Thus the complex interplay of the emotions that we show in our behaviors affects those who are sensitive to these behavioral cues and allows them to prey upon the most vulnerable.

In a very thoughtful analysis of the complexity of emotions, Nico Frijda (this volume) considers "how emotions work." For Frijda emotions are multicomponential phenomena that are best viewed as passions. They are not responses per se, but are rather tendencies to act. They are states that "clamor for action [or] impose inaction." His analysis is compatible with that discussed by Nęcka (e.g., Chuderski & Nęcka, 2010; Nęcka, 2000), who views executive control as a process of organizing actions when faced with multiple goals that are often incongruous or mutually exclusive. For Nęcka we must consider both the horizontal and vertical control of action. Horizontally refers to the queuing of actions in time and the setting of priorities with the appropriate triggering of actions; vertically refers to one's hierarchy of actions. One can have one goal that is achieved through many actions, as well as one action that achieves many goals.

Both Nęcka and Frijda's analysis are reminiscent of the work by Atkinson and Birch (1970) on the dynamics of action (DOA). The DOA introduced the dimension of time to the analysis of motivational strength and direction. The fundamental idea was that analysis of choice, persistence, latency, frequency, and time spent can be done in a common framework: the analysis of actions over time. For example, the initiation of an activity should be analyzed in the same manner as the persistence of an activity, for the latency of onset of an activity is equivalent to the persistence of not doing that activity. This was a model with many different motivational states running off in parallel but producing a single chain of behavioral outcomes.

The dynamics of action was a model of how instigating forces elicited action tendencies, which in turn elicited actions. The basic concept was that action tendencies had inertia. This was an outgrowth of earlier work by Gestalt psychologists influenced by Kurt Lewin (e.g., Zeigarnik, 1927/1967), as well as Feather (1961) and Atkinson and Cartwright (1964). In simple terms, a wish persists until satisfied and a wish does not increase unless instigated. (This is, of course, a restatement of Newton's first law of motion that a body at rest will remain at rest, while a body in motion will remain in motion). By considering motivations and actions to have inertial properties, it became possible to model the onset, duration, and offset of activities in terms of a simple set of differential equations. The consummatory strength of doing an action was thought in turn to reduce the action tendency. Forces could either be instigating or inhibitory (leading to negaction).

The relationship between instigating forces (F), changes in action tendencies over time (dT), and the expression of actions (T) themselves was described by a simple differential equation (reminiscent of Newton's second law):

$$dT = F - CT$$

where

$$C = cT$$

and $c = 0$ if an action is not being done; otherwise c is a function of the type of action (eating peanuts has a smaller c than eating chocolate cake).

That is, for a set of action tendencies T, with instigating forces F:

$$dT_i = F_i - cT_i \qquad \text{if } T_i \text{ is ongoing}$$
$$dT_i = F_i \qquad \text{if } T_i \text{ is not ongoing}$$

Unfortunately, the dynamics of action was a theory before its time. With the exception of those who understood control theory (e.g., Carver & Scheier, 1982; Toates, 1975), few psychologists of the 1970s and 1980s were prepared to understand differential equations or do computer modeling of difference equations. However, with a simple reparameterization and modern software and computational power, the model is much easier to simulate and examine. Applications of the revised model may be extended to the dynamics of emotion (e.g., Frijda, this volume), as well as to social behavior. The cues-tendencies-action (CTA) model (Revelle, 1986) considers environmental cues to instigate action tendencies, which in turn lead to actions.

Rather than specifying inertia just for action tendencies and a choice rule of always expressing the dominant action tendency, thinking of actions themselves also as having inertial properties leads to a simpler model. In an environment that cues for action, cues (**C**) enhance action tendencies (**T**), which in turn strengthen actions (**A**). This leads to two differential equations, one describing the growth and decay of action tendencies (**T**), the other of the actions themselves (**A**):

$$d\mathbf{T} = s\mathbf{C} - c\mathbf{A} \qquad (1)$$
$$d\mathbf{A} = e\mathbf{T} - i\mathbf{A} \qquad (2)$$

There are several interesting implications of incorporating inertial properties into our theories. Perhaps the primary implication from a personality perspective is that trait stability is seen in the rates of change in affect and cognitive states. In the DOA/CTA model, traits act as coefficients in Equations 1 and 2. Thus sensitivity (**s**) to environmental cues (**C**) as well as rates of consummation (**c**) from doing an action, the strength of association (**e**) between a tendency and an action, and the inhibitory connections (**i**) between actions are all individual differences parameters.[1]

While tendencies may rise and fall independently, actions are frequently mutually incompatible and thus occur sequentially. There is no need for a homunculus to make decisions between action tendencies, for actions themselves are mutually incompatible. Perhaps the most vivid example of conflicting needs affecting the patterning of behavior is sexual behavior (which occurs underwater) for the air-breathing newt. Increasing the amount of oxygen available at the surface for breathing prolongs underwater sexual bouts (Halliday, 1980; Halliday & Houston, 1991). A less dramatic example of competing needs is being at a reception following a scientific convention. That is, while optimizing one goal (paying attention to what a colleague is saying) that is compatible with another goal (quenching one's thirst with a beer), one is not optimizing another goal (the growing need to micturate given all that beer). For both the newt and the scientist, dynamic models predict alteration of behaviors even in a stable environment.

This complex stream of affect, desire, thought, and behavior while satisfying a desire is just one example of why Frijda (this volume) believes that emotion cannot be adequately defined, for a full-fledged emotion is a continuous mixture of all these elements.

CONCLUSION

The authors of the chapters in this book were presented with the ambitious challenge of providing a forum for those interested in integrating theories of personality with theories of cognition and affect. They achieved that goal. Although each chapter emphasizes a particular aspect of the problem, the coherent themes of the entire volume form a whole that is more than a mere sum of the details. Just as the study of cognition is enhanced when considering affect, so is the study of affect enhanced when studying cognition. The personality researcher who focuses on just one of these aspects is missing the integrative whole known as personality. By considering the broader coherency over time and space of how people feel, think, want, and act, and by looking at the big picture rather than focusing on the details, the volume editors were able to organize such seemingly disparate work into an integrated whole. All the contributors appreciate the efforts of the editors, as well as those of their fellow authors.

---

[1] To allow researchers to explore the applications of this model, computer code simulating the revised model is available in the cta function in the psych package (Revelle, 2011), which is written in the open source language R (R Development Core Team, 2011). Applications of this dynamic model have been used to simulate behavioral and emotional expression in the interactions of several children and adults in a playground (Fua, Horswill, Ortony, & Revelle, 2009; Fua, Revelle, & Ortony, 2010).

REFERENCES

Abele, A. E., & Wojciszke, B. (2007). Agency and communion from the perspective of self versus others. *Journal of Personality and Social Psychology, 93*, 751–763.

Anderson, K. J., & Revelle, W. (1982). Impulsivity, caffeine, and proofreading: A test of the Easterbrook hypothesis. *Journal of Experimental Psychology: Human Perception and Performance, 8*, 614–624.

Apter, M. J. (1984). Reversal theory and personality: A review. *Journal of Research in Personality, 18*, 265–288.

Apter, M. J. (Ed.). (2001). *Motivational styles in everyday life: A guide to reversal theory.* Washington, DC: American Psychological Association.

Atkinson, J. W., & Birch, D. (1970). *The dynamics of action.* New York: Wiley.

Atkinson, J. W., & Cartwright, D. (1964). Some neglected variables in contemporary conceptions of decision and performance. *Psychological Reports, 14*, 575–590.

Barrett, L., & Russell, J. A. (1998). Independence and bipolarity in the structure of current affect. *Journal of Personality and Social Psychology, 74*, 967–984.

Block, J. (1995). A contrarian view of the five-factor approach to personality description. *Psychological Bulletin, 117*, 187–215.

Block, J. (2010). The five-factor framing of personality and beyond: Some ruminations. *Psychological Inquiry, 21*, 2–25.

Blodgett, H. (1929). The effect of the introduction of reward upon the maze performance of rats. *University of California Publications in Psychology, 4*, 113–134.

Bodenhausen, G. V. (1990). Stereotypes as judgmental heuristics: Evidence of circadian variations in discrimination. *Psychological Science, 1*, 319–322.

Book, A. S., Quinsey, V. L., & Langford, D. (2007). Psychopathy and the perception of affect and vulnerability. *Criminal Justice and Behavior, 34*, 531–544.

Broadbent, D. (1971). *Decision and stress.* London: Academic Press.

Carver, C. S., & Scheier, M. F. (1982). Control theory: A useful conceptual framework for personality-social, clinical, and health psychology. *Psychological Bulletin, 92*, 111–135.

Carver, C. S., & Scheier, M. F. (1990). Origins and functions of positive and negative affect: A control-process view. *Psychological Review, 97*, 19–35.

Chuderski, A., & Nęcka, E. (2010). Intelligence and cognitive control. In A. Gruszka, G. Matthews, & B. Szymura (Eds.), *Handbook of individual differences in cognition: Attention, memory, and executive control* (pp. 263–282). New York: Springer-Verlag.

Cooper, R. M., Rowe, A. C., Penton-Voak, I. S., & Ludwig, C. (2009). No reliable effects of emotional facial expression, adult attachment orientation, or anxiety on the allocation of visual attention in the spatial cueing paradigm. *Journal of Research in Personality, 43*, 643–652.

Corr, P. J. (2008). Reinforcement sensitivity theory (RST): Introduction. In P. J. Corr (Ed.), *The reinforcement sensitivity theory of personality* (pp. 1–43). Cambridge, UK: Cambridge University Press.

Corr, P. J., & Fajkowska, M. (2011). Introduction to special issue on anxiety. *Personality and Individual Differences, 50*, 885–888.

Derakshan, N., & Eysenck, M. W. (2009). Anxiety, processing efficiency, and cognitive performance: New developments from attentional control theory. *European Psychologist, 14*, 168–176.

DeYoung, C. G. (2010). Toward a theory of the Big Five. *Psychological Inquiry: An International Journal for the Advancement of Psychological Theory, 21*, 26–33.

Digman, J. M. (1990). Personality structure: Emergence of the five-factor model. *Annual Review of Psychology, 41*, 417–440.

Digman, J. M. (1997). Higher-order factors of the Big Five. *Journal of Personality and Social Psychology, 73*, 1246–1256.

Easterbrook, J. (1959). The effect of emotion on cue utilization and the organization of behavior. *Psychological Review, 66*, 183–220.

Eysenck, H. J. (1952). *The scientific study of personality*. London: Routledge & Kegan Paul.

Eysenck, H. J. (1967). *The biological basis of personality*. Springfield, IL: Charles C. Thomas.

Eysenck, M. W. (1979). Anxiety, learning, and memory: A reconceptualization. *Journal of Research in Personality, 13*, 363-385.

Eysenck, M. W. (2000). A cognitive approach to trait anxiety. *European Journal of Personality, 14*, 463–476.

Eysenck, M. W., & Derakshan, N. (2011). New perspectives in attentional control theory. *Personality and Individual Differences, 50*, 955–960.

Eysenck, M. W., Derakshan, N., Santos, R., & Calvo, M. G. (2007). Anxiety and cognitive performance: Attentional control theory. *Emotion, 7*, 336–353.

Eysenck, M. W., Lister, R. G., & Weingartner, H. J. (1991). Anxiety and cognitive functioning: A multifaceted approach. In *Perspectives on cognitive neuroscience* (pp. 314–324). New York: Oxford University Press.

Feather, N. T. (1961). The relationship of persistence at a task to expectation of success and achievement related motives. *Journal of Abnormal and Social Psychology, 63*, 552–561.

Fleeson, W. (2001). Toward a structure- and process-integrated view of personality: Traits as density distributions of states. *Journal of Personality and Social Psychology, 80*, 1011–1027.

Fleeson, W. (2007). Studying personality processes: Explaining change in between-persons longitudinal and within-person multilevel models. In R. W. Robins, R. C. Fraley, & R. F. Krueger (Eds.), *Handbook of research methods in personality psychology* (pp. 523–542). New York: Guilford Press.

Fua, K., Horswill, I., Ortony, A., & Revelle, W. (2009, November). Reinforcement sensitivity theory and cognitive architectures. Paper presented at the First International Conference of Biologically Inspired Cognitive Architectures. Washington, DC.

Fua, K., Revelle, W., & Ortony, A. (2010, August). Modeling personality and individual differences: The approach-avoid-conflict triad. Paper presented at the annual meeting of the Cognitive Science Society, Portland, OR.

Funder, D. C. (2006). Towards a resolution of the personality triad: Persons, situations, and behaviors. *Journal of Research in Personality, 40*, 21–34.

Gasper, K., & Clore, G. L. (2002). Attending to the big picture: Mood and global versus local processing of visual information. *Psychological Science, 13*, 34–40.

Goldberg, L. R. (1990). An alternative "description of personality": The Big-Five factor structure. *Journal of Personality and Social Psychology, 59*, 1216–1229.

Gray, J. A. (1981). A critique of Eysenck's theory of personality. In H. J. Eysenck (Ed.), *A model for personality* (pp. 246–277). Berlin: Springer-Verlag.

Gray, J. A. (1982). *Neuropsychological theory of anxiety: An investigation of the septal-hippocampal system*. Cambridge, UK: Cambridge University Press.

Gray, J. A. (1991). The neuropsychology of temperament. In J. Strelau & A. Angleitner (Eds.), *Explorations in temperament: International perspectives on theory and measurement* (pp. 105–128). New York: Plenum Press.

Gray, J. A., & McNaughton, N. (2000). *The neuropsychology of anxiety: An enquiry into the functions of the septo-hippocampal system* (2nd ed.). Oxford, UK: Oxford University Press.

Gurtman, M. B. (1994). The circumplex as a tool for studying normal and abnormal personality: A methodological primer. In S. Strack & M. Lorr (Eds.), *Differentiating normal and abnormal personality* (pp. 243–263). New York: Springer Publishing.

Gurtman, M. B. (1997). Studying personality traits: The circular way. In R. Plutchik & H. R. Conte (Eds.), *Circumplex models of personality and emotions* (pp. 81–102). Washington, DC: American Psychological Association.

Halliday, T. R. (1980). Motivational systems and interactions between activities. In F. M. Toates & T. R. Halliday (Eds.), *Analysis of motivational processes* (pp. 205–220). London: Academic Press.

Halliday, T. R., & Houston, A. I. (1991). How long will newts wait? An experiment to test an assumption of a causal model of the courtship of the male smooth newt, triturus v. vulgaris. *Behaviour, 116*, 278–291

Herbert, R. L., Seurat, G., & Art Institute of Chicago. (2004). *Seurat and the making of La Grande Jatte*. Chicago: Art Institute of Chicago.

Higgins, E. T. (1998). Promotion and prevention: Regulatory focus as a motivational principle. In M. P. Zanna (Ed.), *Advances in experimental social psychology* (Vol. 30, pp. 1–46). Academic Press.

Hilgard, E. R. (1980). The trilogy of mind: Cognition, affection, and conation. *Journal of the History of the Behavioral Sciences, 16*, 107–117.

Hofstee, W. K., de Raad, B., & Goldberg, L. R. (1992). Integration of the Big Five and circumplex approaches to trait structure. *Journal of Personality and Social Psychology, 63*, 146–163.

Humphreys, M. S., & Revelle, W. (1984). Personality, motivation, and performance: A theory of the relationship between individual differences and information processing. *Psychological Review, 91*, 153–184.

Leary, T. (1957). *Interpersonal diagnosis of personality*. New York: Ronald Press.

Leon, M. R., & Revelle, W. (1985). Effects of anxiety on analogical reasoning: A test of three theoretical models. *Journal of Personality and Social Psychology, 49*, 1302–1315.

Liberman, N., Molden, D. C., Idson, L. C., & Higgins, E. T. (2001). Promotion and prevention focus on alternative hypotheses: Implications for attributional functions. *Journal of Personality and Social Psychology, 80*, 5–18.

MacKinnon, D. P. (2008). *Introduction to statistical mediation analysis*. New York: Erlbaum.

MacLean, P. D. (1990). *The triune brain in evolution: Role in paleocerebral functions*. New York: Plenum Press.

MacLean, P. D., & Kral, V. A. (1973). *A triune concept of the brain and behaviour*. Toronto: University of Toronto Press.

Matthews, G., Campbell, S. E., Falconer, S., Joyner, L. A., Huggins, J., Gilliland, K., et al. (2002). Fundamental dimensions of subjective state in performance settings: Task engagement, distress, and worry. *Emotion, 2*, 315–340.

Matthews, G., Panganiban, A. R., & Hudlicka, E. (2011). Anxiety and selective attention to threat in tactical decision-making. *Personality and Individual Differences, 50*, 949–954.

Matthews, G., Zeidner, M., & Roberts, R. D. (2002). *Emotional intelligence: Science and myth*. Cambridge, MA: MIT Press.

Mayer, J. D. (2001). Primary divisions of personality and their scientific contributions: From the trilogy-of-mind to the systems set. *Journal for the Theory of Social Behaviour, 31*, 449–477.

Mayer, J. D., Salovey, P., & Caruso, D. R. (2002). *Mayer-Salovey-Caruso Emotional Intelligence Test (MSCEIT) item booklet*. Toronto: MHS Publishers.

Mayer, J. D., Salovey, P., Caruso, D. R., & Sitarenios, G. (2003). Measuring emotional intelligence with the MSCEIT V2.0. *Emotion, 3*, 97–105.

McAdams, D. P. (2008). Personal narratives and the life story. In O. P. John, R. W. Robins, & L. A. Pervin (Eds.), *Handbook of personality: Theory and research* (3rd ed., pp. 242–262). New York: Guilford Press.

McAdams, D. P., & Pals, J. L. (2006). A new Big Five: Fundamental principles for an integrative science of personality. *American Psychologist, 61*, 204–217.

McAdams, D. P., & Walden, K. (2010). Jack Block, the Big Five, and personality from the standpoints of actor, agent, and author. *Psychological Inquiry, 21*, 50–56.

Mitchell, R. L., & Phillips, L. H. (2007). The psychological, neurochemical and functional neuroanatomical mediators of the effects of positive and negative mood on executive functions. *Neuropsychologia, 45*, 617–629.

Nęcka, E. (2000). Intelligence, cognitive strategies, and arousal: Can we control non-cognitive factors that influence our intellect? In U. Hecker, S. Dutke, & G. Sedek (Eds.), *Generative mental processes and cognitive resources: Integrative research on adaptation and control* (pp. 95-122). Dordrecht, The Netherlands: Kluwer Academic Publishers.

Neshat-Doost, H. T., Dalgleish, T., & Golden, A.-M. J. (2008). Reduced specificity of emotional autobiographical memories following self-regulation depletion. *Emotion, 8*, 731–736.

Oatley, K. (2009). Communications to self and others: Emotional experience and its skills. *Emotion Review, 1*, 206–213.

Oehlberg, K. A., Revelle, W., & Mineka, S. (in press). Time-course of attention to negative stimuli: Negative affectivity, anxiety, or dysphoria. *Emotion*.

Ortony, A., Norman, D. A., & Revelle, W. (2005). Affect and proto-affect in effective functioning. In J. Fellous & M. Arbib (Eds.), *Who needs emotions? The brain meets the machine* (pp. 173–202). New York: Oxford University Press.

Ortony, A., Revelle, W., & Zinbarg, R. (2007). Why emotional intelligence needs a fluid component. In G. Matthews, M. Zeidner, & R. D. Roberts (Eds.), *The science of emotional intelligence: Knowns and unknowns* (pp. 288–304). New York: Oxford University Press.

Pelli, D. G. (1999). Close encounters: An artist shows that size affects shape. *Science, 285*, 844–846.

R Development Core Team. (2011). R: A language and environment for statistical computing [computer software manual]. Vienna: R Foundation for Statistical Computing.

Rafaeli, E., & Revelle, W. (2006). A premature consensus: Are happiness and sadness truly opposite affects? *Motivation and Emotion, 30*, 1–12.

Rafaeli, E., Rogers, G. M., & Revelle, W. (2007). Affective synchrony: Individual differences in mixed emotions. *Personality and Social Psychology Bulletin, 33*, 915–932.

Reisenzein, R. (1992). A structuralist reconstruction of Wundt's three-dimensional theory of emotion. In H. Westmeyer (Ed.), *The structuralist program in psychology: Foundations and applications* (pp. 141–189). Toronto: Hogrefe & Huber.

Revelle, W. (1986). Motivation and efficiency of cognitive performance. In D. R. Brown & J. Veroff (Eds.), *Frontiers of motivational psychology: Essays in honor of J. W. Atkinson* (pp. 105–131). New York: Springer-Verlag.

Revelle, W. (1995). Personality processes. *Annual Review of Psychology, 46*, 295–328.

Revelle, W. (2011). *psych: Procedures for personality and psychological research* [computer software manual]. Evanston, IL: Northwestern University.

Revelle, W., Wilt, J., & Condon, D. (2011). Individual differences and differential psychology: A brief history and prospect. In A. F. Tomas Chamorro-Premuzic & S. von Stumm (Eds.), *Handbook of individual differences* (pp. 3–38). Oxford, UK: Wiley-Blackwell.

Richeson, J. A., & Shelton, J. N. (2003). When prejudice does not pay: Effects of interracial contact on executive function. *Psychological Science, 14*, 287–290.

Russell, J. A. (1980). A circumplex model of affect. *Journal of Personality and Social Psychology, 39*, 1161–1178.

Russell, J. A., Lewicka, M., & Niit, T. (1989). A cross-cultural study of a circumplex model of affect. *Journal of Personality and Social Psychology, 57*, 848–856.

Scherer, K. (1995). Plato's legacy: Relationships between cognition, emotion, and motivation. *Geneva Studies in Emotion and Communication, 9*, 1–7.

Schimmack, U., & Reisenzein, R. (2002). Experiencing activation: Energetic arousal and tense arousal are not mixtures of valence and activation. *Emotion, 2*, 412–417.

Spence, K., Farber, I., & McFann, H. (1956). The relation of anxiety (drive) level to performance in competitional and non-competitional paired-associates learning. *Journal of Experimental Psychology, 52*, 296–305.

Stöber, J., & Pekrun, R. (2004). Advances in test anxiety (editorial). *Anxiety, Stress, and Coping, 17*, 205–211.

Storr, R., Close, C., Varnedoe, K., & Wye, D. (1998). *Chuck Close*. New York: Museum of Modern Art.

Strelau, J. (1987). Emotion as a key concept in temperament research. *Journal of Research in Personality, 21*, 510–528.

Strelau, J. (1998). *Temperament: A psychological perspective*. New York: Plenum Press.

Tangney, J. P., Miller, R. S., Flicker, L., & Barlow, D. H. (1996). Are shame, guilt, and embarrassment distinct emotions? *Journal of Personality and Social Psychology, 70*, 1256–1269.

Tellegen, A. (1985). Structures of mood and personality and their relevance to assessing anxiety, with an emphasis on self-report. In A. H. Turna & J. D. Maser (Eds.), *Anxiety and the anxiety disorders* (pp. 681–706). Hillsdale, NJ: Erlbaum.

Tellegen, A., Watson, D., & Clark, L. A. (1999). On the dimensional and hierarchical structure of affect. *Psychological Science, 10*, 297–303.

Thayer, R. E. (1989). *The biopsychology of mood and arousal*. New York: Oxford University Press.

Thayer, R. E. (2000). Mood. In A. E. Kazdin, Ed.), *Encyclopedia of psychology* (Vol. 5., pp. 294–295). Washington, DC: American Psychological Association; New York: Oxford University Press.

Toates, F. M. (1975). *Control theory in biology and experimental psychology*. London: Hutchinson Educational.

Tolman, E. C., & Honzik, C. (1930). Introduction and removal of reward, and maze performance in rats. *University of California Publications in Psychology, 4*, 257–275.

Wachtel, P. L. (1973). Psychodynamics, behavior therapy, and the implacable experimenter: An inquiry into the consistency of personality. *Journal of Abnormal Psychology, 82,* 324–334.

Weiner, B., & Schneider, K. (1971). Drive vs. cognitive theory: A reply to Boor and Harmon. *Journal of Personality and Social Psychology, 8,* 258–262.

Wheeler, S., Book, A., & Costello, K. (2009). Psychopathic traits and perceptions of victim vulnerability. *Criminal Justice and Behavior, 36,* 635–648.

Wiggins, J. S. (1996). An informal history of the interpersonal circumplex tradition. *Journal of Personality Assessment, 66,* 217–233.

Wilt, J., Funkhouser, K., & Revelle, W. (2011). The dynamic relationships of affective synchrony to perceptions of situations. *Journal of Research in Personality, 45,* 309–321.

Wilt, J., Oehlberg, K., & Revelle, W. (2011). Anxiety in personality. *Personality and Individual Differences, 50,* 987–993.

Wilt, J., & Revelle, W. (2009). Extraversion. In M. Leary & R. H. Hoyle (Eds.), *Handbook of individual differences in social behavior* (pp. 27–45). New York: Guilford Press.

Wine, J. (1971). Test anxiety and direction of attention. *Psychological Bulletin, 76,* 92–104.

Woodworth, R. S., & Schlosberg, H. (1954). *Experimental psychology* (rev. ed.). New York: Holt.

Wundt, W. (1904). *Principles of physiological psychology.* London: Swan Sonnenschein. (Translated from the fifth German edition, 1902)

Yerkes, R., & Dodson, J. (1908). The relation of strength of stimuli to rapidity of habit-information. *Journal of Comparative Neurology and Psychology, 18,* 459–482.

Zeelenberg, M., Nelissen, R. M. A., Breugelmans, S. M., & Pieters, R. (2008). On emotion specificity in decision making: Why feeling is for doing. *Judgment and Decision Making, 3,* 18–27.

Zeigarnik, B. (1967). On finished and unfinished tasks. In W. D. Ellis (Ed.), *A source book of Gestalt psychology.* New York: Harcourt Brace. (Reprinted and translated from *Psychological Forschung,* 1927, 9, 1–85)

Name Index

Z

Subject Index

A

Ability. *See* Cognition, as ability; Emotional intelligence (EI), as ability

Accuracy
  aging's effects on, 55, 55*f*, 58–61
  anxiety's effects on, 164
  task engagement correlated with, 38–39, 40

Achievement motive, 32

Action(s), 17, 50
  agentic *vs.* communal construal of, 127, 133–137, 134*f*, 135*f*
  emotion's relationship to, 93–97, 112, 165–166
  goal-oriented, 73–78, 80, 96
  guilt *vs.* shame related to, 142–146
  initiated, 67, 69, 169
  See also Agency; Behavior

Action readiness, 6–7, 93–97, 99, 100, 101, 107, 108

Activation, modes of, 80, 94

Adaptation, 32, 108

Affect, 28, 76, 94, 101, 149
  aging's relationship to, 49, 50–51
  behavior's relationship to, 158–161, 163, 169–171
  cognition's relationship to, 163–166, 170, 171
  creative intuition and, 83–84
  emotion's relationship to, 160, 165, 171
  See also Emotion(s); Feeling(s); Moods; Negative affect; Positive affect

Affective coherence principle, 82

Affective maps, 6, 68, 80–81

Affective priming paradigm, 81

Affective Shift Task, 20

Affiliation, 110, 111

Agency, 7–8, 9, 166, 167
  See also Perception, agentic *vs.* communal content in

Aggression, guilt *vs.* shame's relationship to, 8, 144–147, 151–152

Aging
  cognition and, 5, 9, 47–48, 49, 52–56, 58–61, 62
  decision making and, 5, 47–52, 53, 62, 163

Agreeableness, 8, 36, 166, 167
  guilt *vs.* shame's relationship to, 146, 168
  task engagement and, 30, 115, 116

"Aha" moments, 68, 69

Alcohol abuse, guilt *vs.* shame's relationship to, 8, 147

Amygdala, emotions' activation of, 2

Anger, 2
  actions based on, 93, 99, 112
  guilt *vs.* shame's relationship to, 8, 144–146, 151–152, 168
  social contexts of, 34, 108, 109, 110, 111

Anhedonia, 20

Antipathy, 124

Antisaccade task, 17

Anxiety, 2, 20, 22, 93
  central executive impacted by, 14, 15–16, 18, 20, 21, 165